The

NATURAL
RIGHTS
REPUBLIC

FRANK M. COVEY, JR.
Loyola Lectures in Political Analysis

THOMAS S. ENGEMAN
General Editor

Our late colleague Richard S. Hartigan founded the Frank M. Covey, Jr., Lectures in Political Analysis to provide a continuing forum for the reanimation of political philosophy. The lectures are not narrowly constrained by a single topic nor do they favor a particular perspective. Their sole aim is to foster serious theoretical inquiry, with the expectation that this effort will contribute in essential ways to both human knowledge and political justice.

The

NATURAL RIGHTS REPUBLIC

STUDIES IN THE FOUNDATION OF THE AMERICAN POLITICAL TRADITION

Michael P. Zuckert

UNIVERSITY OF NOTRE DAME PRESS

© 1996 by University of Notre Dame Press
Notre Dame, Indiana 46556
All Rights Reserved

Manufactured in the United States of America

Paperback 1998
ISBN 0-268-01487-6

Book design by Wendy McMillen
Set in 10.5/13 New Baskerville by Books International
Printed and bound by McNaughton & Gunn, Inc.

Library of Congress Cataloging-in-Publication Data

Zuckert, Michael P., 1942–
    The natural rights republic : studies in the foundation of the
American political tradition / Michael P. Zuckert. — [Rev. ed.]
        p.   cm. — (Frank M. Covey, Jr., Loyola lectures in political
analysis)
    Includes bibliographical references
    ISBN 0-268-01480-9 (alk. paper)
    1. Natural law.   2. Political science—Unites States—History.
3. United States—Politics and government.   I. Title.   II. Series.
JC571.Z833   1997
323'.01—dc20   96-9756
                                                                    CIP

To Rachel, Lara, and Emily.

Something of the wisdom of the fathers—
to my children.

Contents

Acknowledgments

—————————————————————————————————&

The chapters which make up *The Natural Rights Republic* are a revised version of the 1994 Frank M. Covey, Jr., Lectures in Political Analysis. It was not only an honor for me to be part of this lecture series, but it gave me a tremendous feeling of vindication as well. Over twenty-five years ago, as a fledgling graduate student about to leave the nest and (I hoped) find a job, I read in place after place that political philosophy, my main field, was dying, or perhaps already dead. The American Political Science Association suggested as much in a poll it published of its members' rankings of the relative importance of the various fields within political science. Political philosophy was at the bottom. Even the political theorists were saying so. The Covey Lectures, I take it, prove that the accounts of the death of political philosophy, like those regarding the death of Mark Twain and God, were much exaggerated. The first debt I would like to acknowledge, then, is to Frank Covey for recognizing and contributing to the continued vitality of political philosophy, and to Tom Engeman for skillfully organizing the Covey lectureship. The second is to all the others who have been responsible for the survival of political philosophy, including, especially, some of the men with whom I studied as a graduate student—Leo Strauss, Joseph Cropsey, Herbert Storing, and before them my undergraduate teachers, Walter Berns and Allan Bloom. The late Herbert Storing was the man who introduced me to the thought of the American founders, and although I have come to disagree with some of his conclusions about the American founding, he has always stood as a model for me of what a scholar, a teacher, and a human being could be. His name will appear from time to time in my notes, but this does not begin to acknowledge the debt I felt then and feel still. His too early death was a great loss to me, as it was to all who knew him.

This book has been many years in the making; some of the ideas in it first broke water in the first class I taught at Carleton, in the fall of 1968. To my Carleton students and colleagues, to other professional colleagues and friends who have shared in these inquiries in one way or another I thus acknowledge many more and deeper debts than a brief page can accommodate.

I am especially grateful to two scholarly colleagues who read the manuscript through from beginning to end, Vickie B. Sullivan of Skidmore College, and Catherine Zuckert of Carleton College. Both made suggestions that have helped make this a better book than it otherwise would have been. Since I did take nearly all their suggestions, I cannot claim they had ways to make it better yet, but perhaps they were holding out on me.

Catherine has been with the project from the beginning; she has willingly listened to the ideas herein contained, all the way back to the first one in 1968. She has also willingly contributed her critical and creative mind and eye to my thinking and writing over these many years. She has combined encouragement and criticism to a degree I do not think could have been more perfect or helpful. One could certainly not ask for more from a colleague, but as chief intellectual companion, best friend, and wife she has given very much more. "But the greatest of these is love."

A number of institutions have been instrumental to the writing of this book. Carleton College, in addition to supplying me with guinea pigs on whom to try out some of these ideas, was also generous with its support in time, money, and encouragement. Part of this book was written during a very productive year at the Newberry Library in Chicago, another part during an equally productive year at the Woodrow Wilson Center in Washington, D.C. The National Endowment for the Humanities supplied indispensable aid. Finally the Earhart Foundation made possible the last half year free from teaching duties, which allowed me to complete the volume.

Certainly not least of those who have contributed to the completion of this book are the hearty souls who helped this small-motor-skills-challenged-pre-typist turn a (pretty illegible) handwritten text into a beautiful word-processed manuscript. The bulk of the typing of the original Covey lectures was done by

Christianne Walker; most of the manuscript of the book as it stands was typed by Barbara Moore and Rachel Zuckert. All three were patient and skillful beyond measure.

Various parts of this book have appeared in somewhat different form in earlier publications. Chapter 2 appeared in the *Review of Politics* for 1987, chapter 3 in a book edited by Robert Licht, *The Framers and Fundamental Rights* (1992), published by the American Enterprise Institute. Part of chapter 4 has been adapted from my *Natural Rights and the New Republicanism* (1994), published by Princeton University Press. My gratitude to all the copyright holders who gave permission to reprint here.

This book is dedicated to my three children, all of whom typed some parts of it, but whose claims on the book go well beyond that. As the American framers well understood, politics is about the creation of stable structures, stable over time and continuous over generations, structures productive of such goods as can be handed down from generation to generation to those near and dear. These three young women are that to me—my near and dear. Although I suspect all three of them will find this book wanting in some way or other—it won't be Kantian enough for Rachel, psychological enough for Larissa, or contentious enough for Emily—yet I hope and trust they will find something to please them, if nothing else the love and affection with which it is dedicated to them.

Introduction

─────────────────────

I heard that you ask'd for something to prove this puzzle the New World,
And to define America, her Athletic Democracy.

Walt Whitman, "To Foreign Lands"

Defending himself in almost the last year of his life from accusations that he had, in effect, cribbed the Declaration of Independence from other sources—from Locke, or Sidney, or earlier colonial documents—Thomas Jefferson responded by urging that such criticism altogether missed his point in drafting the document.

> This was the object of the Declaration of Independence. Not to find out new principles, or new arguments, never before thought of, not merely to say things which had never been said before, but to place before mankind the common sense of the subject. . . . Neither aiming at originality of principle or sentiment, nor yet copied from any particular and previous writing, it was intended to be an expression of the American mind.[1]

Jefferson as scrivener to the American mind—that and only that.

In those later years Jefferson fairly frequently had to parry angry or resentful or envious comments about his role in drafting the Declaration. Some men ungraciously wondered why Jefferson was receiving so much credit for drafting a statement that did indeed "express the American mind" and not any views peculiar to Jefferson himself. The resentment, of course, stemmed from the fact that the Declaration had come to be accepted not only as the most authoritative statement of "our rights and the acts of the British government contravening those rights" at the time of the Revolution, but as the most perspicuous statement of the philosophy that had come to be the American political creed. As such, it

1

became a matter of moment, also, who wrote the Declaration. To receive credit for formulating the national creed—that was something other men could understandably envy.

Despite his modesty about his role as chief drafter of the Declaration, Jefferson himself placed that act as his first and chief accomplishment in the epitaph he composed for himself. It wasn't that Jefferson was incorrect or insincere when he said he had merely captured "the common sense of the subject," when he said he wrote out merely what "all American whigs thought . . . on these subjects"; as will be made clear below, Jefferson was indeed quite correct. Yet he had given an expression to the American mind that surpassed in concision, euphony, and dramatic power any of the other statements of the same philosophy produced during that era. The world has much noted and long remembered what Jefferson wrote, not only for its content but for the elegance and economy with which he said it.

Although Americans still read the Declaration (in school at least), it is not so clear it is any longer the "common sense of the subject." The language of rights and the appeal to rights remain important in American political life, but both as historians and as political thinkers and actors, Americans are less clear about the philosophy of the Declaration itself. As historians, we are no longer certain how important the Declaration's natural rights philosophy actually was in the era of the revolution and of the formation of the new republican governments in state and nation thereafter. As political thinkers and actors, Americans also appear uncertain about what the Declaration means and whether they still believe it.[2]

Whether the philosophy can again become the common sense of the matter I do not know, but my goal is to explicate and defend that philosophy so far, I hope, as to make it at least intelligible and plausible again as a statement of the principles of political right.[3] At the same time I mean to defend the old and traditional view, now somewhat discredited, that the natural rights philosophy as articulated in the Declaration was indeed the understanding of political right on which the founding was conducted and which has served as the cornerstone of the American political tradition.

Jefferson did not understand himself to be saying anything novel in drafting the Declaration, but the "American mind," whose amanuensis he professed to be, apparently understood itself in terms of novelty and innovation. References to the innovativeness of American thoughts and deeds abound through the era. This understanding came to set the mark on the entire founding enterprise when the new nation adopted the motto *Novus Ordo Seclorum*, "a new order for the ages," printed on the back side of all dollar bills, the new order dated to have begun in 1776.[4] James Madison, not a man often given to rhetorical rhapsodies, waxed downright enthusiastic about the devotion of his fellow countrymen to the new. He almost sang in *The Federalist* of the "glory of the people of America," who "have not suffered a blind veneration" to stand in the way of great and truly memorable political innovations "in favor of private rights and public happiness." The Americans, he said, made a "revolution for which a precedent could not be discovered"; they made new governments for their states with "no exact model" to pattern themselves after; and, he implied, they were about to innovate even more dramatically in their new national constitution.[5]

Americans were "glorious," the constitutional experiment was "memorable" because they trod new paths, innovated so that politics the world over was irrevocably transformed. The exemplary power of the American model shone especially vividly one day in the spring of 1989 when the Chinese, in the midst of their democracy movement, rallied around their Miss Liberty, loosely adapted from the American Statue of Liberty, itself a gift from the French in recognition of the American model of free politics. On that same day Mikhail Gorbachev, still in power in what was still the Soviet Union, defended part of his proposal for a new constitution with an observation that he clearly considered would be the last word on the subject—his was the correct way to do it, because, after all, this was the way it was done in the American Constitution! These are just two almost random examples, of course. Perhaps the single most revealing fact, however, is this: before the American founding, democracy was mostly a term of opprobrium; since America, even the most undemocratic systems must attempt to present themselves as democracies—the compliment vice pays to virtue, certainly, but more significantly, an indication of how political virtue has come to be redefined.

The notion of the "natural rights republic" captures the specific character of the most important of the American innovations. This notion can best be explicated in terms of a distinction frequently drawn by political thinkers of the seventeenth and eighteenth centuries. In the preface to his massive book *On the Law of War and Peace*, the Dutch philosopher Hugo Grotius distinguished between two kinds of inquiries: political science as practiced by Aristotle and legal science as practiced by himself. Political science takes up such topics as "showing what course of action is practically advantageous," that is, questions of prudence or expediency, whereas legal science addresses "the question of what is lawful," particularly what is lawful under the law of nature. Where political science examines the advantageous, legal science explores the right: what, for example, is the nature and origin of sovereign authority, of property; what are the duties of submission a citizen owes his prince; what obligations do promises engender, and so on.[6]

Half a century later, John Locke stated a distinction not quite identical to the one Grotius had earlier propounded, but recognizably similar. According to Locke, "politics contains parts very different the one from the other, the one containing the original of societies and the rise and extent of political power, the other, the art of governing men in society." He placed his own *Two Treatises of Government* in the first, but not the second, category.[7] A century later, Thomas Jefferson restated and further modified the distinction. He identified two classes of political writing, "theory" and "practice." The first promulgates "the general principles of liberty and the rights of man, in nature and in society." He neglected to provide a general description of the second kind, but he supplied examples of each—again Locke's *Treatises* in the first class, and *The Federalist* in the second. Although the fit is not perfect, the distinction all three are making corresponds rather closely to the divide in current academic disciplines between political philosophy and political science.

We can employ this recurrent way of dividing up political knowledge in order to identify the particular innovations the

American founding generation instituted. At the level of "theory" (to use Jefferson's terminology), the Americans committed themselves to the natural rights or social contract theory of "the original of societies and the rise and extent of political power." The Americans surely did not invent or first discover the natural rights philosophy—they learned it from distinguished forebears such as Locke and the English "Cato"—but they made the most explicit and thoroughgoing commitment to that philosophy that had yet been carried out in practice anywhere. On the fiftieth anniversary of the Declaration of Independence, Jefferson identified that document as "an instrument pregnant with our own and the fate of the world," precisely because in it are proclaimed "the rights of man."[8]

At the same time, the Americans embarked upon a most thoroughgoing exploration of the political science suited to this new political philosophy. They developed a new science of institutions meant to embody and realize the principles of the natural rights theory of legitimacy. Again, they were not the first to pursue a new political science in service of the new political philosophy, for they had important predecessors in that enterprise; two who were especially important for the Americans of the founding era were Cato and Montesquieu. Important as these two were, they were unable to pursue the new political science as far as the Americans could, mainly because they were not writing on a clean slate. Both were heirs to political systems that did not leave them the freedom of speculation the Americans later had. The "new order of the ages" was possible in part because the new world supplied far greater opportunity for something like a new beginning.

The Americans developed a new political science in two areas in particular. In the first place, they, or rather chiefly, James Madison, discovered a new federalism, a new principle of union among quasi-independent political member units. The Americans also developed a new republicanism. Not only did they draw the conclusion that as a matter of practice republican (or, in our contemporary jargon, democratic) regimes were required in principle by the new philosophy of rights, but they also developed an almost altogether novel understanding of how institutions might be structured "in order to secure these rights." Here was where their relatively clean slate helped the Americans follow up uncompromisingly on the constitutional and institutional implications of the new rights philosophy while Locke, Cato, and Montesquieu, monarchies at their backs, were unable to do so.[9]

The present set of studies addresses for the most part only the first of these major American founding innovations: the natural rights philosophy. To a lesser extent, the New Republicanism, or one form of it at least, is also presented. These studies thus emphasize the political philosophy as opposed to the political science of the founding, but an implicit reference to the latter informs them throughout.[10]

In committing myself to the centrality of the natural rights orientation, I am implicitly locating myself within a more or less raging scholarly Battle of the Books over the initial character of the American regime. The debate is complex and the contestants ill-defined, but for present purposes it will suffice to accept the categories as most frequently found in the literature: was the American founding inspired by classical republican, Christian, Whig historical, Scottish enlightenment, or modern liberal conceptions?[11] Each of these alternatives has its champions and partisans, and like a thread of gold or, if you prefer, like a bad penny, the themes raised by this debate recur regularly throughout this book.

Thomas Pangle's recent review of these debates reminds us of the scholarly consensus prior to the emergence of the current dissensions. An earlier generation "attempted to interpret the thought of the Founders . . . in the light of a supposedly uninterrupted, steadily evolving Western tradition." This "tradition" traced back to Plato and Aristotle, gathered up Christianity (Thomas Aquinas, Richard Hooker), then early modern philosophy (Locke, Montesquieu) on its way to America; the tradition was held to be a continuous and harmonious if not quite seamless whole.[12] This consensus tradition has been too much undermined by subsequent research and reflection to be taken entirely seriously; the various elements have been shown to be more different and more hostile to each other than the consensus view allows. Yet the present formulation of the alternatives is too rigid. In terms of the debate my emphasis on natural rights positions me as a partisan of liberal modernity; that is neither an inaccurate nor an unwelcome categorization. Yet, without returning to the old eclecticism, I think the affirmation of liberal modernity need not imply the simple rejection of the other options. Like several other recent writers on the founding, I have my reservations about the terms of the debate. What are taken to be exclusive alternatives often are not. In sorting through the issues raised by the scholarly debate, the distinction between political philosophy and political science proves of great value, for systems of political thought taken to be political philosophy opposed to liberal modernity and natural rights (e.g., republicanism) are less that than systems of political science complementary to the natural rights/social contract theory.[13] Moreover, although liberal modernity at bottom derives from a different impulse than classical antiquity or Christianity, and indeed opposes some aspects and versions of both, it yet proved able to make peace with and indeed to assimilate important aspects of both.[14]

Indeed, in addition to explicating the natural rights/social contract theory as the founding generation understood it (Part I), and in addition to making a case for the primacy of natural rights liberalism for understanding the American founding (Part II), these studies attempt to bring out the truly remarkable occurrence that stands at the opening of the tradition: the assimilation by the natural rights philosophy of a variety of what are often thought to be competing traditions of political thought. Thus the question is not so much, is America liberal or Christian, old Whig or republican, as it is, how did the amalgam which swept up elements of all these traditions come to be, and just how do the various elements in the amalgam relate to each other? Thus Part II contains a complex double movement: it insists, on the one hand, on the differences between natural rights liberalism and these other positions, and it shows, on the other hand, how natural rights liberalism nonetheless was able to incorporate versions of them. My overall thesis is that the uniqueness of the American political tradition consists precisely in the unique amalgam so constructed. It is also my claim, only lightly developed here, that our understanding of the course of American political history is enriched not only by perceiving this amalgam but by perceiving the tensions that occur when various elements within the tradition pull away from each other. In the late twentieth century we surely have much experience of the latter. For instance, one of the "great debates" within our recent political life concerns the place of rights and rights-enforcing institutions like the Supreme Court vis-à-vis republican or democratic political institutions. This is a conflict to which we have found no clear answer because it involves two elements of the traditional amalgam moving out of harmony with each other. Likewise, the ongoing debate about abortion and other "life-style" issues at least in part reflects a similar disharmony among elements of the traditional amalgam. These studies do not explicitly address either historical or current instances of such disharmonies except in passing, but they do supply some insights into the why and wherefore of some of the most typical tensions that recur in American political life. Perhaps for a creative reader they supply some materials for fruitful reflection on how to respond to these disharmonies. Such at least is my hope.

Part One

A Political Philosophy of Natural Rights

No thread runs through the tangle of American politics more clearly than rights. When the Americans came to the most solemn moment of their founding activity, when they took the irrevocable step that they knew put at hazard their "lives, fortunes and sacred honor," they spoke the language of rights in order to justify themselves. The king's failure to "secure these rights" was precisely the ground for their right, even their duty, "to throw off [his] government."

Rights are not merely the oldest theme in our constitutional order, but the newest as well. The most important and far-reaching current constitutional controversy also centers on the question of rights: do citizens have rights beyond those explicitly embodied in the Constitution and laws? If so, does the Supreme Court have a warrant to enforce them? The current agitation of the question of rights in constitutional circles is matched by parallel concerns for human rights in the sphere of international relations and for the development of a theory of rights in the philosophic sphere. In all three arenas such questions as, What is a right? Where do they come from, and What rights are there? press themselves upon thoughtful persons.

At the same time, our national obsession with rights is paradoxical. Although the theme of rights obviously goes back to the founding era, those who are concerned with rights in the contemporary context hardly look to the founding period on the question, while those who study the founding have more or less abandoned the perspective of rights. Current discussions of "theories of rights" show remarkably little concern for the indigenous sources of the doctrine. While such a wide variety of rights theories have been developed in the recent philosophic literature that it would be difficult indeed to characterize what they all share, it is easy to notice what most omit: a consideration of rights in the perspective of the American founders. One is far more likely to find Kant cited as an authority than the Declaration of Independence. Indeed, one is nearly certain to find the one and not the other.

On the other hand, many leading students of the founding era have abandoned the perspective of rights in favor of a very different focus on republicanism, the latter understood in terms of a special tradition of "civic humanism" traced by its discoverers back to the Italian Renaissance and thence to Aristotle. In this light the Americans are seen not as political innovators but as the last flowering of an old tradition, itself antimodernist in character. Others look not to republicanism but to a "Protestant communalism," different from and even hostile to natural rights liberalism.

We lose something important on both sides of this paradox. By excluding the founders from our reflections on rights, we forsake potentially valuable guidance as we make our own attempts to "take rights seriously." We need not believe that we are bound to follow the doctrine of rights held by the framers in order to see the value of looking to their thoughts on the question. At the very least it can provide us a view with strong roots in our traditions, and with a real embodiment in the Constitution. Equally important, the original doctrine raises a strong claim to philosophical adequacy.

We lose something historically, also, when we attempt to grasp the founding without central reference to rights. The fact is, rights were the dominant and central political focus for the thinking and acting that produced the Constitution. As Forrest McDonald says, "Almost to a man, patriots were agreed that the proper ends of government were to protect people in their lives, liberty, and property."[1]

Central as rights have been to the American political experience, there is nonetheless reason to believe that they have been ill-understood. Current controversies over "fundamental rights" in constitutional law and "human rights" in international relations, as well as the shyness historians show towards the idea suggest intellectual confusion. Although we continue to speak the language of rights, it has to some degree become what Latin became to Catholic laypeople or Hebrew to most American Jews. We say the words but we are not quite certain what they mean.

Although the theme of rights recurs throughout the writings of the founding generation, one statement has achieved particular authority: the Declaration of Independence. As James Kloppenburg says, it is the "central document of the Revolution."[2] With that, we begin.

Chapter One

ON THE DECLARATION
OF INDEPENDENCE

I begin my treatment of the founding with the Declaration of Independence. There is good precedent for doing this, the most famous probably being Abraham Lincoln's Gettysburg Address. Lincoln's best explanation for identifying the Declaration as the beginning of the nation appeared in a lovely and quite moving meditation he wrote on a saying from the Book of Proverbs: "A word fitly spoken is like an apple of gold in a frame of silver." According to Lincoln, this proverb suited America perfectly: the frame was the Constitution, the apple of gold was the Declaration. The Declaration is thus the more precious thing, because, as Lincoln put it, "the frame is made for the apple, not the apple for the frame." The Declaration, suggests Lincoln, or the truths and principles of the Declaration, state the ends, the Constitution the means, of American political life.

Thus, Lincoln has led to the Declaration as the statement of the ends of American political life, at least as understood by the founders. But Lincoln's was perhaps an old-fashioned view, an overly reverent one. He never knew, for example, the historical work of Charles Beard. Beard's book, *An Economic Interpretation of the Constitution*, appeared in 1913, and after his book it is difficult to accept a naive and sentimental view of the founders, or to accept Lincoln's view of the relation between the Declaration and the Constitution. Beard denied that the Constitution is the means to the philosophical ends set forth in the Declaration. Rather, he argued, the Constitution is the means to the economic ends set forth in the framers' bank accounts and property portfolios. Beard and his followers concluded that the Constitution was not a fulfillment of the political aspirations of the Declaration but a rejection or falling away from them, and thus the Declaration, according to this view, is not the proper beginning point for a study of the constitutional order.[1]

A second challenge to beginning with the Declaration must be noted as well. It is almost the opposite of the first: the Declaration is not the beginning, for the beginning occurred long before the Declaration with, let us say, the Puritans or the Pilgrims or the English Whigs. The true and proper beginning is, then, perhaps, the Mayflower Compact, or the Declaration of Rights from the Glorious Revolution. Both challenges require serious consideration, but for now I will accept Lincoln's guidance, and begin with the Declaration.

An early editor of Thomas Jefferson's writings attested to our familiarity or even overfamiliarity with the Declaration of Independence when he called it "the paper which is probably the best known that ever came from the pen of an individual."[2] We have memorized it as school children, we have read it and listened to it on public holidays, we have looked to it when seeking to understand ourselves, taken refuge in it when seeking to justify ourselves, and argued about its meaning and application when facing divisive political questions. The traditional place of the Declaration in our national life has perhaps never been stated better than by Ralph Barton Perry:

> The Declaration of Independence contains the essential ideas of American democracy, and has remained its creed and standard throughout the years of its subsequent development. . . . These principles . . . have invariably been invoked in times of crisis or of patriotic fervor as constituting the mutual bond of American nationality.[3]

Yet this familiarity has had its negative effects as well. Long ago, already, Moses Coit Tyler claimed the Declaration suffered "the misfortune of being read too much," with the result, he thought, that it had become "hackneyed."[4] The Declaration's overfamiliarity has not made it any easier to understand, either, if we are to judge by a sampling of the recent literature on the document. That literature, taken as a body, shows almost no agreement as to its meaning. Some argue the Declaration is a democratic, even a "radically democratic" document;[5] others that it is aristocratic at core;[6] yet others that it is monarchic;[7] and finally some maintain it is politically neutral.[8] Some find the Declaration to be essentially radical and transforming;[9] others, essentially conservative.[10] Some find natural rights primary over duties;[11] others that duties retain a primacy over rights.[12] One recent interpreter identifies the Declaration as resting on a theory of the moral sense type, while others maintain that it rests on the kind of rationalist theory which was the chief opponent of moral sense thinking in the eighteenth century.[13]

The present state of confusion derives from a variety of causes, some of which are intrinsic to the Declaration itself. The Declaration, especially its theoretically most interesting parts, proceeds with the utmost concision; it seems, moreover, to pronounce its chief propositions to be self-evident truths, a claim which is not only difficult to understand in itself but which also appears to have discharged Jefferson from any felt obligation to explicate at greater length and with fuller defense the key points of the Declaration's theory. Moreover, concepts as notably equivocal as equality, natural law, unalienable right, and consent figure prominently in the Declaration without the kind of discussion which could serve to fix their meanings more precisely. Since the Declaration is so brief, since its key terms are so controversial yet so unexplained, it is no wonder that different readers should find different things in it.

Notwithstanding this confusion, I believe a persuasive and coherent account of it can be generated if we avail ourselves properly of appropriate aids to understanding. The Declaration may be concise in the extreme and its terms uncommonly equivocal, but they appear in a set context and structure which goes far towards fixing a meaning for the document. Through structure, each element provides a context for every other, and context supplies meaning. Structureless reading presents an open invitation—accepted far too frequently—to read out of context, or to read in.

Two other aids are also helpful. One is John Locke's political philosophy, especially his *Second Treatise of Government*. Many scholars deny the propriety of looking to Locke, but I hope to show that the Declaration, when structurally read, yields up an essentially Lockean teaching.[14]

A second aid derives from the character of the Declaration as shown by Jefferson's description of its "object": "Not to find out new principles, or new arguments, never before thought of," but rather to express "the American Mind." It rests, he said, on the "harmonizing sentiments of the day."[15] As Robert Webking points out, the Declaration's very language offers testimony to Jefferson's "harmonizing aim:

> the clarity of [the natural rights] doctrine in the minds of the Americans is indicated by the first phrase. The statement that "we hold these truths to be self-evident" . . . indicates that to the colonists the principled argument is well known and widely accepted.[16]

If that is true, then other expressions of the same theory ought to be visible in the public discourse of the day, as indeed is the case. Among other places, those "harmonizing sentiments" can be found in public documents, which, like the Declaration itself, clearly seek to express "the American mind" at the time of the Revolution. Particularly valuable are the Virginia Bill of Rights, drafted by Jefferson's friend George Mason in the same year that Jefferson wrote the Declaration, and the Massachusetts Bill of Rights, written in 1780 by John Adams, himself a member of the drafting committee for the Declaration.[17] These documents, like Locke's writings, can be helpful in corroborating and filling in the understanding we may achieve through a structural reading of the Declaration.

REREADING THE DECLARATION

The Declaration's first paragraph announces the intention of the document as a whole: to "declare the causes which impel [the Americans] to the separation" from Britain. The presentation of these causes occurs as a syllogism with the conclusion that "these

United Colonies are, and of Right ought to be, Free and Independent States." The major premise of that syllogism consists of a series of propositions, which, if true, would yield under certain conditions the conclusion that separation is legitimate or even necessary.

The minor premises are supplied by the list of acts of the king, often called the grievances. These are "facts" to be "submitted to a candid world," which are to establish that "the present King of Great Britain" has "in direct object the establishment of an absolute Tyranny over these States," a shorthand description for the situation held in the major premise to justify "altering or abolishing" an established political order.

Thus the parts of the Declaration are not disparate or disjointed as often asserted,[18] but are tightly constructed, like a geometric proof. The first paragraph announces what is to be proved, the second presents the major premises of the syllogism, or the "axioms" of the proof, the series of paragraphs detailing the grievances presents the minor premises, and the final paragraph draws the conclusion from the two sets of premises. The theoretical part of the Declaration cannot be seen as it sometimes is, as a series of glittering sentiments mainly present as a showpiece or introduction to the heart of things in the list of grievances.[19]

The Natural State: Equality

The theoretical paragraph setting forth the major premise of the Declaration's syllogism is itself tightly structured; it consists of six interrelated "truths" "held" by the Americans to be "self-evident." These truths on examination also prove to have a deductive structure. Nothing in the Declaration is more familiar or more vital than the first truth—"all men are created equal." And nothing in the Declaration is more controversial. Nor does any doctrine in it suffer so much from a failure to attend to the structure of the text, for the bare assertion of equality, when read out of context, together with the later reverberations of equality in American political life, has invited readers to project onto the text whatever meanings of equality appeal to them. So it has been asserted in the recent literature that equality means equality in rights, which the text pointedly does not say; that equality means equal in possession of the moral sense, which the Declaration nowhere mentions; equal in subjection to the moral law, equal in moral dignity, equal in claims on the public fisc, equal in claims to "life chances," equal in claims to political power (and thus that it mandates political democracy), or equal in wealth (and thus that it mandates socialism or a heavily redistributive state).

Such a carnival of speculation is unnecessary, however, if one attends to the other "truths" with which the "truth" about equality is juxtaposed, for these set a precise context and meaning for it. The series of six truths presents a temporal sequence, a kind of mini-historical narrative of the political experience of the human race. It begins with a prepolitical condition, that is, the condition before governments are "instituted among men"; tells of the institution (how and why governments come to be made); and then tells of the postinstitution phase (the corruption or falling away of government from its ends, followed by an altering or abolishing that culminates in a new institution). We have three distinct phases, then: civil society, precivil society, and for want of a better term, postcivil society. We might present the three phases, and the corresponding truths schematically as follows:

Pre-political	All men are equal	and endowed with certain unalienable rights
Political	Governments are instituted to secure these rights	deriving their just powers from consent of the governed
Postpolitical	If government becomes destructive of those ends, there is a right to alter or abolish it	and institute new government

Properly set in its context, "created equal" becomes distinctly less mysterious. By nature, or in nature, human beings are equal, that is, not subject to the rightful authority of any other human being. Neither God nor nature has established rule among human beings; they do this for themselves. Human beings, in other words, are not naturally political. By stating that men are created equal

in this sense, the Declaration is saying what some political philosophers said when they posited the original condition as a "state
of nature," a state in which no rightful authority exists by nature.

There is little foundation for the suggestion often made that
"created equal" means "possessing equal rights." Not that the Declaration denies equal rights for all, but it affirms them when it says
that all men "are endowed" with the same rights. If all men possess them, then it is superfluous to say that they are equal in possessing them.[20] The Declaration means something more precise
by "created equal" than that. Likewise, it means something more
precise than the claim that the "equality of human beings . . .
must lie in the simple fact of their humanity, of their belonging to
the same species."[21] This fact does not in any evident way imply
equality, nor does this interpretation adequately explicate the way
equality functions structurally in the Declaration.

In his rough draft of the Declaration, Jefferson is perhaps
clearer: "all men are created equal and independent." John
Adams very closely echoed this phrasing in the Massachusetts
Bill of Rights: "all men are born free and equal." The Virginia
Bill of Rights has the very similar "All men are by nature equally
free and independent." All four texts in turn follow Locke. In
claiming that "all Men by Nature are equal," Locke insists he
does not mean to affirm "all sorts of Equality." "Age, virtue, merit,
high birth, or benefits given or received may distinguish one
person from another. Yet all this consists with the equality, which
all Men are in, in respect of Jurisdiction or Dominion one over
another, which was the Equality I there spoke of." Thus, affirming
that men are created equal does not contradict Jefferson's well-
known commitment to the existence and political role of a "natural aristocracy."

> There is a natural aristocracy among men. The grounds of this
> are virtue and talents. . . . The natural aristocracy I consider as
> the most precious gift of nature for instruction, the trusts, and
> government of society.[22]

So long as the natural superiority of the natural aristocrats does
not generate a natural right to rule others, then this kind of
human inequality is perfectly compatible with the fundamental
equality affirmed in the Declaration.

Being equal means, then, that by nature no man is "subjected to the will or authority of any other man."[23] Locke in several places uses more or less the identical formula that appears in some of the American documents: "Men being . . . by Nature, all free, equal, and independent."[24] The point Locke and the Americans are making is a simple yet powerful one: whatever the many inequalities among human beings may be, whether of intelligence, virtue, beauty, or strength, none of them gives a rightful claim of authority over another.[25]

The Declaration is not saying that all men are equal in the sense that they should necessarily have an equal share of political power and, thus, that the only legitimate form of government is a strongly egalitarian democracy. A reading like that (in part) led Beard to deny the continuity between the Declaration and the Constitution, for the latter clearly did not institute as egalitarian a democracy as Beard's egalitarian understanding mandated. Yet he based his judgment on a misinterpretation of the Declaration, for according to it the very existence of government, i.e., of rightful authority, nullifies of itself the original equality.

The same democratic misreading pervades the classic study of the Declaration by Carl Becker. He believes that the egalitarian philosophy of the Declaration is democratic and anti-monarchical in principle, but then has difficulty understanding the Declaration's failure to denounce monarchy as such: in the list of grievances, it says only that "a prince whose character is thus marked by every act which may define a tyrant is unfit to be the ruler of a free people," implying that a king of another character, a nontyrannical king, would be fit. Likewise, the Declaration displays a remarkable flexibility regarding legitimate forms of government: it affirms a right in the people to make government "in such form, as to them shall seem most likely to effect their safety and happiness."[26]

As we shall see, the founders themselves engaged in a complex and deeply thoughtful debate over the implications of natural equality for civic life. The egalitarian answer certainly had its partisans, yet in no case did they understand the demands of political equality so simplistically and so inflexibly as some of their twentieth-century heirs.

It should also be apparent that the Declaration's proclamation of human equality is not a mandate for equality of condition. Inequalities of wealth, for instance, do not of themselves violate the principle of equality contained in the Declaration. Whatever merit this more egalitarian standard may have, it can not claim the authority of the Declaration.

The structural reading of the Declaration also raises serious questions about the adequacy of two important and closely related approaches to the American tradition, classical republicanism and communitarianism. The two overlap in their common opposition to liberal political philosophy. To simplify matters a bit, we might say the republicans object to the insufficiently political character of liberalism while the communitarians object to the insufficiently social character of liberalism. The republicans harken back to Aristotle and affirm the view they find in him of the dignity and human significance of political life and political participation.[27] Where liberalism speaks of abstract persons and their natural rights, republicanism would speak of citizens, their duties, and their civic virtue. Communitarians also frequently look back to Aristotle and his heirs and to their notion that the "human being is a social animal," social in nature, social in duties, attachments, and satisfactions. Like the republicans, the communitarians object to the individualism of liberalism, to "the picture of the freely choosing individual it embodies."[28]

The clash between liberalism and its opponents occurs along a number of fronts, only one of which implicates issues such as the meaning of equality in the Declaration of Independence. The republicanism thesis is the more historically oriented of the two and, because it has a comprehensive historical analysis attached to it, it will require more systematic attention later on, but here we might pause to note one piece of republican textual interpretation. Gordon Wood, one of the outstanding analysts of republican themes in the founding era, supplies a republican reading of the Declaration on equality as follows:

> a rough equality of conditions was in fact essential for republicanism. Since antiquity theorists had assumed that a republican state required a general equality of property-holding among its citizens. . . . Equality was related to independence; indeed,

> Jefferson's original draft for the Declaration of Independence stated that "all men are created free and independent." Men were equal in that no one of them should be dependent on the will of another.[29]

Wood correctly relates equality to independence, but he incorrectly identifies it as a description of a republican civil condition rather than an assertion of a precivil condition. He thus makes hash of the very language of the clause; not that all men *should be* equal, but that "all men *are created* equal." Wood has taken a descriptive statement and transformed it into a "should", and he has completely lost sight of "created," of the reference to the origin or initial situation it contains.[30]

Partisans of communitarianism have, for the most part, made much less strenuous efforts to claim the American tradition as their own; they more often concede it to have been liberal in inspiration, to have been, in Alasdair MacIntyre's phrase, part of "the Enlightenment project," and thus fundamentally individualist in character.[31] Yet a branch of communitarians does interpret the tradition, including the Declaration of Independence, as essentially communitarian.[32] Wilmoore Kendall, for one, concludes that

> the equality clause of the Declaration . . . simply asserts the proposition that all people who identify themselves as one . . . are equal to others who have likewise identified themselves. . . . The Declaration asserts that Americans are equal to, say, the British and the French. If the British and French can claim equality among the sovereign states of the world, so, too, can the Americans.[33]

When the Declaration declares all men to be created equal, it is not referring to individual human beings but to peoples, to communities. Such an interpretation, it should be clear, cannot survive a structural reading of the text, for that reading reveals equality to characterize the situation prior to the existence of peoples. Moreover, the same "men" who are said to be "created equal" also are said to be prepolitical possessors of rights. Surely these possessors of rights are human individuals. When Jefferson wished to speak of peoples, he knew perfectly well how to do so;

in the opening paragraph of the Declaration, for example, he spoke of the occasion when "it becomes necessary for one people to dissolve the political bands which have connected them with another." The juxtaposition of the first paragraph's "people" and the second paragraph's "all men" in such close contiguity surely signifies a difference in reference. Jefferson responds to a question about peoples—when can one people rightly sever its bonds with another?—with a statement about individuals. This is not such a non sequitur as it might appear, for Jefferson seeks natural principles of right, which leads him to seek the natural as such: human individuals are more natural than such human artifacts as states.[34]

For better or worse, then, the Declaration does appear to line up on the liberal rather than the republican or communitarian side of the battles over the character of America. Of course, this does not of itself imply that the theory of the Declaration suffers from the deficiencies imputed to it by the republicans and communitarians. One such deficiency frequently emphasized by critics of liberal individualism is the ahistorical character of the liberal position, well epitomized by the Declaration's notion of "created equal." Human beings never have lived in a state of nature; they are born into society and social life, they are born under subjection to authority. If the Declaration presents, as I said above, a "mini-history" of the race, it is frightfully bad history, say the communitarians.

This is a much misguided criticism, however, for the Declaration does not present literal or empirical history, but moral history. It is speaking of rightful or "just power," not power simpliciter. Nobody is merely born into moral subjection to political power, no matter how civilized and political their origins. The Declaration is not speaking of some primordial prepolitical condition in which human beings wander the forests "lonely as a cloud." "All men are created equal"—those born into society right under our noses just as much as those born in prehistory. The sociological or historical facts to which the above-mentioned critics advert are simply irrelevant to the Declaration's claim about equality and rule.[35] Here again Locke is helpful in understanding the point, for the Declaration follows the English philosopher in his revision of the late-sixteenth-century natural law theories of Richard Hooker. Hooker had spoken of "a time before civil society," identified by him with earliest biblical times, but a time abrogated with finality by the institution of government. For Hooker, the prepolitical was a once and nevermore condition, emphatically not shared in by his fellows of postbiblical times. Locke, on the other hand, "affirms that all men are naturally in that state, and remain so, till by their own consents they make themselves members of some political society."[36] He obviously is not referring to some mythical prehistory.

To affirm the state of nature, or this original equality, thus does not entail affirming some historically dubious condition; nor does it necessarily commit one to the view that human beings are naturally asocial. They are without political order by nature, but the Declaration makes no commitment regarding natural society, other than to imply that natural sociality, if there be such, is defective, for it requires supplementation by government, that is, by law backed up by force.[37]

The Natural State: Rights

The first characteristic of human beings in the state of nature is a lack, the lack of relations of rightful authority, of superiority and subordination, which lack constitutes the original equality or independence. But the second characteristic of persons in the state of nature is a possession; they are endowed with "unalienable rights." These rights precede the institution of government and exist prior to all human law. They are said in the sequel to be that for the sake of which human law and government exist. While human beings have rights in the state of nature, the Declaration makes no mention of their having duties or obligations or limits upon them in the state of nature. The Declaration thus provides no explicit support for the view, sometimes expressed, that the rights in the Declaration derive from prior duties or obligations.[38]

An unalienable right is one that cannot be taken away or given up, and a fortiori cannot be presumed to have been given up. Thus human beings should never accept any argument that they ought rightfully submit to any authority which threatens their rights on the grounds that they or their ancestors have somehow given up their rights.[39] Accordingly, the Virginia Bill of Rights speaks of "certain inherent rights, of which, when they enter into a state of society, they cannot by any compact deprive or divest their posterity" (Art. 1). Even if they consciously wish to give up their rights or their posterity's, they cannot do so. It is possible that men, wallowing in "monkish ignorance and superstition" consented and thereby made a government which neither they nor it understood to rest on their consent, nor to have as its purpose the securing of their rights. They might even have understood themselves to owe it unconditional obedience. The moment they come to understand their unalienable rights, that is, that there are certain claims they may always rightfully assert, they may rightfully take whatever action is needful, including withdrawing their consent and altering or abolishing the government, precisely because their rights are inalienable. The rightful power to unmake and remake government is the strongest and most persistent token of the inalienability of rights.

The source of the rights is somehow the Creator, but the text is quite inexplicit in saying how. Surely we do not learn of these natural rights to life, liberty, and the pursuit of happiness from the Bible, for in the biblical account we learn not of rights or claims that human beings have or raise in the original condition, but of free gifts to them from the Creator God and an injunction or duty laid on them.

Harry Jaffa has suggested that "the Declaration has reference to natural, not to revealed theology," which seems a very good suggestion in the light of the text's reference in its first paragraph to the "laws of Nature and of Nature's God."[40] The "Laws of Nature's God" are not quite identical to the "Laws of God."[41] The laws of God might, for example, include laws pertaining to nonnatural subjects (e.g., salvation, grace), and be known in nonnatural or nonrational ways (e.g., revelation). The God who legislates in the Declaration is a God who speaks through reason and acts in nature. His laws, then, are none other than the laws of nature themselves, as understood by human reason. If God acts only through the mediation of nature, then the Creator would seem to be nothing other than "Nature's God," and his action the action of nature.

That does not necessarily mean, however, that the rights with which human beings are endowed derive from the laws of nature and nature's God, even though some scholars do not hesitate to assert that they do.[42] The text, for one thing, does not say so. The Americans are entitled to a "separate and equal station among the Powers of the Earth" by the laws of nature and of nature's God, but nowhere does it say that these laws are the source of rights.

It does seem, however, that natural equality derives from the natural rights. Each person has rights to life, liberty, and the pursuit of happiness, his or her own life, liberty, and pursuit of happiness. With each person possessing these natural rights, it is impossible that any other person could naturally be the ruler of any individual, for a natural or rightful ruler would have authority inconsistent with such wide-ranging natural rights. That someone possessed a natural right to rule would imply that the ruled do not have full rights to determine the shape of their own lives. Thus the primordial possession of such wide-ranging natural rights implies natural equality.[43]

The Declaration unequivocally asserts that the purpose of government is the securing of rights, and only the securing of rights. Law, not the duties of others, is the source of security for rights. Only the rights of others are a proper boundary and limit on rights. A political society organized according to the principles of the Declaration is a society dedicated to servicing or allowing the pursuit by individuals of their rights. We need not pursue here the implications of this orientation to rights in the limited character of the government, in the essentially secular character of the society, in the primacy of the private sphere—in short, in the liberal polity that would result. The Declaration's rights doctrine empowers such features of liberalism as individualism, constitutional government, privatism, and the embrace of the idea that liberty, not virtue as such (the good state of soul of the individual), not salvation, and not glory form the legitimate end of the liberal state.[44] Political life conducted under the auspices of the rights philosophy is in principle open to the potentially varied and variable goals of its citizens; within limits about which neither the founders nor we have arrived at a consensus, human beings are to be left free to "pursue" their own happiness, to follow their own bent. This principled commitment to liberty has produced, among other things, a tremendous economic development, for when left to their own bent Americans sought material betterment.[45]

For all their importance, however, the Declaration is noticeably reticent on the source, nature, and specific contours of the rights. For more light on these topics we must consider reasonings not contained in the Declaration. The Declaration's near silence about the source and nature of rights also limits what one can say about the table of rights provided. Why these rights? Since the three rights specified in the text are said to be "among" the inalienable rights, it is clear there must be others, but what they are or how we discover others is not stated. In other places, Jefferson mentions other rights—a right to property, to expatriate, to freedom of conscience. The Declaration itself provides little further insight on this point, however.

The Political State

Everything about the institution of government follows deductively from the truths about the prepolitical state we have already discussed. Government is instituted to secure rights: that follows not only from the fact that rights are insecure without government, but also from the fact that there is no supervening claim over rights in the name of which coercion could rightfully be employed. The security of rights can be the only legitimate end of political society. Likewise, since neither God nor nature provides for rule, this must be done by human beings themselves: governments must derive "their just powers from the consent of the governed," a derivation known in the philosophic tradition as a social contract. Since government exists to secure rights and only for that purpose, governments which fail to secure rights can have no legitimacy. The people, therefore, must possess "the right to alter or abolish governments" that have lost legitimacy. This so-called "right to revolution" must be "among" the other rights not earlier specified in the list of primary rights. Given its relation to the primary rights, it too must be an "unalienable right." Thus the right to alter or abolish is a universal right, valid for all political societies, quite independent of their particular histories. A nation with a history of absolutist and tyrannical rule is therefore not morally disbarred by its own history and traditions from reclaiming its inherent rights. It is as legitimate for France or Haiti to assert the right to alter or abolish, as it is for the English colonies in America. Altering, and especially abolishing, government leaves rights once again insecure, as they were prior to the existence of government. The new situation of no government implies the same "right to institute new government" as the "original" situation did.

Governments are needed to secure rights because they are otherwise insecure. What makes them insecure is not stated. Within the social contract philosophic tradition there were a variety of answers given to that question, and the Declaration pointedly withholds judgment. The character of the government needed as a remedy for the insecurity of rights depends, to some degree, on the nature of the threats. For example, so deep in the nature of man is the source of rights-threatening behavior, according to Thomas Hobbes, that only a very powerfully armed state can hope to secure rights. On the other hand, Locke finds threats to rights to be less severe and to be more related to natural scarcity. The political solution for Locke is a far milder government with greater emphasis on securing the conditions for overcoming natural scarcity. And of course other alternatives existed as well. Perhaps the Declaration remains silent on the nature and severity of the threat to rights because that topic escaped the "harmonizing sentiment of the day."

The Declaration's silence on the nature of the threat to rights may have something to do with the openness on kinds or forms of legitimate government that we have already noticed. The Declaration is open on form notwithstanding its pronouncement that governments "derive their just powers from the consent of the governed." As Martin Diamond points out, and as the structure of the text confirms, this affirmation of consent applies particularly to the origin or institution of government.[46] However, governments do not "derive" their power once and for all at some originating moment.[47] Governments exercise powers derived or delegated from their constituents, and thus all just power is always derived from the "consent of the governed." That a government derives its powers from the consent of the governed does not mean, however, that governments necessarily operate democratically or through representative assemblies.[48] Again, Locke helps make clear what the Declaration might mean by "consent":

> What shall be understood to be a sufficient Declaration of a Man's consent, to make him subject to the Laws of any government. . . . Every man, that hath any possession, or enjoyment, of any part of the Dominions of any Government, doth thereby give his tacit consent, and is as far forth obliged to Obedience to the Laws of that Government, during such Enjoyment, as any one under it; whether this his Possession be of Land, to him and his Heirs for ever, or a Lodging only for a Week; or whether it be barely travelling freely on the Highway; and in Effect, it reaches as far as the very being of any one within the Territories of that Government.[49]

So far is this from being a democratic doctrine, that it hardly seems to be a doctrine of consent at all. It is worth noting that the consent, such as it is, outlined by Locke is not limited to the originating moment of a government, or even to that one moment when some person becomes a member of or consents to a civil society.

But why make so much of consent if there is so little to it? Is there any condition or act which counts as not consenting? Locke's doctrine of consent, bare as it might be, yet implies an affirmation of some real significance: that all governments rest on consent is another way of saying that all government is a human artifact, constructed from human agreement or conventions, and, when the human situation is properly understood, serving certain ends only. Nonconsent, or the withdrawal of consent, is precisely what happens when the government is perceived no longer to serve the purposes for which it has or should have been constructed, and people act to alter or abolish it. Another implication of the Lockean doctrine of consent would appear to be an inalienable right to emigrate.

Thus the Declaration, following Locke, can affirm the continuing basis of political power in consent and yet not commit itself to democratic forms. The Declaration, of course, is not anti-democratic. It endorses whatever form the people settle on as "most likely to effect their safety and happiness." It is well known that Jefferson and many other founders judged that popular or republican government was the form most likely to satisfy the ends set forth in the Declaration, but they did not render that judgment in the Declaration itself.

To say, as one scholar does, that from the point of view of the principles of the Declaration the English monarchy is itself a form of republicanism obscures as much as it elucidates.[50] According to the social contract theory of the Declaration and of Locke, it is true, the king's authority rests on the consent of the people governed. Thus, Jefferson could refer to the king, in his *Summary View of the Rights of British America*, as "no more than the chief officer of the people." Nonetheless, neither the Declaration, nor Locke, nor common sense itself finds it valuable to blur the real difference between a monarchy, or "mixed regime," *jure populo*, and what Madison in the *Federalist* calls "wholly popular forms." Harry Jaffa well summarizes the state of the issue: "This does not mean, however, that the Declaration did not envisage that a variety of forms of government—including a variety of forms of republicanism—might from time to time receive the people's sanction" and thus be legitimate under the principles of the Declaration.[51]

It is striking how far we in the late twentieth century tend to reverse the Declaration's priorities regarding government. The ends of government—the security of rights—are, according to the Declaration, set and certain; the means of government, the form, however, may vary. The criterion of good government has far more to do with securing the end than with some universal test of form. We, on the other hand, are uncertain about the ends that legitimate government should pursue but are far more certain of the necessity of the democratic form. This shift in emphasis is in part a result of the further reflections the founders brought to bear on the problems of "the natural rights polity" (the subject of Part II of this study).

The Declaration's affirmations regarding such matters as consent and the right to revolution indicate with special clarity what kind of historical narrative the Declaration is presenting. It is a "history" to be sure, and not a mere "ought," but it is a history of a peculiar kind. The founders knew that the historical record of mankind did not entirely support the account of the origins they were providing. Many political communities, for example, lack the self-understanding that political authority derives from the consent of the governed, or that political authority exists "to secure these rights." The Declaration gives a history as that history would be lived by human beings who understood the truth of their situation in nature correctly; the Declaration's history is thus a rational reconstruction rather than literal history; it is not, for all that, utopian, however, for it can become literal history the moment people understand and act on the fundamental truths of politics and morality.[52]

As rational reconstruction, the Declaration implies a theory of justice relevant to the civil societies established according to its precepts. Human beings who knew what they were doing would consent only to a government that promised to secure their rights; they would not consent to a government that threatened to subordinate their rights to the rights of others or the welfare of others per se. Each would require that each get out of government what each is in it for—security of his or her own rights. This implies that everyone has an equal claim on the government for protection; it means government has an obligation not to sacrifice some to the others. Both majority and minority tyranny are abhorrent. The Declaration stands prima facie against class or race politics.

The so-called right to revolution is straightforward enough but indicates how different the point of view and political attitude of the Declaration is from the attitudes about politics prevailing earlier. According to the earlier view, the most pressing need was to teach not rights but duties, to teach men to defer to their "betters."[53]

REREADING THE READERS OF THE DECLARATION

A responsible effort to interpret the Declaration as the foundation statement of the American political order requires a consideration of other recent efforts to construe the Declaration. Such a consideration has two purposes. Because so much novel, interesting, and varied work has appeared in the past two decades, any new interpretation must learn from and establish itself in relation to this work. Secondly, a consideration of the other readers of the Declaration will allow me to expand and deepen a few of the most significant topics developed earlier.

Equality

Two of the more interesting of the recent studies of the Declaration, Garry Wills's *Inventing America* and Paul Eidelberg's *On the Silence of the Declaration of Independence,* raise important alternative understandings. Wills quite explicitly attempts to free the Declaration from all ties to John Locke, and instead to trace Jefferson's chief inspiration back to the Scottish Enlightenment thinker Francis Hutcheson. Wills's goal is at least partly political in the mode of contemporary communitarianism—to challenge the received view of America as Lockean in its origins and therefore as individualistic and "proto-capitalist" at its roots. The Hutcheson with whom he would replace Locke, provides, Wills believes, a more communitarian and moral foundation for the American polity than Locke does.[54]

Wills's intention is serious, but his interpretation of equality in the Declaration stands as a particularly egregious example of the dangers of structureless reading. In line with his general attribution of authority to Hutcheson, Wills relates the Declaration's claim about equality to the "moral sense," a natural faculty Hutcheson posits as the source of moral knowledge. As the eye, the visual sense, perceives color, so the moral sense perceives moral qualities: so argues Hutcheson. Wills maintains that "created equal" in the Declaration means equality in the moral sense, "man's highest faculty."[55]

> To say that men are equal in their exercises of this faculty is to define them as *essentially* equal. . . . This separate faculty, equal in all, makes differences in other capacities comparatively minor, unable to reach the rights of self-regulation.[56]

Wills rests his case, however, on often only peripherally relevant evidence. For example, Jefferson frequently speaks of the moral sense or "the heart" as the basis of moral behavior and moral judgment; Jefferson found the black slaves unequal to whites in many physical and intellectual matters, but their equal in heart, a finding that Wills believes to have been decisive for Jefferson's strong denunciations of slavery. But Wills fails to produce any evidence that Jefferson saw equality in the moral sense to be the sort of equality he meant in the Declaration. For that matter, he never produces any evidence that Jefferson finds human beings equal in the moral sense; he himself quotes in his text passages in which Jefferson unmistakably speaks of inequalities in the moral sense. Jefferson writes in one place of "the want or imperfection of the moral sense in some men."[57] Wills points out also that according to Jefferson the moral sense may be "stunted" in some.[58] How this conforms to Wills's insistence on "literal equality" is difficult to say.[59]

Moreover, Wills's identification of equality in the Declaration with equality in the moral sense conflicts with many pieces of evidence about what the Declaration's text means. It misses the structural features of the text; it conflicts with Jefferson's rough draft, with its "equal and independent"; it ignores the parallel texts of the time, e.g., the Virginia and Massachusetts bills of rights, which quite clearly do not mean equality in the moral sense when they affirm equality.

Paul Eidelberg also goes astray through failure to attend to structure. "Before the laws of nature, before a universal moral law," Eidelberg says, "all men are necessarily equal."[60] Or, as he restates his point, "Since the law of nature is 'diffused among all men,' all men are to that extent equal."[61] But this has much the sound of a trivial proposition: men are equal to the extent of being equally under the moral law and so "necessarily equal" only in the sense in which one could say that since all men are under the moral law, all men are under the moral law.

Eidelberg attempts to draw a less trivial conclusion when he later restates his position: "The Declaration proclaims that all men are subject to the same universal moral law, as a consequence of which no group of men can rightly rule other men as if they were an inferior species."[62] He comes closer here to the authentic sense of equality in the Declaration, but his formulation nonetheless has two serious difficulties. First, the Declaration does not say that men are equal in being equally subject to the law of nature. The text applies the law of nature to peoples but not to all men. It also attributes to all men certain "unalienable rights," but these are not said or implied to be derivative from the laws of nature. It attributes to all men an equality, but neither is this said to follow from the law of nature.

The second difficulty with Eidelberg's version of equality appears if one notices that it does not follow from the proposition that all men are equally subject to "the same universal moral law" that none can rightly rule any other, unless the moral law in question specifies that. What Eidelberg says makes about the same sense as saying, "since all employees are under one salary schedule, they all receive equal salaries." Something more than the mere existence of the moral law must establish equality; it must be shown to be the content of the moral law, and Eidelberg has not done that.

Rights

The most interesting as well as the most challenging of recent discussions of rights in the Declaration of Independence is contained in Morton White's *Philosophy of the American Revolution.* The great interest of his argument lies in his strenuous effort to elucidate the meaning, foundation, and source of the rights affirmed in the Declaration. White finds the rights to be derivative from duties established by the moral law of nature, a not uncommon conclusion in itself, but he goes further in explicating and defending that view than anyone else who has advanced it.

White looks to the Swiss eighteenth-century natural law writer Jean Jacques Burlamaqui as the source of "the logical substructure upon which Jefferson built." It must be said at the outset that the external evidence connecting Burlamaqui to Jefferson and the Declaration is hardly even slender. Jefferson owned Burlamaqui's book, but he never singled it out for explicit mention in connection with the Declaration, nor did he recommend it to others as valuable reading in law or politics. Probably more of the writers of the revolutionary generation cited Burlamaqui than Wills's favorite, Hutcheson, but he still does not have the stature, for Americans, of Locke, Sidney, and the writers of the Whig tradition, or of Blackstone in the juridical literature.[63] The strongest connection White can show between Jefferson and Burlamaqui lies in the fact that Jefferson put extracts into his commonplace book from James Wilson's 1774 pamphlet, "Consideration on the Nature and Extent of the legislative Authority of the British Parliament." According to White, Wilson "leaned heavily on Burlamaqui" in that pamphlet, but, while it is well known that Wilson was an admirer of the Swiss jurist, White's claim is quite untenable for this particular work.[64] In a rather long and learned work, Wilson cites Burlamaqui only twice, on points far removed from the matters for which, White claims, Jefferson relied on Burlamaqui. Wilson relies, rather, on Blackstone and other expositors of English law, quite understandably, considering the topic of his pamphlet. Jefferson could hardly have imbibed Burlamaqui's doctrines on moral rationalism and the moral sense, on the content and basis of the law of nature, or on the nature of rights from this work by Wilson, nor could he have been led to Burlamaqui's work itself by any special prominence or interest Wilson took in him.[65]

Despite the absence of direct evidence of a link between Burlamaqui and the Declaration, White looks to him as the source and best explication of its doctrine of rights. The Swiss jurist supplied a natural law teaching of the rationalist sort in which he claimed to be able to deduce the precepts of the law of nature from rational knowledge of God and of the essence of man. For Burlamaqui, the precepts of the law of nature are derivative from more fundamental knowledge of God and of human essence.

According to Burlamaqui, human beings can acquire rational knowledge of a creating God, benevolent and legislative. God is the source of human nature or essence, and has endowed humanity with certain promptings towards fulfilling that essence. God has left human beings free to fulfill their nature through choice in a way that he has not left other beings free, but it is nonetheless God's will that human nature be fulfilled.

Human nature and the nature of its fulfillment can be grasped by looking at three "states" or conditions, or relations, in which God placed humanity and from which derive the main precepts of the laws of nature. Human beings (1) stand in relation to God as creatures, and from that derive certain duties toward God; (2) exist as individuals with certain strivings toward preservation and happiness, from which derive duties to self; (3) exist as part of the human race, from which derive certain social duties.[66]

White gives a detailed example of the derivation of the duty to preserve life.

> He [Burlamaqui] first asserts that God made life *part of the essence of man*—that being his version of the statement that God created man. He next asserts that God is good, wise, omnipotent, and does nothing in vain. Therefore, Burlamaqui is able to assert that since God made life part of the essence of man, God must have proposed the preservation of life as an end of his creature, man, because God would have given man life in vain if God had not proposed man's preservation of that life as one of man's ends. Burlamaqui's next step is to assert that since God proposed the preservation of life as an end of man, God *wills* that man should preserve his life. . . . We are now at a point where we may assert that since man has been created as an essentially living being, he has the duty to preserve his life.[67]

White then finds it but a "trifling step" from this argument to what Jefferson said in his rough draft: "from that equal creation they derive rights inherent and unalienable, among which are the preservation of life."[68]

But that mere "trifling step" appears to be more like a long leap, for it requires moving from the duties that Burlamaqui derives to the rights that Jefferson announces. White attempts to make that leap by means of a simple but ingenious argument. Every duty to do "x" implies also a right to do "x," according to the principle that what one ought to do, one may do.[69] The sort of right that derives from a duty obviously differs from the sort of right Hobbes had in mind when he defined right as "a liberty to do or to refrain from doing something." A right derivative from a duty would not involve a liberty to do or to refrain, only a right to do or to refrain, whichever one's duty prescribed.[70] White believes then that he has found a way to take that "trifling step" from a Burlamaquian duty to a Jeffersonian right.

But one may trip even in taking a short step, and much evidence conjoins to indicate that White has lost his footing here. First, his construction does not mesh well with the text of the Declaration. The text, after all, says "right" and not "duty." Why would Jefferson, his drafting committee, the Congress, the men responsible for all the similar documents and statements produced at the time continually use the weaker and more derivative expression, rights, over the stronger and more primary expression, duty? If they meant to endorse a system of thought which derived their rights from their duties in the way White describes, would they not be far more likely to make the argument in terms of the much stronger claims available to them, given the fact that right so understood merely means that one may do one's duty? Did the Americans mean to say "all men are endowed by their Creator with certain inalienable permissions to do their duties, that among these permissions are the permissions to do our duty to preserve our life, to do our duty to preserve our liberty, and to do our duty to pursue happiness?" Merely to restate the text read in White's way is to reveal the rhetorical and psychological senselessness of stating the Burlamaquian doctrine in this way. So much better would it be to say it in a more Burlamaquian way: according to the law of nature, men possess certain duties, and our actions here must be understood as our effort to fulfill our duties. That they did not say it that way suggests very strongly that that is not what they were attempting to say.

White anticipated this kind of criticism by raising "the interesting question whether, if a right is implied by a corresponding duty, we are obliged to make that implication explicit."[71] The answer to White's question might depend on circumstances, I suppose, but under the circumstance of the Declaration I should think that a person would "make that implication explicit," for the Declaration responds to an implicit challenge: by what warrant do you take the step of separating from Great Britain? The warrant, according to White's construction, is supplied by the duty; the right is simply and weakly derived from it. Again we can see the point if we translate "right" in White's way: we are taking this step because we have a warrant to do our duty, and doing our duty requires taking this step. That is, under challenge the proper response is the warrant, and the warrant is the duty.

White, to the contrary, sees this as a case which raises the question, "If you know that you may assert the logically stronger of two propositions, should you always assert the stronger?"[72] He answers his own question by saying that "under certain circumstances one is entitled to say less than what one knows about a certain matter."[73] Although it is difficult to argue with White's general claim here, my point is that the circumstances of the Declaration cannot reasonably be held to be among those where one would be entitled to say "logically less, or weaker."

White finds much support for his Burlamaquian reading of rights from the rough draft's claim "that from that equal creation they derive rights inherent and inalienable." He reads that clause so as to emphasize the "creation": the rights derive (via unstated duties) from the creation, roughly on the model of Burlamaqui's argument outlined above. But White almost certainly misreads this passage from the rough draft, for in its context it is the *equality* at the beginning from which Jefferson attempts to derive the rights rather than from the creation itself. If the text meant what White wants it to mean, it would much better read as follows; "that all men are created, and from that creation derive rights [or better yet, duties]."

As little supportive of his reading as the rough draft is, nonetheless it is far more so, by his own testimony, than the final draft. That in itself speaks with great authority against his construction (for why would the drafters change the text so that it no longer makes the point they wish to make?). White's reading of rights does not sort well with the parallel statements in the Virginia and Massachusetts bills of rights. The one document says that "all men are by nature equally free and independent, and have certain inherent rights"; the other document says that "all men are born free and equal, and have certain natural, essential and unalienable rights."[74] Neither document mentions the creation at all, but rather speaks of equality by "nature," or "by birth." In both documents it is the original equality that is carefully being affirmed, as it appears was also the case in both versions of the Declaration.

Probably the most significant difference between what a genuinely Burlamaquian Declaration of Independence might look like and the one Jefferson actually wrote lies in what each says about the ends of government. It is altogether implausible that Burlamaqui could affirm that the end of government is the securing of rights in general, and in particular the rights of life, liberty, and the pursuit of happiness. The almost total differences in character and spirit of the doctrines of Burlamaqui and the Declaration appears clearly if we listen to the Swiss writer's discussion of the "end of law:"

> Laws are made to oblige subjects to act according to their real interests and to choose the surest and best way to attain the end they were designed for, which is happiness. With this view the sovereign is willing to direct them better than they could themselves, and gives a check to their liberty, lest they should make a bad use of it contrary to their own and the public good.[75]

Burlamaqui's notion of the ends of law is more or less what we would expect from a thinker who adheres to a natural-law teaching of the sort to which he adheres. The law, or civil society, rather, has the purpose of enforcing the "duties of man," and in particular that most comprehensive duty to happiness, rather than securing the "rights of man." Accordingly, the law does not take its task to protect individuals in their own pursuits of happiness, as freely and individually sought, but rather "directs them better than they could themselves" toward happiness. Laws do not have as a primary goal the securing of the right to liberty, but rather give "a check to their liberty" for their own good as well as the good of others.

We can again perceive the distance between Burlamaqui and the Declaration when we look to some of the natural duties (translatable easily, according to White, into rights) which he derives from the natural law. White dwells on the relationship to God only in order to develop some of the Burlamaquian duties to self and others, but it is worth looking at that relationship for what it says about duties to God. Once we understand the nature of God, and of ourselves as creatures, "we ought necessarily to acknowledge the sovereign perfection of the Supreme Being, and our absolute dependence on him. . . . they should honor, love, adore, and obey him." Piety, according to Burlamaqui, is "the assemblage of all these sentiments, well engraved in the heart." There is then a natural duty to piety.

> Piety, if it be real, will show itself externally two different ways, by own works, and by outward worship. . . . External worship, as well public as private is derived [from piety]. Reason presents it as a duty of indispensable necessity.[76]

Now surely this "duty of indispensable necessity" would find a place in a general statement like the Declaration if written by a convinced Burlamaquian, but the Declaration, and the American polity built upon it, are chary, to say the least, about arming government with any duties to promote and establish "external worship."

If the Declaration is a version of Burlamaqui it is a highly selective one, omitting matters of the highest importance in Burlamaqui's doctrine and affirming things that Burlamaqui was altogether unwilling to affirm. Burlamaqui as inspiration for the Declaration works as little as Hutcheson does.

We appear then to be left with the old view as the most plausible view, that Locke inspired the Declaration and that it has a basically Lockean meaning. That conclusion is important not because one ought to read the Declaration by reading Locke; to the contrary, a structural reading of the Declaration can take us very far towards an understanding of the Declaration. The Declaration presents a structurally and logically coherent set of propositions, but it nowhere makes clear the source and foundation of the rights that it proclaims. Instead of giving further reasons for the most fundamental of its truths, the Declaration announces, "We hold these truths to be self-evident."

Chapter Two

NATURAL RIGHTS AND THE
QUESTION OF SELF-EVIDENCE

In the Declaration of Independence, Jefferson declared the existence of rights, along with the related propositions about equality and so on, to be "self-evident truths." That claim of self-evidence has puzzled most readers who have paused to reflect on it. Could Jefferson really believe that such theses about politics as he proceeded to list were "self-evident"? As Dennis Mahoney has well pointed out: these truths were "foreign to the opinions of most of the people and peoples in the world" when Jefferson pronounced them "self-evident."[1]

Jefferson's claim is often taken today as evidence of the intellectual and political innocence of the simpler days of the Founding. Says Henry Steele Commager, for example, "There was indeed a simplicity in the moral standards and in political faith—a simplicity reflected . . . in the language of the time: 'we hold these truths to be self evident.'"[2] Since 1776, political developments have made it clear that the founders' Enlightenment principles would not sweep all before them, and various intellectual developments have made it difficult to affirm confidently any moral or political truths, much less "self-evident" ones. "We would not today," says Commager, "assume a body of 'self-evident truths,' certainly not in the arena of government or politics."[3] Sanford Levinson puts it even more strongly: "it is simply not open to an intellectually sophisticated modern thinker to share Jefferson's world."[4] Unable to believe in the "self-evidence" of those truths, a friendly critic of the Declaration like Eva Brann finds Jefferson to be "un- or anti-philosophical." She claims that

41

the Declaration "does not contain coherent, deep-rooted truths." It is rather, she says, "a benign text" written in a "peculiar, curtailed or shallow mode." What Jefferson takes to be self-evident truths are, she says, no more than opinions, "unthought out thoughts."[5] Does the appeal to self-evidence mean, then, as Sanford Levinson seems to think it means, that "to believe in Jefferson's Declaration of Independence [today] . . . would require a leap of faith indeed"?[6]

PRACTICAL SELF-EVIDENCE

What does Jefferson mean by "self-evident truths"? One interpretation that comes readily to the minds of modern readers, including some of those who have been critical or bemused by Jefferson's use of the term, is self-evident in the sense of evident or obvious to all. Jefferson himself gave much warrant for this reading, for in an 1825 letter to Henry Lee he recounted "the object of the Declaration of Independence" not to be "to find out new principles, or new arguments, never before thought of," but rather "to place before mankind the common sense of the subject, in terms so plain and firm as to command their assent." Above all, he meant the Declaration "to be an expression of the American mind" and to rest it on "the harmonizing sentiments of the day."[7]

And yet there are two good reasons at least to pause before accepting self-evidence in the loose sense of "obvious to all." That interpretation conflicts with another important piece of testimony from Jefferson on the truths of the Declaration. In the very last letter of his life, regretfully declining an invitation to appear in Washington at the fiftieth anniversary celebration of the Declaration of Independence, Jefferson restated his view of the lasting significance of that document:

> May it be to the world, what I believe it will be . . . , the signal of arousing men to burst the chains under which monkish ignorance and superstition had persuaded them to bind themselves. . . . All eyes are opened, or opening to the rights of man. The general spread of the light of science has already laid open to every view the palpable truth, that the mass of mankind has

not been born with saddles on their backs, nor a favored few booted and spurred, ready to ride them legitimately, by the grace of God.[8]

The truths about rights are not obvious or evident to all, are not the universal "common sense of the subject," but come after the sway of "monkish ignorance and superstition," which still rules those parts of the world not yet sufficiently enlightened. The "light of science," not "common sense," brings acceptance of these truths. And in 1776 Jefferson had even less reason to believe that the Declaration's principles could appear "the common sense of the subject" to all human beings, for by 1826 those principles were established in a far wider area—because of the American and then the French Revolutions and their aftermaths—than they were in 1776.[9]

A second consideration that speaks against interpreting "self-evident" as "obvious or evident to all," is the fact that "self-evident truths" had a significance as a technical philosophic term in the eighteenth century that it has lost for most twentieth-century readers. Indeed, the nature of self-evidents was one of the matters greatly in dispute during the titanic philosophic battles of the seventeenth and eighteenth centuries, of which Jefferson and the Americans were to some degree the heirs.

Jefferson probably first learned a philosophic doctrine of self-evidence in the important eighteenth-century logic text by William Duncan, one of the teachers of his teacher, William Small. According to Wilbur Samuel Howell, Duncan's logic text identified self-evidents in terms of their function in syllogisms—they serve as the most fundamental sort of premise, what in mathematics are called axioms.[10] The usage of the "self-evident truths" idea in the Declaration comports very well with that thrust of Duncan's text, as the overall structure of the Declaration makes clear. The whole is in form a syllogism, intending to establish the conclusion that "these United Colonies are, and of Right ought to be Free and Independent States." The theoretical paragraph contains the "major premise" of the syllogism. Those propositions are labeled by Jefferson, in accordance with Duncan's presentation of "self-evident truths," as the axioms or most basic premises from which deductive reasoning may proceed.[11]

Duncan's functional notion of self-evidents parallelled some very traditional ideas. Thomas Aquinas, for example, had said that "the precepts of the natural law are to the practical reason what the first principles of demonstration are to the speculative reason, because both are self-evident principles."[12] There must be some starting point for valid reasoning which is valid prior to reasoning, and the truth of which must be self-evident. Thus the motive for calling the fundamental premises of an argument "self-evident truths."

Beyond that functional parallel, however, there was important conflict within the philosophic tradition over the status of self-evidents. Where Thomas, for example, had maintained that "the precepts of the natural law, . . . are the self-evident principles" for the practical (i.e., moral) reason, John Locke had insisted that there are "no innate practical principles," a claim meant to reject the Thomistic version of natural law.[13] Locke also contested Thomas's view of the role of self-evidents in theoretical reasoning.[14]

Duncan sided with Locke in this dispute, for he defined self-evidents just as Locke had done. Duncan:

> When any Proposition is offered to the view of the Mind, if the Terms in which it is expressed are understood; upon comparing the Ideas together, the Agreement or Disagreement asserted is either immediately perceived, or found to be beyond the present reach of the understanding. In the first case the Proposition is said to be *self-evident* and admits not of any Proof, because a bare attention to the Ideas themselves, produces full conviction and Certainty; nor is it possible to call in anything more evident, by way of Confirmation. . . . From what has been said it appears, that Reasoning is employed only about demonstrable Propositions.[15]

Locke:

> Knowledge . . . consists in the perception of the agreement or disagreement of *ideas;* now where that agreement or disagreement is perceived immediately by itself, without the intervention or help of any other, there our *knowledge is self-evident.*[16]

Then, much nearer in time to the Declaration, the idea of self-evident moral principles had a great revival in the philosophies of English dissenters like James Burgh and Richard Price. To these writers, self-evidents were not merely the immediately grasped agreement or disagreement of ideas of things but were the source of genuine knowledge of the things, moral things included. There is a "power within us that *understands;* the *intuition* of the mind."[17]

However much these notions of self-evidence differed from each other, they all shared one defining element: self-evidents are underived and underivable from any other truth, proposition, or idea. Price, for example, spoke of "self-evident truths" as all ideas "we discover without making use of any process of reasoning." Duncan had also emphasized that "reasoning is employed only about demonstrable propositions." It is this quality of underivability that led these otherwise different authors to retain the term "self-evident."

Given the prominence of the discussions of self-evidence in the philosophic literature, much of which Jefferson certainly knew, it is likely that he had in mind a relatively precise notion of self-evidence when he put the phrase in the Declaration. What Jefferson must have meant, at a minimum, is captured in Martin Diamond's formulation of "self-evidence" in the Declaration:

> it means that the evidentness of the truth is contained within the truths themselves. That is, these truths are not to be reached at the end of a chain of reasoning: they are not the fruit of supporting evidence, inference and argument.[18]

Through the years, of course, most famously by John C. Calhoun, and by various writers cited above, the self-evidence and often even the truth of the Declaration's principles have been doubted.[19] Remarkably, the language and structure of the Declaration itself, if read attentively, support some of those doubts. We must first listen to the text: "We *hold* these truths to be self-evident. . . ." Not only is the "we" who holds them emphasized, but so is the fact of holding them to be self-evident. To say "we hold these truths to be self-evident" is not the same as to say "these are self-evident truths." "We hold" insinuates a doubt as to the status of the truths; it brings to the fore the "we" in their act of "holding" the truths to be self-evident, not the truths themselves in their self-evidence. An element of subjectivity and an element of hesitation are introduced into a judgment which should be the most epistemologically solid possible. It is almost as though the text says, "We believe or judge these truths to be self-evident." But truly "self-evident truths" have no room for "belief." There either is "immediate perception of agreement of ideas," that is, self-evidence, or there is not. As Robert Ginsberg well says of the "we hold": "The famous self-evident truths are not presented as self-evident truths. To do such would obviate the necessity of saying one believes in them."[20]

Similarly, Hannah Arendt comments on the "incongruous phrase Jefferson used."[21] On the other hand, however, "we hold these truths to be self-evident" does not properly translate into "these are our strongly held convictions," as focusing on the "we hold" might lead us to attempt. The text states quite clearly that they are truths, not merely convictions or deep beliefs. They are truths, held to be, or as if "self-evident." They are truths which function as the ultimate premises for the Declaration's syllogisms, and perhaps for the political life to rest on the principles of the Declaration. But the truths are not affirmed to be in themselves self-evident, only to be held as such by the Americans.

If the truths are not themselves self-evident, then whence derives knowledge of their truthfulness? How would the Americans prove or establish them? On the basis of the text of the Declaration itself we are simply unable to say. In his letter to Roger Weightman, Jefferson suggested that "the light of science" might be the source of knowledge of some truths similar to those affirmed in the Declaration. The Declaration necessarily points beyond itself, for it rests on premises which are not themselves defended there, although Jefferson vouches for his belief in their truth by insisting that they are truths.

As Jefferson's letter to Weightman makes clear, the truths about politics announced in the Declaration must be "held" in order to achieve their maximum efficacy. "Monkish ignorance and superstition," that is, false opinions, have led human beings to construct chains for themselves rather than to secure the "rights of man." The truths must be held to be achieved, but the truths are themselves the product of "the light of science." But Jefferson believed that not everyone could be a scientist or a philosopher.

"For one man of science there are thousands who are not."[22] All must hold the truths, but not all can hold them as truths. Not all persons can be in possession of the reasoning that establishes their truth.[23] Some people, perhaps most people, must *hold* them, in the emphatic sense, as opinions, not knowledge. For most, the truths must be as if self-evident, the basic premises or touchstones for all political reasoning.

The Declaration adopts a position between that of Socrates in the *Republic* and that associated with the Enlightenment. According to Socrates, the citizens of the just city must "hold" a lie, albeit a "noble lie"; the citizens of the Declaration's regime "hold" the truth, but they hold it in less than a fully enlightened way. The Declaration's teaching on the role of truth in politics poses especially interesting questions of whether and in what ways truth requires the aid of nontruth, and even of whether effective political truth requires limitations on the open pursuit and dissemination of truth in society.[24]

Support for this interpretation of "self-evident" in the Declaration emerges from an examination of the truths so denominated. A self-evident truth properly so-called bears its truth in itself, and neither can nor need be derived from other, anterior truths. But some of the so-called self-evident truths clearly derive from others of them.[25]

The Declaration asserts as a truth that "to secure these rights governments are instituted among men, deriving their just powers from the consent of the governed." Governments are institutions made by human beings, and have no other bases for existence but their having been made and constituted by men for the specified purpose of securing rights. If these claims are true, then the next assertion denominated a "self-evident truth" follows deductively from them: "whenever any form of government becomes destructive of these ends, it is the Right of the people to alter or to abolish it, and to institute new government." The "self-evident" truths about the altering or abolishing of government follow from the truths about the institution and ends of government, and therefore cannot be properly self-evident.[26]

Likewise the truths about the ends of government and the role of consent follow from the truths that precede them in the list. If "created equal" means that by nature there is no subjection or subordination of one to another, then if there is to be just subjection, it must derive from an act of submission by the people themselves. That is, "governments derive their just powers from the consent of the governed."

The truths about the institution of government then follow from the truths about prepolitical society as the truths about the postpolitical situation follow from the truths about the institution of government. Therefore, neither the second nor the third set of "self-evident truths" is properly speaking self-evident. Thus Mortimer Adler and William Gorman rightly insist that the "clauses" in the Declaration subsequent to "created equal" "are not self-evident in the strict logical sense. That men are endowed with certain inalienable rights, . . . that governments derive their just powers from the consent of the governed—these propositions can be staunchly defended as true, but precisely because they need to be and can be defended by arguments, they are not "self-evident."[27]

Yet Adler and Gorman mean to retain the claim for the self-evidence of "created equal." The text does not support this reading, however, for in the Declaration all three sets are equally said to be "held as self-evident." That suggests that the first set of truths, the truths about the prepolitical situation, are no more inherently self-evident than the others.[28] The text cannot mean to affirm that only the first or "prepolitical" truths are affirmed as self-evident, for that is not grammatically possible. All the truths are presented in perfectly parallel clauses so it is impossible to read the text as granting some a different status from others.

That these truths were not understood as self-evident in themselves, but functionally and politically self-evident only, is suggested by a variety of other facts. Neither Jefferson nor any other thinker of his generation referred to these propositions as self-evident in any other place, so far as I know, or so far as any other scholar of the period has shown, even though the members of the revolutionary generation frequently discoursed on the very truths outlined in the Declaration.[29] For example, the closely parallel statements in the Virginia and Massachusetts bills of rights do not designate their corresponding propositions as "self-evident truths." Nor did the "self-evident truths" formula appear in Jefferson's rough draft of the Declaration, a most striking omission if he believed the propositions to be epistemologically grounded in their self-evidence. Rather, he said in the earlier version: "We hold these truths to be sacred and undeniable."[30]

The language, the logic, and the historic connections of the Declaration all point to the same conclusion: the truths announced in the Declaration are not self-evident, nor are they pronounced to be. They are rather to be held as if self-evident within the political community dedicated to making them effective. The truths must serve as the bedrock or first principles of all political reasoning in that regime. While they stand as the conclusion of a chain of philosophical or scientific reasoning, they must stand at the beginning of all chains of political reasoning.

Contrary to first appearances, the Declaration does not mean to address the cognitive or theoretical status of the truths involved at all but what we might term their political or practical status. Right opinion is the most—and the least—that one can achieve by way of intellectual support for the politics of rights. The Declaration, therefore, is not the product of "unthought-out thought" but of deeply thought-out practice. Nor is it, as Hannah Arendt speculated, the result of being produced "in a period of transition."[31]

EPISTEMOLOGICAL SELF-EVIDENCE

The account of self-evident truths presented here differs entirely from that of Morton White, who makes the theme of self-evidence central to his account of *The Philosophy of the American Revolution* and who develops most fully the real alternative, that the Declaration's appeal to self-evidence is to be understood literally as an epistemological thesis, rather than politically and practically, as above.[32]

At stake in White's interpretation is not only the philosophy of the Declaration but that of Locke as well, for White traces the language of self-evidence to the latter's philosophy. He thus departs from many recent scholars who doubt the importance of Locke for the Declaration.[33] White has "little doubt . . . that Jefferson had read Locke's *Second Treatise* carefully before writing the Declaration and that he had been influenced by what Locke had said there, in particular by passages in which Locke *freely uses* the concept of self-evident truth."[34] White claims that "Locke's rationalistic doctrine of self-evident moral principles was accepted by Jefferson when he was writing the Declaration"; he concludes quite confidently that "when the word 'self-evident' appeared in the Declaration, it was used as it had been by Locke and by other rationalistic theorists of natural law."[35]

Given the connection he sees between the Declaration and Locke, he attempts to understand the doctrine from Locke's philosophic and political writings. That is, he attempts to show how Locke's doctrine of natural law relies on self-evident truths.

Contrary to White's repeated claims, however, Locke does not identify the fundamental truths of the law of nature or, more broadly, of politics, as self-evident truths. The evidence shows, I think, that with only one possible exception, White has systematically misread Locke's texts. For example, he finds Locke's early *Essays on the Law of Nature* to present a "doctrine of self-evident principles," wherein moral truth is grasped by "intuitive reason."[36] But Locke never said that. The closest he came is the claim that the natural law is "discernible by the light of reason," that "our mental faculties can lead us to the knowledge of this law." Locke emphasized, even in the very passages White quotes, that the laws of nature are "secret decrees of nature"; he referred to them as "the secret and hidden laws of nature . . . much less easy to know" than "matters that relate to the practice of ordinary life."[37] Now to say that a certain kind of knowledge is available to human reason, rather than being altogether unknowable, or available only through revelation, is surely not ipso facto to say that the knowledge is self-evident. To emphasize that the knowledge in question is very difficult to come by and that it is hidden and secret, argues strongly that it is not self-evident. Indeed, Locke affirmed that reason "attains" to knowledge of the law of nature, "through sense experience," not through an immediate intuitive grasp.

Locke's explicit testimony shows that when he spoke of the natural law as accessible to reason he did not mean accessible as self-evident principles to the intuitive reason:

Reason is here taken to mean the discursive faculty of the mind, which advances from things known to things unknown and argues from one thing to another in a definite and fixed order of propositions. *It is this reason by means of which mankind arrives at the knowledge of natural law.*[38]

White claims in one place that Locke "often said" that the law of nature can be seen "by intuition."[39] In fact, White can find him doing so "often" (or at all) only by sliding across the gap between a law of nature accessible to reason, which Locke often affirmed, and a law of nature which was self-evident, which he often denied.

Only one Lockean passage provides any support for White's efforts to find in Locke self-evident truths about politics. Very early in the *Second Treatise* Locke said:

> *there being nothing more evident,* than that Creatures of the same species and rank promiscuously born to all the same advantages of Nature, and the use of the same faculties, should also be equal one amongst another without Subordination or subjection, unless the Lord and Master of them all, should by any manifest Declaration of his will set one above another.[40]

White concludes that the emphasized phrase in the passage means "self-evident," on the basis of the observation that for Locke, "a self-evident truth possesses the greatest amount of evidence that can be supplied for a truth."[41] However that may be, it is nonetheless as certain as anything can be that the proposition Locke finds "nothing more evident than" is not a self-evident truth.

We can restate the passage more schematically to make this clear: (1) If human beings are "creatures," that is, the product of a creating and willing God, whose will sets the moral standards to which human life should conform; and (2) if that God has made all human beings of "equal rank," etc., and not by a declaration of his will set one above another, then (3) human beings are of equal rank and should recognize themselves to be so. To put the point most simply: the assertion that "men should also be equal one amongst another" is the conclusion of an argument with the other propositions as its premises. But a proposition deduced from other propositions is not self-evident. Or, to restate the point in more strictly Lockean terms: "Where the agreement or disagreement [of ideas] is perceived immediately by itself, without the intervention or help of any other, there our knowledge is *self-evident*."[42] Now the agreement of the ideas of "equality" and of "man" is not direct and immediate in this way, but rather depends on the intervention of a variety of other ideas, such as the idea of a creating God, of a divine will, of divine appointment, and so on. Moreover, Locke would not consider these premises or intervening ideas to be themselves self-evident, as can be seen from his effort to derive the idea of a creating God in book 4 of the *Essay*.[43]

White's interpretation derives its plausibility from a simple logical error. Even if no truth can have more evidence than a self-evident truth, it does not follow that every truth than which none is more evident is self-evident. Perhaps Locke meant that truths clearly supported by a chain of deduction bear as much evidence as self-evident truths themselves. White needs, moreover, to notice Locke's distinction between self-evident propositions and self-evident truths. Locke has a great deal to say about the former, much of the point of which is to demonstrate that these are not necessarily identical to the latter.[44]

Our analysis of this passage from the *Second Treatise* certainly coheres better with Locke's settled conviction (which White himself notes) that "there could be no self-evident practical principles" than does White's analysis.[45] Unless Locke could forget what he had written so recently and so assuredly in his *Essay*, he could hardly have developed the doctrine of self-evident political principles White claims to find, with so little textual support, in the *Treatises* and elsewhere.

When White comes to elucidate the thought of the Declaration and the Americans, he reveals the central incoherence in his own position. As hard as he had tried to turn Locke into a theorist who relied on self-evident moral and political principles for the sake of thereby explaining the Declaration's position on self-evidence, he nonetheless finds that the Americans did not understand the truths in the Declaration to be what Locke (or anybody) would call self-evident. Rather "they accepted their so-called self-evident truths on the basis of an argument that they did not make explicit in the Declaration. That argument . . . rested on other premises."[46] But an argument which "rested on other premises"—or on any premises—is not self-evident.

Although White spends much space attempting, or seeming to attempt, to establish that the Declaration is Lockean in its appeal to self-evident truths, his real concern is not to establish that thesis at all but rather the claim that the Declaration was "rationalist" in a sense he never explains very clearly, but which he associates with a deductive ethic in which a "natural morality" is derived from claims about the "essence of man" and natural theological claims about God. According to White's real view, the rough draft of the Declaration better captured Jefferson's underlying thought when it called the truths "sacred and undeniable," for while (White believes) the truths were derivative and thus clearly not self-evident, they were thought to be demonstrable and therefore "undeniable" in the sense that a theorem derived from axioms is undeniable.[47] White thus makes his own point best when he says, "Jefferson would have been better off if he had let 'sacred and undeniable' stand."[48] White insists then on the moral rationalism of the documents and allows the self-evidence to drop off, or rather pushes it over the cliff himself. According to White, "Jefferson probably believed that many of his truths were theorems," and therefore "he should not have made this change [from 'sacred and undeniable' to 'self-evident'] nor acquiesced in it from a philosophical view. . . . I believe that Jefferson, under the influence of Burlamaqui, appealed to more fundamental truths than those that in the Declaration are finally called self-evident."[49]

But his analysis of the self-evidence issue in the Declaration is no more persuasive than his analysis of Locke. For one, it requires seeing the rough draft as not only importantly different from the final version but as philosophically much truer to the doctrine meant to be expressed. White seems to favor the view that Franklin, not Jefferson, made the textual change.[50] But Jefferson's own recollection of what happened when he submitted his rough draft to his fellow committeemen, based on notes he took at the time, runs altogether counter to this view: Jefferson called their alterations "merely verbal"; they did not, in his opinion, reach the sense or meaning of what he had intended to say.[51]

While Jefferson complained more than a little over the changes Congress made in the draft the committee reported out, he never complained or even remarked on the changes made by the committee. Would Jefferson allow to pass unnoticed, to pass as a mere matter of wording, a change made by others that got his philosophic point entirely wrong? Or, alternatively, would he himself make a change that got his own philosophic point entirely wrong, and not notice?

White's interpretation as a whole leaves us with a quite incomprehensible document, a document which says one thing and means quite another, and does so for inexplicable reasons.[52] The failure of White's reading is instructive, for his is the most serious and strenuous effort to take the Declaration's affirmation of self-evidence as an epistemological thesis. That failure lends support to the effort above to take the self-evident truths as an indication of a practical imperative. Not only does this interpretation make better sense of the various texts in question, it points us toward an understanding of the imperatives of the American polity as Jefferson (at least) understood them.

The Declaration implies that the cognitive status of its truths is not the important, or at least not the politically important, question. The true ends of political society can be achieved only in a regime in which the citizens hold those truths, but necessarily hold them in the mode of "self-evident truths." But how is this produced? Who has the public responsibility for the character of the opinion that prevails in society? Jefferson's own political career, with its constant and overriding concern for tending to opinion, represented one extended mode of answering these questions, as these questions provide a key for understanding his career: for Jefferson, the highest task of statesmanship in this regime is the cultivation of the necessary kind of opinion.

This line of argument gives insight into Jefferson's almost obsessive concern with education, a concern which culminated in his founding of the University of Virginia. It also explains one feature of Jefferson's thinking on education which has puzzled more than one thoughtful modern reader:[53] he had no hesitation whatever in having the state prescribe the curriculum on politics and the American regime. He may have believed in the grand virtues of free inquiry, but in the political sphere he favored something very like indoctrination, even for the elite students of his university. Nothing captures Jefferson's position better than his "Report" on behalf of the Board of Visitors of the University of Virginia, which reads, in relevant parts:

> It is the duty of this Board to the government under which it lives, and especially to that of which this university is the immediate creation, to pay especial attention to the principles of government which shall be inculcated therein, and to provide that none shall be inculcated which are incompatible with those on which the Constitution of this State, and of the United States were genuinely based.[54]

To that end, the board listed the texts that were officially approved for instruction. In no other branch of study did the board presume so much. The text first among those which were to present "the distinctive principles of our State, and that of the United States" was none other than the Declaration of Independence. Such are the ways in which the truths of the Declaration are to remain "self-evident" practical axioms for Americans.

Understanding "self-evident truths" as a practical but not an epistemological thesis gives purchase on the practical tasks facing the natural rights polity, but it sheds little light on the set of theoretical issues the natural rights philosophy raises: what are the nature, source, and foundation of rights?

Chapter Three

ON NATURE AND NATURAL RIGHTS

The American polity began with an appeal to rights, and that appeal has remained a particularly potent one throughout American political history; the debates over slavery, over labor unions, over race, over women have occurred largely in terms of rights.[1] The idea of rights has not, however, led a trouble-free life in America. In the late twentieth century especially, a series of strong challenges to the idea of rights have emerged on a number of quite different fronts. Some challenges have been essentially historical: from the perspective of classical republicanism, scholars like J. G. A. Pocock have questioned the importance of rights at the time of the founding. From the perspective of legal history, scholars like John Phillip Reid have questioned their centrality as well. From a philosophical perspective, thinkers like Jacques Derrida or Richard Rorty have challenged the idea that nature can be the source of standards for rights, or that there are universal standards for rights to be found anywhere. Finally, from a political point of view, critics of the contemporary "rights revolution" have wondered whether rights can supply an adequate grounding for a healthy political life. Rights, Mary Ann Glendon or Amitai Etzioni argue, are too absolute, too individualistic, too blind to the necessity for responsibility in social life.[2] Some, although not all, of these challenges receive especial force from the Declaration of Independence's appeal to practical self-evidence and its silence on the grounding of rights.

The Americans of the founding generation appear to have shared none of the perplexity about rights characteristic of the twentieth century. Although, as James Madison said, the Americans had no precedent for the revolution they made they nonetheless spoke with great confidence in the document that purported to explain and justify that revolution.[3] They rested their actions on truths they "held to be self evident" and trusted that "a candid world," to say nothing of "divine providence," would respect the reasons for their actions. The very language and rhythms of the Declaration of Independence reinforce the impression of confidence—stately yet simple, firm and even passionate yet not shrill.

The Americans spoke with such authority, it seems, because they found warrant for what they did in the "ultimate realities" of God or nature. The rights on behalf of which they acted were the gifts of "the creator," and they appealed to "the laws of nature and of nature's God." God and nature—not the uncertainties, ambiguities, and groundlessness of human laws or human history.[4] The founders apparently believed they understood the ground of the truths they affirmed in the Declaration.

Nature

Since the Declaration was a political document, it could only deploy, not discuss, the philosophical and theological ideas it invoked.[5] Yet its author, Thomas Jefferson, was a philosophically minded man, as well as a politician, whose only book was largely an attempt to explore those same ultimate realities appealed to in the Declaration. His *Notes On the State of Virginia* seems at first to be anything but a philosophical work. Both in origin and in ultimate form it presents a series of answers to the set of quite specific questions about Virginia posed to Jefferson (and to leading figures in the other new states) by François de Marbois, the secretary of the French legation in America. He asked about Virginia's geography, climate, products, inhabitants, and so on. As Merrill Peterson puts it, "viewed in one aspect, the *Notes On Virginia* was simply a glorified guidebook, descriptive, crammed with facts, informative on a broad range of subjects from cascades and caverns to weights and measures."[6]

But as Peterson also notes, that aspect does not exhaust the riches of the book; it is also "touched with philosophy." More than that, it is philosophical, if not philosophy, through and through. Jefferson had a precedent for the kind of combination of information and philosophy he presented. At this time, apparently, he first became familiar with the French *Encyclopédie*. According to Douglas L. Wilson, "the all-encompassing character of the *Encyclopédie*, which aimed at nothing less than the presentation of knowledge in all its dimensions, clearly captivated Jefferson, as did the philosophical aims and orientation of the compilers."

The *Notes* may have been responsive to Marbois's questions, but there is much evidence that Jefferson reframed them for his own purposes. He thoroughly reordered the whole and even changed the number of questions around which he organized his essays.

> Marbois' twenty-two queries came to Jefferson's hand in a jumble. Questions on colonial laws and charters and the constitution preceded questions of a geographical nature, for instance, and some questions combined incongruous subjects. Jefferson sorted and arranged the whole under twenty-three heads, the order proceeding from the natural through the civil to the generally social and moral.[7]

Peterson very well captures the principle of Jefferson's reordering: "he thought it important to begin with nature." The distinction between the natural and the nonnatural governed Jefferson's presentation, a theoretically informed order that implies an altogether different purpose than a "glorified guide-book."

Although the topics covered are nominally governed by Marbois's queries, Jefferson obtrusively digresses or wanders off into issues not obviously necessary to answer his questions. One such digression relevant to our concern for the Declaration's appeal to the "ultimate realities" of God and nature occurs in Query VI: in the midst of a catalogue of the minerals of Virginia, Jefferson launches a substantial discussion of shells or shell fossils found far from the seashore, and even in the Andes—far from Virginia as well. Jefferson considers the question, certainly foreign to the spirit of Marbois's inquiries, of how shells came to such unlikely places.

The chief point of his interest in this question is clearly if cautiously put: the fact that shells have been found on mountain tops "is considered by many, both of the learned and the unlearned, as a proof of a universal deluge."[8] Of course, Jefferson is thinking of those who accept the biblical account of the flood in the book of Genesis.

> And the waters prevailed so mightily upon the earth that all the high mountains under the whole heaven were covered; the waters prevailed above the mountains, covering them fifteen cubits deep.[9]

While showing that a "universal deluge" could not account for the presence of shells on mountains, Jefferson shows by a very ingenious argument that there could not have been a universal flood at all. There is not enough water in the whole heavens to cover the earth. Although a "universal deluge" could not have occurred, Jefferson thought it quite likely that there were "partial deluges" in the Mediterranean region, and these were probably the basis for Hebrew and Greek "traditions" about a flood.

Jefferson thus demotes the Bible to the level of a "tradition," one with a character and authority no different from other ancient traditions. Like those other traditions, it is of questionable authority. The biblical account was based (at best) on an undisciplined inference from a partial experience, generalized beyond the bounds warranted by the experience itself into a claim that went beyond the bounds of natural possibility. And, Jefferson insists, natural possibility is all there is: the universal deluge is rejected because it would be "out of the laws of nature."[10]

Because there is no mode of divine action other than nature, the "laws of nature" are identical to the "laws of nature's God," and there is no mode of knowing God other than through nature.[11] Jefferson underlines his rejection of the truth-revealing character of the Bible by entertaining another hypothesis regarding the placement of the shells, a hypothesis which "supposes" events to have occurred "in times anterior to the records either of history or tradition."[12] According to this hypothesis, the earth is much older than the Bible says, and has a history of which the Bible knows nothing. Jefferson did not accept that hypothesis, but he had no problems with the idea of prebiblical times.[13] In sum, he approaches the Bible himself just as he later advised the young Peter Carr: "Read the Bible then, as you would have read Livy or Tacitus."[14]

In accord with his understanding of the nature of divine action, Jefferson cannot understand the creation in anything like the biblical manner. In a subsequent discussion he interchangeably speaks of "nature" and "creation"; at first he says nature was responsible for the characters of the mammoth and elephant, but then he says it was the creator, and then nature once again. Only if nature is the creator does his apparently wavering language make sense.[15] When he says in the Declaration that men "are endowed by their Creator with certain unalienable rights," he means, we now see, that nature, or nature's God is the source of rights.[16] The "unalienable rights" are indeed natural rights.[17] Nor does a later and very important passage in the *Notes* derogate from that conclusion: "And can the liberties of a nation be thought secure when we have removed their only firm basis, a conviction in the minds of the people that these liberties are of the gift of God?"[18] This later passage speaks of the convictions necessary in the minds of the people; it does not speak of Jefferson's own view of the origins of rights, of liberty, or of the character of God. The passage helps, however, to account for Jefferson's employment of the potentially misleading term "creator" in the Declaration. If it has produced a misunderstanding, it is a misunderstanding he would have welcomed.[19]

Jefferson seems to have followed a principle in his own writing which he discovered in one of his early intellectual heroes, Bolingbroke. Of the latter he once wrote: "His political tracts are safe reading for the most timid religionist, his philosophical, for those who are not afraid to trust their reason with discussions of right and wrong."[20] Jefferson firmly believed that certain things were properly said in some places and others not, as his views on the limits of enlightenment imply. That principle surely must be recalled when considering his most public, that is, his political writings, but it ought also to be kept in mind when considering the great variety of different things Jefferson said on moral and political topics in his voluminous correspondence. It made a difference to him whether his correspondent was a "timid religionist" or a "philosopher"—or one of the innumerable human types between those two poles.[21]

The "ultimate reality" to which the Declaration appeals is thus nature. But what do we know of nature? And how does nature ground the political truths announced in the Declaration? The *Notes on Virginia* constitutes a sustained meditation on these questions. As we have already seen, the book begins with the natural and is organized around the distinction between the natural and the nonnatural. That theme appears from the very outset of the book in the first query, on the boundaries of Virginia. As a physical entity, Virginia is in some sense a natural object. Yet even as a merely physical entity, Virginia is hardly natural. Its boundaries are in part natural boundaries, such as the Atlantic Ocean, but more frequently humanly drawn lines such as that "which was marked by Messrs. Mason and Dixon."[22] And, he points out, all the boundaries, including the "natural ones," derive their existence as boundaries of Virginia from legal actions such as ancient charters, compacts between the colonies, and treaties. Virginia as a physical entity is thus a complex intermixture of nature and artifice: nature cannot so readily be extricated from nonnature.

The character of the intermingling of nature and human artifice becomes clearer in his treatment of the rivers of Virginia in the second query. He presents them above all in terms of their navigability, that is, in terms of their fitness for human commerce, travel, and exchange. Human purpose or use dominates. But what of the rivers in themselves? What about nature not viewed in terms of human purposes?

Mountains, the subject of the next query, do not seem to be so useful; at least Jefferson forbears from presenting them in terms of their usefulness. Mountains do not appear to be raw material for human use in the same way rivers are. Here nature is more natural, belongs more to itself, is not so much appropriated for human purposes. The mountain is not something to use, but rather presents something to see: it is, he says, "one of the most stupendous scenes in nature." The perspective Jefferson takes on the mountains is far more theoretical, in the original sense of a viewing rather than a doing or making, than is the account of rivers. Furthermore, the mountain scene suggests to his mind a geological (that is, nonbiblical) account of the history of the earth, and reveals "the most powerful agents of nature," the creating or making forces, and their astonishing power.[23] When all use is stripped away, "the effectual truth" of nature stands revealed as an awesome array of forces. "This scene," Jefferson wistfully concludes, "is worth a voyage across the Atlantic." Yet even people who live very near to the scene do not come "to survey these monuments of a war between rivers and mountains, which must have shaken the earth itself to its center."[24] When people cross the Atlantic, it seems, they do so for reasons of use. Nature, which seems to reveal itself only to a more theoretical attitude, thus goes largely unknown.

But if nature is revealed only if one puts aside all questions of human use, then how can nature be the source of guidance for human life? How can nature be the ground of natural right? The discussion of mountains cannot exhaust the problem of nature.

In the next query, Jefferson turns to the natural bridge, "the most sublime of nature's works." He concedes that this discussion too is a digression—it is "not comprehended under the present head"—but nonetheless it "must not be pretermitted."[25] Like the mountain scene from the previous query, the natural bridge also shows the signs of "some great convulsion," which has "determined" its chief features. The bridge results from natural forces, and yet it is, or can be taken to be, a bridge, a product "made" by nature that resembles a product made by human beings for human use. The bridge stands between the natural and the human and connects them.[26]

The bridge is remarkable because it combines two very different views. There is an experience of the bridge from its top, looking over its edge; and there is an experience from the bottom, looking up. Here is Jefferson's description of the view from the top:

> Though the sides of this bridge are provided in some parts with a parapet of fixed rocks, yet few men have resolution to walk to them, and look over the abyss. You involuntarily fall on your hands and feet, creep to the parapet and peep over it. Looking down from this height about a minute, gave me a violent headache.

But the view from beneath is entirely diferent:

> If the view from the top be painful and intolerable, that from below is delightful in an equal extreme. It is impossible for the

emotions arising from the sublime to be felt beyond what they are here; so beautiful an arch, so elevated, so light, and springing as it were up to heaven! The rapture of the spectator is really indescribable![27]

One stands before this passage almost with the same sensation as Jefferson had atop the bridge. Something unexpected and almost dangerous comes to light here. Nature reveals itself in two guises. From the top of the bridge nature is "painful and intolerable," from below "delightful." It takes great "resolution" to look nature in the face from the top; from beneath, the spectator is in "indescribable rapture." Can there be two such truths about nature? Is nature an "abyss" or does it point to heaven?

Jefferson presents two perspectives on nature, one looking down and one looking up, but the truly decisive difference between the two lies in the different situation of the spectator. In the one case he is exposed, vulnerable. The danger is so great that Jefferson reacts in a most extreme manner—the involuntary falling onto hands and feet, the creeping to the edge, the violent headache. He experiences his—or humanity's—radical exposedness. Just as in the mountains, nature lies before him as blind, cold, and cataclysmic forces. But in the mountains he sees evidence of those forces at work in the distant past and far away. He does not feel the threat of nature. Here atop the bridge there is a more immediate vulnerability to the great uncaring natural forces.

Jefferson becomes dizzy at the prospect of nature so understood.[28] He emphasizes the exposedness: he first speaks generally of "men," then of the more personal but still indefinite "you," but finally of "me." It is one of the very few moments in this very scientific book when Jefferson as unique individual allows himself to be caught sight of. In the experience of facing his exposed situation in nature, Jefferson is most emphatically an individual. That experience breaks through all disinterest, every merely aesthetic attitude. He reacts to the natural bridge as Pascal's *libertin* reacts to nature as conceived in the new science: "le silence éternel de ces espaces infinis m'effraye."[29] For Pascal, as for Jefferson, the same "me." The bridge, unlike the mountain of the preceding query, once again juxtaposes nature with human concerns but not, like the rivers, as an object of use. The bridge reveals the limits of human domination and use of nature. From the perspective of human insecurity, the bridge shows the terrors of nature.

Beneath the bridge is security. From the perception of security achieved or promised, the bridge appears to soar towards heaven and testify to providence. This purely natural entity presents a form, an arch, that human beings produce in their own makings, and the intelligibility of which they discover in their mathematics. Beneath the bridge stands not the "I" but once again the impersonal "spectator," who can afford to indulge himself in an intensely aesthetic reaction, which converges with a moral or religious experience as well. Beneath the bridge humanity, nature, and heaven are all joined in a beneficent harmony.

Jefferson's quest for nature gives him double vision. There is no "nature-in-itself," for the truth of nature varies with the perspective—secure or insecure—of the investigator. Nature must inevitably be juxtaposed with the human concern for security— all knowing is, after all, human knowing. The human drive for security, that which orients the two human perspectives, is itself natural.[30] Human beings, too, are part of the natural kingdom. The natural bridge proves be a bridge to nature not so much because it uncovers nature-in-itself, but because it uncovers the natural ground for what Jefferson saw as a necessary, and a true, bifurcated grasp of nature. Security as the natural ground, moreover, provides the rationale and ultimate justification for a utilitarian orientation toward nature.[31]

Beneath the bridge is the source of the rational theology that Jefferson from time to time propounded, very little in *Notes on Virginia* but at greater length in some of his correspondence. Probably the best example is contained in an 1823 letter to John Adams.

> I hold (without appeal to revelation) that when we take a view of the universe, in its parts general or particular, it is impossible for the human mind not to perceive and feel a conviction of design, consummate skill and indefinite power in every atom of its composition. The movements of the heavenly bodies, so exactly held in their courses by the balance of centrifugal and centripetal forces . . . , it is impossible, I say, for the human

mind not to believe that there is, in all this, design, cause and effect, up to an ultimate cause.[32]

This passage, I believe, expresses exactly what Jefferson means when he says of the arch of the natural bridge that it "springs as it were up to heaven." A natural theology of order and final cause, of intelligence and purpose, is the truth from beneath the bridge.

But that truth coexists with the other truth, the top-of-the-bridge view of nature. Jefferson does not present so detailed and explicit a statement of this alternative perspective, but he supplies many indications that the natural theological view from beneath the bridge is not the exclusive truth.[33] The natural theological "proof" he gives in his letter to Adams depends on the claim that "it is impossible for the human mind not to perceive and feel a conviction of design, consummate skill and indefinite power. . . . It is impossible . . . for the human mind not to believe that there is, in all this, design, cause and effect, up to an ultimate cause." But Jefferson knew very well of thinkers whose minds found no such impossibilities. In an earlier letter to Adams he had spoken of "the school of Diderot, D'Alembert, D'Holbach," which accepted a "system of atheism." These atheists "agreed" with theists "in the order of the existing system," but drew different conclusions. These atheists "supposed" the order of nature "from eternity" rather than "having begun in time." They "descanted on the unceasing motion and circulation of matter thro' the animal vegetable and mineral kingdoms, never resting, never annihilated, always changing form, and under all forms gifted with the power of reproduction."[34] It cannot, therefore, be an "impossibility," strictly speaking, for the human mind to fail to conceive of Jefferson's rational God and deistic system of nature. Perhaps it would be more accurate to say that the human mind can scarcely help but entertain such a hypothesis and that it cannot definitely disprove the hypothesis—or its atheistic counterthesis.[35]

Natural theology and atheistic or materialist cosmology together are but another way to state what Jefferson conveys in his parable of the natural bridge: there exist two irreducible perspectives, and a thoughtful person stands undecided before them. A yet more thoughtful person, perhaps, affirms the deeper truth beneath the two: the point of reference for both is the human drive for security, and nature presents itself in these two guises as security is promised or threatened. Jefferson, it seems, is not quite the Enlightenment rationalist he is most often taken to be.

HUMAN NATURE

Human beings first come into view in the *Notes* not so much as part of nature but as knowers of nature; Jefferson shares the perspective of modern, or post-Cartesian philosophy, which is not surprising, given his "trinity of the three greatest men that have ever lived, without any exceptions, Bacon, Locke, and Newton."[36] But what comes into view about human beings as knowers is the determinative character of their security-seeking. All animals seek their own survival; only human beings seek security, the reasonable confidence in the prospect for survival and the allaying of the anxieties arising from threats to existence. The truth uncovered in the discussion of the natural bridge necessitates a more particular discussion of human beings as a special species of natural being.

Jefferson begins that discussion in the next query (IV), on natural productions: human beings, too, can be seen among nature's productions or creations. It is obviously a very important discussion, for it contains the first mention in the *Notes* of two themes central to the Declaration of Independence—natural equality and rights.[37] Jefferson himself emphasizes the importance of the discussion when he suggests that it will vindicate "the honor of human nature."[38]

Human nature required vindication from the slur cast upon it by the French naturalist Comte de Buffon. Buffon aroused Jefferson's indignation with his assertions about the unfriendliness of nature in America to "the production and development of large quadrupeds" and of human beings as well.[39] Jefferson considered Buffon's theories an insult not merely to America but to human nature; according to his own testimony, it was the honor of human nature itself rather than of America which was to be the chief beneficiary of his rebuttal of Buffon.[40]

The core of Buffon's position, as identified by Jefferson, is that "*heat* is friendly, and moisture adverse" to animal development.[41]

The relative lack of heat and the surplus of humidity in America manifest themselves first and foremost in the deficient sexual powers of those human beings native to America. According to Buffon, adverse climate produces lowered sexual capacity, which produces lower sexual interest; since sexual drives appear to be the root of both individual energy and sociability, the Indian shows little of either individual or social development. As Jefferson quotes the French naturalist: "This indifference to the other sex is the fundamental defect which weakens their nature, prevents its development, and—destroying the very germs of life— uproots society at the same time."[42]

Buffon had insulted human nature, for he had made it a reflex of climate and sexual drive, two subhuman forces. Jefferson vindicates human nature by showing that Buffon's description of the Indians is quite mistaken factually and that his explanation for what he finds is quite misguided.[43] Jefferson observes that the Indians are affectionate, even indulgent toward their children, and that in general their affections operate just as do those of Europeans. The Indian "is neither more defective in ardor nor more impotent with his female, than the white reduced to the same diet and exercise."[44] The Indians have fewer children than whites not for Buffon's reasons but because of "circumstances." Their way of life makes childbearing "inconvenient," planting "obstacles . . . of want and hazard." When these obstacles are removed, they produce as many children as the Europeans.

Jefferson thus rejects both of the chief links in Buffon's deterministic explanation. The sexual characteristics of the Indian do not derive from climate but from "way of life." And their other qualities do not, in turn, derive from their lack of "sexual ardor" but also from way of life, or circumstances. Jefferson vindicates the honor of human nature in large part by showing that nature is directly responsible for much less about human existence than Buffon had said. Morever, nature operates on human beings not mechanistically, but through human adaptation to circumstances. Like Buffon, Jefferson was indeed an environmentalist, in the sense that he thought environment had a shaping influence on mankind, but he saw it operating in a very different way.[45] For Buffon, nature, in the form of climate, acted directly—physiologically and mechanistically—on human beings, making them a part of nature and the chain of natural causes no different from other parts of nature. For Jefferson, nature or environment operates on humanity through human intelligence, through the more or less conscious adaptation of ways of life in rational response to circumstance. Human nature is much less fixed, much more flexible and variable, much more human and intelligent than Buffon had thought. Buffon, one might say, had a top-of-the-bridge view only.

Jefferson's discussion of the Indians provides the occasion for considering human nature or, more broadly, what nature supplies to human beings. The Indians were as close to nature or natural man as Jefferson thinks he can get. Yet even here, the line between nature and "education" is very obscure. He finds himself unable to distinguish between the roles of nature and education in the production of several important Indian practices.[46] Obscure and remote as pure nature remains, the Indians nonetheless seem to provide insights into the natural truths about politics. According to Jefferson's account, they live in the condition the philosophers had called the state of nature. They have "never submitted themselves to any laws, any coercive power, any shadow of government."[47] This corresponds precisely to the state of nature, as defined by John Locke, Jefferson's philosophic authority on "the general principles of liberty and the rights of man, in nature and in society."

> Those who are united into one body and have a common established law and judicature to appeal to, with authority to decide controversies between them and punish offenders, are in civil society one with another; but those who have no such common appeal, I mean on earth, are still in the state of nature.[48]

For Jefferson, the state of nature is prepolitical, but not necessarily presocial. In place of law, government, and coercion, the Indians live under control of "their manners, and that moral sense of right and wrong, which, like the sense of tasting and feeling, in every man makes a part of his nature."[49] Life in the state of nature is thus governed by a complex amalgam of nature and manners. Nature does not supply government, but does supply a guide for human life, the moral sense. But even in the state of nature, nature does not serve as sole guide: manners or customs, too, play their part, and these are certainly not entirely natural. As Jefferson insists in his attack on Buffon's environmental determinism, human beings are rational and conscious creatures and their ways of life always show the marks of these qualities. This is perhaps why Jefferson believed he never could reach a state of pure nature, it being the nature of human beings always to add something to their strictly natural endowment, and why he tended to eschew the terminology of the state of nature.

In crucial respects, however, the guidance supplied by nature is inadequate. That inadequacy appears most clearly in Jefferson's discussion of the "unjust drudgery" to which Indian women are subjected. "This I believe is the case with every barbarous people. With such force is law. The stronger sex therefore imposes on the weaker."[50] Nature may provide the moral sense, but that is insufficient to produce just or moral social relations. The rule among peoples most exclusively dependent on the moral sense (and on nature) is force.

Jefferson draws a most paradoxical conclusion: "It is civilization alone which *replaces* women in the enjoyment of their natural equality."[51] The state of the Indians obviously is not a pure state of nature, for Jefferson measures their condition against a yet more primordial one in which, he insists, all human beings, emphatically including women, were truly equal. The Indians lack government, but their life does not fully embody the original natural equality. There can be subjection to forces other than governments. Only further progress away from nature and into civilization can bring a return to natural equality. Civilization is thus in one sense at least a restoration of a purer natural condition.

Civilization restores the natural situation because it "first teaches us to subdue the selfish passions, and to respect those rights in others which we value in ourselves."[52] The moral sense fails because the "selfish passions" overpower it. Again, a bifocal view of nature's endowment for humanity: in accord with the view from beneath the bridge, the moral sense; from above, the selfish passions. But the two aspects of nature are quite unequal here. What comes to view from the top is far more powerful.

The taming of the selfish passions occurs not through the unvarnished or even strengthened moral sense but through the discovery of rights. Rights appear to replace the moral sense as a more effective source of just social relations. As opposed to the moral sense, which operates directly like any other sense, rights require some sophisticated figuring out. That is why rights operate in civilized and not in barbarous conditions. Both the moral sense and the system of rights counter the natural selfish passions, but the system of rights makes peace with the passions in a way the moral sense does not. Like the moral sense, the system of rights leads to consideration of others, but it allows people also to consider themselves, and even builds on that consideration. We come "to respect those rights in others which we value in ourselves."

The moral sense is deficient in at least two different ways: practically, as a motive to moral action; and epistemologically, as a source of moral knowledge. Jefferson addresses the first insufficiency quite explicitly in the *Notes on Virginia*. It is tempting to understand his discussion in terms of a hard-and-fast distinction between the practical and epistemological: the moral sense is a faculty for knowing or perceiving, not for doing. That is why it is so easily overpowered by the selfish passions, which emphatically provide motives for action. An analogy from the sphere of the senses may make the point clearer: the senses of taste and smell allow human beings to identify (within limits) some substances as food and others as not, but supply (of themselves) neither the ability to acquire the food so identified nor even the practical motive to do so. One could imagine a being possessing the power to discriminate agreeable from disagreeable tastes or smells, but, lacking hunger, possessing no particular impulsion to eat.[53] Jefferson's picture of the natural endowment for humanity is thus complex. On the one side nature supplies the moral sense, which points to the moral course of action; on the other side, however, are the selfish passions, which point elsewhere, and are by far the stronger. Despite the very un-Hobbesian moral sense, Jefferson nonetheless concludes this world is a "bellum omnium in omnia."[54]

The moral sense fails to a degree in its epistemological function also: the good varies from time to time and place to place;

the moral sense does not reveal the good action or the good social practice in itself. The moral sense sets up benevolence as such as the standard, a general "love of others, and a sense of duty to them."[55] But which specific actions and practices embody benevolence or genuinely benefit others remains an open question. The moral sense allows for serious error also: witness the Indians who reduce their women to drudgery and claim this to be "right." The moral sense is ineffective not only in producing moral action but in producing valid moral standards.[56]

The system of rights corrects or replaces the moral sense in both respects. With their intimate ties to the passions, rights are more effective than the moral sense; but rights also supply the specific standards of political action, of justice, as the moral sense does not. The moral sense does not entirely disappear from the scene, but it functions as a supplemental support to the system of rights.

Rights as Jefferson understands them make for sociability, for they contain within themselves an accommodation to the claims of others and a tempering of the selfish passions that set human beings against one another. Rights thus understood may be natural, but they derive from nature in a human, as opposed to a mechanistic, manner. The system of rights does not involve a mechanism of causation like Buffon's, which ignores the source of human dignity in the capacity for rational and conscious action. The system of natural rights thus accords more fully with the honor of human nature than does even the vaunted moral sense.[57] Natural rights, as opposed to the moral sense, are compatible with both perspectives on nature that come to view from the natural bridge. As claims justly raised by all, they are appropriately seen as an endowment from the creator, and thus are part of the perspective from beneath the bridge. As responses to and modifications of the selfish passions, they comport with the view from the top of the bridge.[58]

The account of the origin of rights presented here differs entirely from the well-known statement in Garry Wills's *Inventing America.* Wills traces Jefferson's position on rights back to the Scottish philosopher, Francis Hutcheson, who, according to Wills, derived rights directly from the moral sense. "Right was the exercise of the moral sense in some way that affected the lives of others for general good."[59] In so doing, however, Wills fails to bring into focus the distinction between right and rights. From the perspective of a moral-sense theory, it is true, "exercise of the moral sense in some way that affected the lives of others for general good" would be right, could indeed be the very definition of right. But the language of rights came about as a means of saying something different from mere rightness; as one contemporary legal theorist puts it, "Rights-talk is in part a way of talking about discretionary devices—about what one may or may not decline to do as distinct from what one ought or ought not to do."[60]

In addition to his insensitivity to the conceptual distinction between right and rights, Wills's discussion suffers from some fatal historical deficiencies. First, he discusses Hutcheson lengthily on rights, but he makes only the thinnest connection to Jefferson. Wills presents no evidence other than Jefferson's use of the term "unalienable" to establish his claim that Jefferson understood rights as he says Hutcheson did. The notion of "unalienable rights" is not sufficiently Hutchesonian for that purpose, however. Even Hobbes identified some rights as inalienable, and the entire thrust of Locke's liberal version of rights theory rests on an acceptance of inalienability.[61]

More importantly, Wills entirely ignores the crucial discussion of rights in the *Notes on Virginia*, where Jefferson clearly presents rights as a kind of substitute for a more direct natural ordering to justice through the moral sense. Wills thus makes many claims about rights which run counter to Jefferson's discussion. Rights, Wills claims, build entirely on the nonselfish moral sense and not at all on self-interest: "The moral sense," he says, "was directed to others—it was the principle of sociability, of benevolence, not selfishness. No politics built upon the moral sense could make self-interest the foundation of the social contract."[62] But as we have seen, rights are indeed built up from the selfish passions. The morality of rights is not a morality of self-love, but it is a morality that begins with and builds upon self-love. Rights supply a more effective means to achieve security, justice, and equality for all than the moral sense does, for the latter alone is swamped by the selfish passions, while the system of rights enlists those very passions.[63]

NATURAL RIGHTS

We must now attempt to understand Jefferson's teaching on natural rights more precisely. Nature, ironically, is not unequivocally the home of natural rights. Nature is home to "the selfish passions" and to "rights . . . we value in ourselves." At a later stage, a civilized stage, we learn to "respect those rights in others which we value in ourselves." Jefferson thus has in mind three entities: selfish passions, the initial rights, and the later rights. In order to keep these entities disentangled, I propose to refer to the first kind of rights as "proto-rights" and the second kind, as "rights-in-the-proper sense." The reasons for this particular terminology will become clear as the discussion progresses.

In the first instance, rights are claims each is inclined to raise on his or her own behalf, that is, claims based on the selfish passions that are nature's first legacy. The core of the selfish passions derives from the force Jefferson uncovered at the natural bridge: the natural drive to self-preservation in its human form, the natural drive to security. Driven by the desire for security, human beings are far more selfish and contentious than other animals. "In truth I do not recollect in all the animal kingdom a single species but man which is eternally & systematically engaged in the destruction of its own species. . . . Lions and tigers are lambs compared with man as a destroyer."[64]

From this natural drive arise the "proto-rights". These proto-rights are less than rights-in-the-proper-sense because they are fully consistent with rule on the basis of force, or the rule of the selfish passions. These rights fall short of the situation Jefferson sought, rule based on "a right independent of force."[65] Proto-rights are selfish in origin, rooted in the quest for individual security. Proto-rights are the selfish passions decreed rightful. That those who are strong enough to indulge their selfish passions should so decree them is less intriguing than the fact that Jefferson at least partially endorses their doing so: in the *Notes* he says that they come to accept rights in others that they value in themselves. Thus, they claim rights prior to the recognition of similar rights in others, and Jefferson accepts their claim.

Proto-rights fall short of rights-in-the-proper-sense in two respects, however. There is no duty correlative to them, and they are not tailored to the security-seeking that is their actual and legitimate origin. Prior to the stage of mutual recognition of rights, there can only be rights-assertions, with no reciprocal duties attached to the rights. The original proto-rights are thus more or less the same as Hobbes's right of nature—the right of every man to everything. Since each person has a right to everything, no person has an obligation to respect any right of another.

The selfish passions, and thus the proto-rights, do not perfectly align themselves with the means of security, but are, so to speak, imperialistic, seeking more than security. That imperialistic tendency of the selfish passions is checked to some degree by the moral sense, which seems mainly to be a feeling of compassion for others. But, as we have seen, this check is decisively ineffectual. At the same time, the selfish passions are fostered and encouraged by human intellectual errors. Although they are part of a natural order, driven to seek their security, human beings nevertheless participate in that order through intelligence and choice. Prior to the emergence of "science," they are driven by a nature they do not understand. Their errors produce distortions in the natural drives. Under the influence of false ideas, some people come to accept a right by nature to indulge their selfish passions, and, more remarkably, others come to accept "chains," or even come to see themselves as "born with saddles on their backs," and to recognize "a favored few booted and spurred, ready to ride them legitimately, by the grace of God."[66]

These proto-rights, defective as they are, derive so far as they are rights at all from the law of nature which impels human beings to their own security. Such a law is, in the first instance, an amoral law, expressing the necessity of nature. Rights, as Jefferson said elsewhere, are "founded in our natural wants."[67] When rights-in-the-proper-sense arise they remain rooted in "natural wants," or in those claims which are raised "for the relief of sensibilities made a part of . . . nature."[68]

Rights-in-the-proper-sense arise when human beings come to recognize a need for reciprocity in rights, when they recognize that to claim a right for oneself requires accepting the same right in others. That system of mutual recognition constitutes the system of natural duties correlative with natural rights. Human beings, Jefferson says, must recognize "the similar rights of other sensible beings."[69]

But why must they do so? The whole system of proto-rights serves security-seeking, but in fact it is very defective in that respect. It is obviously defective for those whose rights are not respected, that is, for those who are subjected to the rule of force. But it is unsuccessful even for those who rule. They deny the rights of some, of those they subject, and "monkish ignorance and superstition" may even lead the oppressed to accept, or partly accept, their oppression. Nonetheless, nature prompts the oppressed to seek their security also, that is, to assert themselves in the face of their oppression. Their erroneous opinions can mask the rule of nature in them only so far. Thus the rule of the oppressors is always insecure.

Likewise the oppressors suffer from insecurity vis-à-vis each other. They raise claims to more than security, to domination. Their claims inevitably conflict not only with the oppressed but with the claims of other oppressors as well. The rulers in such a system suffer insecurity not only from below, or vertically, but horizontally as well. Human history, under the aegis of proto-rights, is a history of rebellion and civil war. It is not a history of human security. Human security is promised when the drive for security and the rights derivative therefrom are recognized for all, when the oppressed are raised up and the oppressors scale back their claims.[70]

Thus the rights-in-the-proper-sense which replace proto-rights are greater than the latter in at least two ways. First, they are mutually recognized, and thus acquire a genuine moral quality. As recognized claims, they become rights with duties reciprocal to them. To recognize the other's claim as a right is to recognize in oneself (and others) a duty. The rights do not derive from duties, as many contemporary scholars would have it; the duties derive from the rights or, better yet, are co-constituted with rights-in-the-proper-sense in the process of mutual recognition.[71]

Not every claim that an individual might be inclined to raise on his or her behalf can be eligible to become a right-in-the-proper-sense. Not every such claim can reasonably be expected to achieve mutual acceptance by all others. So-called "rights" to dominate others, for example, will not win universal acceptance among those who understand their situation correctly. One can then reverse the Jeffersonian formula: we value those rights in ourselves which we respect in others and expect them to respect in us.

Rights-in-the-proper-sense derive from a relatively complex process of mutual recognition and transformation. Can they really be considered natural rights? It would seem not. What derives from nature are the selfish passions, which in themselves produce only selfish claims, not yet full rights; what transforms the claims of the passions into rights is the "civilized" figuring out of the system of mutual respect for rights, a figuring out no doubt aided by the existence of civilized institutions like government and law, which lend practical effectiveness to the mutual recognition. One might be tempted to adopt the Kantian formula of "rational rights" rather than "natural rights."

Yet Jefferson himself in the Declaration of Independence traced these rights to the creator, that is, nature. Recalling what Jefferson discovered at the heart of nature in his discussion of the natural bridge may help to see how he understood rights to be natural. The core of nature is the human drive for security; the core of rights is the same. The recognition of rights, of mutual claims to security, is the system which both serves and ultimately (but not directly) derives from that same natural drive. A rational or civilized figuring out may intervene, but the natural drive for security guides and grounds that process at every stage. In this quite meaningful sense, the rights thus arrived at are, indeed, natural rights.

The process of mutual recognition is furthered to the degree that human beings become properly self-conscious about the basis for their rights claims. When they recognize that security-seeking is the basis of rights, they not only can become more rationally calculating with regard to the means for the achievement of security; they also pose to themselves the question of why other security-seeking, "sensible beings" do not possess the same rights. If security-seeking is the decisive title to rights, then they are driven by the mere force of reason to recognize that same title in others. Thus the mutual recognition of rights becomes something more than a mere matter of calculation; it becomes a rational principle and can become a matter of conscientious conviction. Certainly for a man like Jefferson himself the recognition of rights stood on this footing. At the same time, the evolution of the system of mutual recognition of rights gives greater play to the moral sense, or natural compassion and benevolence toward fellow human beings. So far as one's own security is part of a system of mutual security, the conflicts between self and others that allowed the selfish passions to overwhelm the other-regarding feelings are muted. Ironically, the moral sense can come most into its own once it has been supplemented by the system of rights and government.[72]

In *Notes on Virginia* Jefferson sketches only the nature of rights in general; he does not pause to derive or list specific natural rights. Of course, in the Declaration of Independence, he has already specified rights to life, liberty, and the pursuit of happiness. But that list is not complete, for the three rights listed are said to be "among" the rights with which men were endowed by their Creator. The treatment of rights in the Declaration is incomplete in yet another respect: it treats the claims about rights as "self-evident truths" and therefore contains no discussion of the basis for affirming these three rights as rights, or for understanding what other rights there may be. Jefferson presented a fuller discussion of the nature of specific rights in a very important letter to his good friend Pierre Samuel Dupont de Nemours in 1816, which remedies some of this incompleteness.

In that letter, Jefferson presents a slightly different list of rights from the one offered in the Declaration: he specifically mentions a right to property and he describes another right which appears to be equivalent to the Declaration's right to liberty. He does not specify either a right to life or a right to the pursuit of happiness.[73]

The difference between the two lists does not imply any inconsistency between them, however; neither claims to be exhaustive and nothing said in either place explicitly or implicitly denies anything said in the other—unless we follow the line of argument taken by some scholars that Jefferson's failure to include the right to property in the Declaration amounted to a rejection of that right. Jefferson's own testimony points to a very different answer:

the two lists are to be added together. That would mean, in effect, that the right to property would be added as a fourth right to the list in the Declaration. No firm reason suggests that these four constitute an all-inclusive list of the natural rights. Indeed, he elsewhere identifies other rights—rights of conscience, rights of emigration, for example. But the current list provides a good beginning point for understanding the nature of specific rights.

The Right to Life

Both the natural rights tradition and Jefferson's Declaration of Independence give pride of place to the right to life. The right to life easily and readily flows from the general description of rights in *Notes*. The natural ground is precisely the drive for security, which is but an extended form of the desire for preservation; the right to life, a "selfish passion," a right we value for ourselves,—this claim appears as a proto-right. It can also be easily redefined into a right-in-the-proper-sense. The right to life clearly is the kind of claim that is restrained enough to be universally and unanimously adopted; it is the kind of claim, in other words, that can satisfy the requirements of mutual recognition. Each person can recognize the right to life of others in return for recognition of his or her own right.

The right to life can be a right-in-the-proper-sense, however, only if it is what some call a negative or a liberty right as opposed to a positive or claim right. The difference between the two types of rights is quite simple: the duty correlative to a negative right is merely negative, the duty to forbear from interfering with the exercise of the right. The duty correlative to a positive right, however, is more active; it demands the duty-bearer to supply that to which the right-holder has a right. An example of each can help clarify the distinction. The right a person has to the funds in his or her bank account is a positive right, because the duty-bearer, the bank, has an obligation to supply those funds when they are properly applied for. The right to freedom of speech, however, is a negative right, for the duty-bearers in this case have no obligation to supply the right-holder with a speech to deliver, or even to listen to a speech. Their obligation extends only to not interfering with valid exercises of the right.

Only a negative right to life can pass the test for becoming a right-in-the-proper-sense. Persons may raise a proto-right claim to a positive right to life, or rather to the means to life, but a positive right to life will not win mutual assent of others: it amounts to a blank check on one's own life and liberty that a rational being would not accept. While human beings are not simply selfish or entirely indifferent to others, they nonetheless are moved most powerfully by self-love, and love of their own.[74] The system of rights counters the ill effects of the selfish passions, but it is effective precisely because it builds on them. Morever, no person who understands property as Jefferson does would accept a positive right to life.

The Right to Property

To many the most striking feature of Jefferson's letter to Dupont is the fact that it asserts, clearly and distinctly, a right to property: "I believe that a right to property is founded in our natural wants, in the means with which we are endowed to satisfy these wants, and the right to what we acquire by those means."[75] Jefferson's affirmation of a right to property, not at all unique to this letter, runs counter to a current scholarly view resting on his modification in the Declaration of the famous Lockean triad of "life, liberty, and property" to "life, liberty, and the pursuit of happiness."[76] As Richard Matthews puts it:

> Jefferson rejects the traditional Lockean triad of "life, liberty, and estate." This omission is significant. While Locke views property as a natural right and its accumulation as the fulfillment of human endeavors, Jefferson does not. Jefferson's vision of man and of man's telos is much grander.[77]

Apparently Jefferson did not agree that substitution of the "pursuit of happiness" for the right to property in the Declaration implies a rejection of the latter right. Indeed, if we consult some of the parallel statements of the day, we see how implausible is the claim that the affirmation of the right to the pursuit of happiness in itself amounts to a rejection of the right to property. Prior to the Declaration, George Mason had written in the Virginia Bill of Rights of "certain inherent rights" human beings possess by nature, "Namely the enjoyment of life and liberty, with the means of acquiring and possessing property and pursuing and obtaining happiness and safety."[78] In the Massachusetts Bill of Rights, the "natural, essential, and inalienable rights" are said to include "the right of enjoying and defending their lives and liberties; that of acquiring, possessing, and protecting property; in fine, that of seeking and obtaining their safety and happiness."[79]

In the letter to Dupont, Jefferson states quite precisely the origin of the right to property: it is in the service of our right to satisfy our natural wants or needs. The right to property is grounded in the right to life, but it marks an important and problematic extension of the latter. The right to life is a right to what is most clearly our own, but the right to property is a right to the external world. This right affirms, in effect, that the external world can become one's own (juridically) just as one's life is. The right to property is thus inherently paradoxical. Jefferson answers this concern along the same lines Locke did. Human beings cannot do without some sort of property in that they must appropriate, make entirely their own, parts of the external world in order to live. The basic metabolism of existence is the first ground of property.[80] Jefferson, concludes Charles Miller, "is surely close to Locke" in his theory of the origin of property.[81]

Even though all living beings appropriate parts of the external world, only human beings have property and a right to property in the strict sense. Moreover, human beings make other animals into property.[82] Humans do not merely share "natural wants" with other living beings, but are, says Jefferson, "endowed" with certain "means . . . to satisfy those wants." The human means are different from other means and are unique. Humans consciously understand their mortality and their vulnerability, and thus consciously shape their world so as to guarantee their survival. Humans project their insecurity into the future. The pervasive rather than intermittent sense of insecurity produces the more or less steady pursuit of security. Human beings labor for the sake of the security they seek. As they have a right to life, they have a right to this unique human means to secure that right, a right to the fruits of their labor, and a right to the wherewithal on which to labor. From the natural right to life arises a natural right to property. Jefferson no less strongly affirms this than does Locke himself.

Driven by their desire for security, human beings invest their labor in the external world. Labor is an investment of what is clearly one's own in that which is not. Labor is also painful; no one would invest it without promise of reward in the form of a right to its fruits, a "right to what we acquire by these means." The investment of labor is necessary not merely because human beings seek security, but because nature of her own accord does not produce enough to satisfy human wants. "A little land culti-vated, and a little labor, will procure more provisions than the most successful hunt; and a woman will clothe more by spinning and weaving clothes than by hunting."[83]

Property is thus both instrumental to human life and expres-sive of the fundamental character of human being. The relation between life, property (the external world), and labor confirms the argument presented in the previous section regarding the right to life as a negative right. Human beings who understand the relationship as Jefferson does would affirm only a negative right to life, for life requires external goods, which in turn re-quire labor, that is, painful interaction with the external world. A positive right to the means of life would not be accepted by all, for it would blur responsibility for labor and would threaten to put one's own labor and the fruits thereof at the service of others indiscriminately. Not merely would this be unacceptable in itself, but a rational person would discern that such a right would un-dermine the very incentive to labor and thereby discourage the activity that makes life more secure. Paradoxically, therefore, a positive right to life would make life generally less rather than more secure.[84]

The Right to Liberty

Jefferson likewise affirmed a right to liberty: "No one has a right to obstruct another, exercising his faculties innocently for the relief of sensibilities made a part of his nature."[85] Again the source is nature. The natural right to liberty is both a broader right than the natural right to property and a narrower one. It is broader in that it arises not merely from "natural wants" but from "natural sensibilities," that is, according to eighteenth-century usage, "instincts of liking or aversion" (*O.E.D.*). An example might be tastes or likings, or pursuits that are not strictly speaking pursuits of needs, such as the sensibility for beauty in art, or chocolate in ice cream. As long as those pursuits are "innocent," in that they do not infringe on rights of others, then there is a right to them, "without hindrance." The right to liberty is an "all things equal" guarantee of freedom of choice and action, without necessary reference to need. The right to liberty is also narrower than the right to property in that it concerns the actions of the individual, "the exercise of his faculties," and not the appropriation of a part of the external world.

The right to liberty as a right-in-the-proper-sense contains within it a tacit reference to the rights of others. As a natural right, the right to liberty is, of course, an inalienable right. But the right only extends so far as it remains "innocent." In a state of nature, where there is no known law or government to draw firm lines establishing where the rights of one end and the rights of another begin, there must be self-definition, self-limitation, and self-defense of rights. Under such circumstances, disagreements over these boundary lines are inevitable; this alone would make a system of rights without government and law a very inconvenient thing. Some relatively neutral party is needed to judge which exercises of liberty are truly "innocent," and which not. The government and laws that do this do not restrict or infringe the inalienable right to liberty but rather define what counts as "innocent" exercise of one's faculties, which is all the inalienable liberty right-in-the-proper-sense amounts to anyway.

The Declaration implicitly retains the old distinction between liberty and license, but the distinction rests solely on whether the parallel liberties and rights of others are invaded. The inherent value or quality of the exercise of liberty is not otherwise a factor in the judgment of whether we are in the presence of a genuine liberty-right or not. In this sense the Declaration clearly articulates a liberal conception of politics and morals.

The rights to life, liberty, and property thus complement each other and form a kind of system. The grounding right is the first, but it is productive of the other two because human beings are part of nature in a unique way, such that the right to life necessarily broadens out to a larger concern for security on the one hand and "sensibility" on the other. The latter leads to a right to liberty, which is not strictly limited to the means to life, but is limited to the use of one's own faculties. The former broadens out to the use and appropriation of the external world. So there is a certain completeness to the triad of life, liberty, and property, which is no doubt responsible for its near universality in rights-thinking.

The Right to the Pursuit of Happiness

But what then is the right to the pursuit of happiness? Forrest McDonald concludes that the introduction of the pursuit of happiness in the Declaration implies the superposition of an "Aristotelian" doctrine, happiness, on what is an otherwise Lockean "enthusiasm for natural law." He bases this conclusion on the assertion that the source for the idea may have been Burlamaqui, who, "it seems evident," was "the first eighteenth century-philosopher to have developed the idea."[86]

The "pursuit of happiness," however, is a Lockean idea, and it was extensively developed in Locke's *Essay Concerning Human Understanding*, a work that even the most devoted anti-Lockeans, such as Wills, concede was important to Jefferson. According to Locke, all animals seek pleasure and attempt to avoid pain, but human beings alone develop a notion of happiness as such that goes beyond the mere satisfaction of individual desires. The idea of happiness "consists in the idea of the enjoyment of pleasure without any considerable mixture of uneasiness."[87] The idea of happiness frees human beings from subjection to individual desires, but they remain emphatically subject to the desire for happiness itself. "Happiness . . . everyone constantly pursues and desires what makes any part of it."[88] Locke emphasized the pursuit of happiness rather than its achievement, for it is a goal that can never be achieved in this life. All happiness is temporary, every satisfaction soon followed by a new unease by which "we are set afresh on work in the pursuit of happiness."[89]

At the same time, Locke used his conception of the pursuit of happiness to give an account and justification "for the various and contrary ways men take, though all aim at being happy."[90] All pursue happiness but the specific objects they pursue necessarily and legitimately vary. Happiness, or its pursuit, stands as the comprehensive object of action within a human life; human beings are unalterably or necessarily directed to this pursuit by their nature.[91] Even though human beings are doomed to frustration in their pursuit of the ever-elusive happiness, they are nevertheless unalterably committed to it. And because different people pursue different visions or objects of happiness, freedom or toleration necessarily characterizes a society that attempts to live according to the guidance of nature as Locke described it in his doctrine of happiness.

The affirmation of a right to the pursuit of happiness in the Declaration entails a commitment to this notion of a comprehensive yet individually variable object of universal human desire and action. It serves as a kind of summation of all the aspirations and strivings which are expressed in the other rights.[92] Recall that John Adams concluded his list of the natural rights in the Massachusetts Constitution as follows: "in fine, that of seeking and obtaining their safety and happiness." Ronald Hamowy captures very well the summative and variable quality of happiness in the Declaration:

> They may act as they choose in their search for ease, comfort, felicity, and grace, either by owning property or not, by accumulating wealth or distributing it, by opting for material success or asceticism, in a word, by determining the path of their own earthly and heavenly salvation as they alone see fit.[93]

The right to pursue happiness, like the rights to property and liberty, derives from the special way in which human beings fit into nature. The idea of happiness, originating in the unique capacity of the human mind to form general ideas, supplies humanity with freedom, or the nearest thing to free will that is attainable. It removes human beings from the chain of stimulus and response to which other animals are bound, and gives human beings the capacity to stand above the particular stimuli they encounter and form a life with some shape or other. As a comprehensive, although variable end of action, happiness stands at a remove from the desire for survival that grounds the right to life.

The right to life is constituted by reference to a passion of antipathy, antipathy to death; in Hobbes's language it is a "fromward." Happiness on the other hand, is a "to-ward," a goal or end to be sought, not merely a fate to be fled. Between these two kinds of rights stands the right to liberty which partakes to a degree of both impulses. As a right, it is constituted by its service as a means to the preservation of life. But it also betokens the human quest toward, the human transcendence of mere survival as an end. Liberty is thus a most comprehensive right. As it often did for writers of the founding generation, it can stand as a short-hand expression for all the rights.

CIVIL RIGHTS AND POLITICAL IMPERATIVES: SOME IMPLICATIONS OF NATURAL RIGHTS

Natural rights are rights human beings possess prior to, that is, independent of, all government. Not only is government not the source of the rights, but the rights do not initially concern government.[94] When government is instituted, however, a new situation arises, for there is now a new kind of entity against which rights hold, namely, government itself. Government can threaten rights, indeed can be a particularly potent threat against rights, because it possesses the organized coercive power of the community. How to protect the people in their natural rights against government became one of the master questions of the philosophy of rights and one of the major issues in contention during the founding era.

That question cannot be adequately approached, however, unless a yet more fundamental fact is recognized: with the institution of government a whole new class of rights emerges, not so much from nature itself, as from the nature of the formation of government, from the universal consent or agreement that institutes government. The individuals, now citizens, have a new right, the civil right to protection in their natural rights. This right, although not natural, is in principle universal, once it is recognized what the purpose of government is.

In addition to not deriving directly from nature as the natural rights do, this fundamental civil right differs from the natural rights in several other important ways. The duty-bearer in this case is not another individual but the new collectivity, the state, brought into existence or rationalized by the "social contract." Secondly, this right, unlike the natural rights, is a claim or positive right. The duty borne by the state is precisely to supply that to which the individuals possess a right—protection by the state. For reasons of justice and safety, protection is to take the primary form of protection by laws. Thus as a first consequence of the making or rationalizing of the state, individuals acquire a right to protection of the laws. Such a right is strictly reciprocal with a duty in the citizens of allegiance. John Adams captured this point exceedingly well in the debates culminating in the resolution to formally break with Britain.

> That, as to the king, we had been bound to him by Allegiance, but this bond was now dissolved by his assent to the last act of Parliament, by which he declares us out of his protection, and by his levying war on us, a fact which had long ago proved us out of his protection; it being a certain position in law, that allegiance and protection are reciprocal, the one ceasing when the other is withdrawn.[95]

The state's duty to supply protection of the laws is not satisfied by any mere act of forbearance as the other duties correlative with the natural rights may be. This duty requires positive acts in order to be fulfilled.

Thus, with the institution of government, two new major rights or sets of rights arise: the right to protection by the state and the right to protection from the state. These rights are the primary civil rights of citizens or persons under the jurisdiction of a government.[96] These two rights are more frequently expressed in a constitutional context as the right to protection of the laws and the right to due process of the law, respectively. Each of these large civil rights implies or is constituted by a cluster of more particular rights, which provide specific ways in which these rights are secured to the individual. These rights also are civil rights, but not generally so universal as their "parent" civil rights; the latter are so universal that they could (and sometimes were) said to be natural rights. The more particular rights may vary somewhat from one political society to another; trial by jury may be considered a necessary part of the right to due process of law in some places, but other means of impartial trial may be accepted elsewhere. The early Americans for the most part clung to the specification of these rights as they had evolved within the English common law and the British constitution.[97]

The two chief civil rights of citizens point in two quite different directions and render the task of governance both complex and difficult. In *Federalist* 51, James Madison gave the nonlegalistic formulation of the two political imperatives corresponding to the two fundamental civil rights. "In framing a government which is to be administered by men over men, the great difficulty lies in this: you must first enable the government to control the governed; and in the next place oblige it to control itself."[98]

These political requirements correspond to the juridical formulation of the right to protection of the laws and the right to due process of law, respectively. The juridical formulations of the rights do not suffice, for the mere declaration of rights does not entail their security. The task of securing the basic civil rights transforms itself into a task of political construction of a government both strong and active enough to "control the governed" in the pursuit of supplying security of rights through protection of the laws, and also one sufficiently controlled that it acts only to secure rights and not to infringe upon them. The Americans pursued that complex task in their efforts to develop a new federalism and a new republicanism.[99]

APPENDIX: ON READING JEFFERSON

Almost the only proposition that most readers of Jefferson can agree on is that he was either very confused or very eclectic. Systematic reflection on how Jefferson wrote, and therefore on how he should be read, helps greatly to diminish the appearance of confusion. Jefferson's comments about Bolingbroke, quoted in the text, indicate that he subscribed to the view that a good writer tailors his writings to the quite different points of view and character types in his audience. Jefferson's writings fall into three main classes: public writings and sayings, undertaken by him in his political capacity and addressed to the community at large;

private writings, mostly correspondence, addressed to particular persons; and his book, *Notes on Virginia*, submitted like his political statements to the public at large, but not submitted in his public capacity.

The audiences differ and the modes of writing differ accordingly. Jefferson's public writings are most like the "political tracts" of Bollingbroke, which he praised as not offending even "the most timid religionist." It is well known that Jefferson frequently wrote in private correspondence of how much he hesitated to have his religious views become public.[100] His public presentations were certainly colored as well by his view that a healthy nation requires "the conviction in the minds of the people that [their] liberties are the gift of God."

His private writings, upon which we are dependent for his views on many subjects, present their own problems, for all were written to specific persons, and what Jefferson said was very much tailored to those persons. A particularly striking example is his exchanges with John Adams and with John Taylor concerning the latter's attack in print on the former. With Adams, Jefferson commiserated: "I hope your quiet is not to be affected at this day by the rudeness of intemperance of scribblers." To Taylor he wrote: "I found here the copy of your [book] for which I pray you to accept my thanks. . . . You have successfully and completely pulverized Mr. Adams' system of orders."[101] In the private correspondence it is not only a matter of Jefferson's concern for sound public opinion at work, but rather tact and good taste, as well as a strong dislike for unnecessary personal conflict. One sees these qualities throughout Jefferson's life: his temperament led him to seek peace, harmony, and easy social relations whenever possible. When personal splits occurred, as for example with Adams, he almost always made it a point to restore good feelings. His great sense of tact is perhaps nowhere more visible than in his long-standing relationship with Madison. Few men have been such close friends over so long a time and yet disagreed so much about the pursuit (politics) to which both devoted their lives. Throughout his private writings, moreover, Jefferson displayed an astonishing tendency to be agreeable to his correspondent. Thomas Law, for example, sent him his book on the moral sense and Jefferson replied that "it contained exactly my own creed on the foundation of morality in man." William Short wrote him about Epicurus and Jefferson replied: "As you say of yourself, I too am an Epicurean."[102] Jefferson chose always to emphasize areas of agreement, and to say as much of what his interlocutor wanted to hear as he felt able. He expressed his own policy in one of those pieces of advice he often gave about life:

> In stating the prudential rules for our government in society, I must not omit the important one of never entering into dispute or argument with another. I never saw an instance of one of two disputants convincing the other by argument.[103]

These qualities of his private writings make for much of the confusion that scholars find in him. They also imply that the correspondence must be interpreted with great caution. It must and can be used, but only with thoughtful analysis, including consideration of the recipient.

Notes on Virginia comes closest to the "philosophic tracts" of Bolingbroke, which Jefferson considered suited "for those who are not afraid to trust their reason with discussions of right and wrong." Since others may also pick up one of these tracts, they must be written with a bit of subtlety, as is *Notes on Virginia*. Nonetheless, by Jefferson's standard *Notes* would appear to bear a specially privileged status among his writings. I, at least, have so treated it.

Part Two

CONVERGENCES

ON THE FOUNDATION OF THE
AMERICAN POLITICAL TRADITION

No thread runs through the tangle of American politics more clearly than rights. Yet rights are not the only thread to run through the tangle, and observers have brought forth at least three others as particularly definitive of American political culture. Perhaps, some have thought, the idea of a *novus ordo seclorum* is a great myth—neither America nor any other nation begins anew; every nation is formed by its history. Tocqueville, for example, thought that "if we could go right back to the elements of societies and examine the very first seconds of their histories, . . . we should there find the first cause of their prejudices, habits, dominating passions, and all that comes to be called the national character."[1] Following Tocqueville's suggestion, many have seen the key to America in its history, or rather, in its prehistory. American civilization was transplanted English civilization in its formative years, and certainly the shape of American political life continues to bear the marks of that origin. Institutions like the jury, representative government, and constitutionalism can all be plausibly placed near the center of the American political experience, and all can plausibly be traced back to prior English practice. The key to the character of the American tradition lies, then, in the past, in the American past and, before that, the English past. The American Revolution, far from being something entirely new, was a replaying on American soil of the Glorious Revolution of the late seventeenth century in England, a revolution that definitively established in England traditions of constitutionalism, rule of law, representative government, and definitively cut back on the pretensions of monarchies, autocracies, and all other forms of arbitrary power. The Glorious Revolution in turn established and confirmed the ancient or inherited or historical English constitution, and along with the constitution, the historical rights affirmed in the constitution and the historical role of parliament in governance. Here, not in the natural rights philosophy, lies the grounding for the American concern with rights, and the seed from which political democracy has grown. America, according to this view, is essentially Burkean—a grown, not made, political society, grown just as its motherland was grown and not made. The mandate of this view is to cherish the past, to look to history, not nature, for guidance, and to retreat from the abstract rationalism of doctrines like the natural rights philosophy. This view of America, this thread in the political culture, we might call, in honor of its Burkean echoes, the Old Whig view.

Others, without denying the presence of some of these elements in the American tradition, still deny the major claim, that the character of America derives from its continuity with the motherland and the Old Whig tradition. America was founded, after all, in a great revolution against the motherland. Even more significantly, however, the revolution did not so much cause as register an earlier disruption and discontinuity. The initial cause of that disruption lies even further back in the settlement of America. That settlement was not quite so smooth an affair as the Old Whig view implies. Those who came to America were dissidents, people setting off to find a new heaven in the new world, or at least to build an unprecedented "city upon a hill," quite different from the corrupt and degenerating country they were leaving in the third and fourth decades of the seventeenth century. Those settlers were not moved by devotion to the past, but by visions of the future—not only the future of their new communities, but the future altogether beyond this world. The Puritans, respectful of the English past, the English constitution, and their rights as Englishmen, nonetheless looked elsewhere for decisive political guidance and understood the foundation of their politics not in a relation to history, but in a relation to the divine.

The Puritans in their time developed a distinctive set of institutions and a distinctive political culture, which, it is sometimes said, were the seed of later, postrevolutionary American politics. As William O. Douglas once said, America is a nation whose institutions presuppose a divine being.[2] It is essential, even today, for political figures to invoke God, and America is said to be a nation marked beyond others by a "civil religion" articulating the divine origin and support for American politics.[3] America, according to this view, owes its specific political character to the religious and theological views and practices of its early settlers and the continuing religious character of its people.

Within Puritanism, it is said, the truly characteristic features of American politics were born. The concern with the individual that is reflected in the American commitment to individual rights, the democracy that flowered in America—these had their source among the Puritans. Tocqueville, too, is a witness on behalf of the Puritans: "Puritanism was not just a religious doctrine; in many repects it shared the most absolute democratic and republican theories." The Puritans, Tocqueville concluded, were the source of that "spirit of freedom" that animates American democracy.[4]

Still others have seen the dominant orientation in America to be neither toward the past in a Burkean manner, nor toward the very distant future in the Puritan manner, but in the present, in a commitment to a democratic form of governance and to the political life that goes with that. America is more secular and less ascetic, more progressive and less attached to the past than the other two points of view would have it. America, like ancient Rome, is defined above all by its political character. America, however, is a thoroughly popular republic, marked by its commitment to equality and democracy. The history of America, according to this view, is the history of the progressive realization of democracy, from the halting steps of the founders through the ideas of Jefferson and Lincoln through the democratizing reforms of the Progressive, New Deal, and Great Society eras.

This commitment to democracy is, in turn, understood by many to be a variant of a classical perspective that saw self-governance as the only calling worthy of human beings. To be a self-governing community, to be a community of citizens, not subjects, not saints—this is America. This commitment to politics, to citizenship, to self-governance, is often seen as a revival and development of a very old orientation, called classical republicanism. It is old, but it is not necessarily backward-looking; not custom but the deliberative judgments of the community governs. The American founders expressed their grasp of America as a revival of classical republicanism when they took as pen names the

names of heroes of Greek and especially Roman republicanism—
Publius, Brutus, Cato. They expressed it also when they chose to
build their public buildings in a classical style, when they portrayed George Washington in a toga and compared him to the
Roman patriot Cincinnatus.

Each of these ways of grasping what is central to the American
tradition has had its champions, both in public life and in the
scholarly literature. The aim of Part II is to explore these three
visions of America, competitors with the natural rights orientation. My argument is a bit complex. On the one hand, I maintain that the claims for primacy of one or another of these three
are misplaced: America is the natural rights republic. Yet these
are genuine threads, and the fact that none is dominant does not
imply that any of them is absent. In fact, I argue, what made
America was the way these four elements—Old Whig constitutionalism, political religion, republicanism, and the natural rights
philosophy—came together. The amalgamation that occurred in
America was unique in the world, and led America to a unique
path of political development and to a particularly tense existence
as these four different and, in some dimensions, incompatible elements fell in and out of harmony with each other. In that amalgam, however, the four elements did not all enjoy an equal status;
the natural rights philosophy remains America's deepest and so
far most abiding commitment, and the others could enter the
amalgam only so far as they were compatible, or could be made
so, with natural rights. The truly remarkable thing is the demonstrated capacity of the natural rights philosophy to assimilate the
other three and hold them all together in a coherent if not always
easily subsisting whole.

I am thus putting forward a kind of answer to the questions
posed in the current battle over the nature of the American tradition. The battle persists because the various partisans all do
have their hands and minds on a piece of the tradition. At the
same time, however, they have but a partial grasp. I thus return in
a way to the old eclectic view of Corwin and others of his generation, but I hope, as in the higher stages of the Hegelian dialectic,
at a higher stage of synthesis. It is surely not, I will argue, a seamless and unproblematical whole. The four elements that came

together at the origin of America and have continued in some form throughout American history are not natural allies and often go into opposition against each other.[5] The tense unity of the four, I would be tempted to speculate, is also the story of the success of America. And their irrevocable splitting apart, should that occur, might be the signal of the decline of America.

Chapter Four

NATURAL RIGHTS AND HISTORY: AMERICAN WHIGS AND ENGLISH WHIGS

By following Lincoln in identifying the Declaration of Independence as the beginning, and by reading the Declaration as a document of the liberal enlightenment, I have taken sides in the great battles over the nature of the American founding. Both judgments are contestable: it might be held that the Declaration should be read in an entirely different way, or it might be held that the Declaration is in no way the beginning.[1] Of course, Lincoln was not alone in testifying on behalf of 1776; the founders themselves did so when they put that date on the base of the weird pyramid with the eye on its top as depicted on the back side of the Great Seal of the United States, available for easy inspection on every one-dollar bill. Nonetheless, other events and moments surely might count as founding moments. We must take note of some of these, for they point toward quite different conceptions of the American regime.

WHIGS

At the time of the movement of opposition that resulted in the Revolution, those Americans who protested British policy most frequently referred to themselves as "patriots" or, more significantly, as "Whigs." This latter term was meant to evoke the memory of the English Whigs of the seventeenth century, the men who had stood for the constitution and resisted the Stuart monarchs, the men who made the Glorious Revolution of 1688-89, the revolution that dislodged King James II from the throne and replaced him with the far more constitutionalist William and Mary. Through their identification with the seventeenth-century Whigs, the Americans perhaps suggest that 1776 is not the beginning but merely a continuation of an older tradition of political thought and action, the nature of which is not likely to be caught in terms of liberal modernity, for this Whig tradition surely predated and was quite independent of the emergence of liberal modernity. Scholars like Randolph G. Adams pick up on the suggestiveness of the Whig name when they trace the Americans' "revolutionary" principles back to the ancient British constitution, itself traceable as far back as the Magna Carta.[2]

Two important claims have frequently been forwarded about the English Whigs and the American revolutionaries: either that the natural rights philosophy is the same as the Whig theory of the Glorious Revolution, or that it is different but essentially irrelevant to what happened in the American Revolution, the relevant things being the old Whig things.[3] Both claims come to the same point, a denial of American innovativeness. Exploring both claims will thus help clarify further the novelty of the Americans, the relevance of the natural rights philosophy to the Revolution, and the understanding on the basis of which the new nation was made. At the same time we will see that despite the novelty of the Americans' position, there is nonetheless much continuity between them and their Whig ancestors. Surely the Americans had good ground for taking the name "Whig." More specifically, if one juxtaposes the list of grievances in the American Declaration of Independence or in other statements of the revolutionary era with the constitutional rights claimed and defended by the English Whigs, it is easy to see the signs of continuity; the affirmations by the earlier Whigs are clearly echoed in those of the later Whigs, and if the Americans understood some things differently, they still found themselves claiming much of what their seventeenth-century English predecessors had fought for. The new natural rights philosophy had an amazing power to sweep up and assimilate these older things; indeed, John Locke, the chief architect of the new philosophy, seems to have gone out of his way to formulate a political philosophy that would do just that. The American Revolution may have been understood to usher in a *Novus Ordo Seclorum,* but it differed from successor revolutionary doctrines in not requiring that a wrecking ball be applied to everything already standing before its new edifice could rise from the ground.

We cannot survey here the wide variety of political writings issued by the seventeenth-century English Whigs, so we must consider the most significant product of their Glorious Revolution. Parallel to the American Declaration of Independence, more or less functionally equivalent to it, stands the English Declaration of Rights, a document explaining and justifying the Glorious Revolution as the Declaration justified the American Revolution. We might anticipate the results of a comparison between the two documents as follows: significant as are the parallels and even continuities, of far greater significance are the differences. Differences show up throughout, but most crucially with respect to the central doctrine of the Declaration of Independence: the Declaration of Rights (despite its name) has nothing at all like the doctrine of natural rights. The English document's complete lack of a doctrine of natural rights is reflected in one great and pervasive difference between the two statements: the English document has nothing analogous to the theoretical "truths" that constitute the center of the American Declaration. Indeed, the question arises regularly about the Glorious Revolution, whether there is any discernible theory implicit in the event or in its justifying document.

Nowhere is the uncertain theoretical rationale of the Declaration of Rights more evident than on the crucial issue of the "revolutionary" character of the action being justified. In the Declaration of Independence, the Americans were unequivocal in affirming a universal right in all peoples "to alter or abolish" governments that failed to accomplish the ends for which government was established. Quite different was the Declaration of Rights: King James is there said to have "abdicated the government," the throne being "thereby vacant." The English pointedly fail to endorse a right in the nation "to alter or abolish" the government and insist instead on the patently fictitious idea of a quasi-voluntary abdication by the king (he had fled the country to escape the army of the invading William of Orange), but they fail even to specify wherein that abdication occurred.[4]

Given the organization of the document, one might be tempted to conclude that the abdication was a consequence of James's alleged abuses of power listed just prior to the assertion that he had abdicated. That long list of actions, introduced as evidence of an "endeavor to subvert and extirpate the Protestant religion and the laws and liberties of the Kingdom," is said to stand utterly and directly contrary to "the known laws and statutes and freedoms of this realm." The juxtaposition of the list of abuses with the assertion of abdication might imply that the abdication consisted precisely in the commission of those great illegal acts. If so, that might amount to something like a right of revolution— the view that political power is held conditionally, and the people have a right to call the king to account if those conditions are violated.[5]

Yet, that would not be a valid conclusion, for the abdication claim is not presented as deriving from the abuses but as a separate item. The illegalities are introduced with one "whereas" and the abdication with a second; the two are presented as parallel and more or less independent facts, the one relevant to the reaffirmation of rights about to be presented, the other to the new settlement of the throne to be established thereafter. As H. T. Dickinson observes, "It was never explicitly stated that James II had been deposed because of his actions."[6]

The Declaration of Rights is studiedly ambiguous; it not only fails to endorse a general right of revolution, it fails to admit that the Glorious Revolution *was* a revolution. Rather, according to the Declaration of Rights, it should be known to history as "The Glorious Abdication." It is no surprise that the authors of the Declaration of Rights hesitated to endorse a right of revolution or unequivocally to identify 1688 as a revolution. As a rule, political societies are or were hesitant to admit a general right of revolution. It is *very* unsettling; it gives people "ideas"; it goes contrary to the view that authority must be secure in order to be effective. The Americans, with their clear affirmation of the right of revolution, introduced a novelty into politics; they were willing to take a chance with the disruptive principle, they were willing to encourage an adversarial or a judgmental attitude by the people toward their government. As Edward Corwin notes, "For the first time in the world, the principles of revolution are made the basis of settled political institutions." This was a great innovation, and a great act of daring (although since the American Revolution it has become far more commonplace).[7] Thus Edmund Morgan contrasts the two revolutions by calling the one "the cautious revolution" and the other "the incautious revolution."[8] The affirmation of the right of revolution constitutes no small part of the American *Novus Ordo Seclorum*.

The first of the Declaration of Independence's "self-evident truths" is the claim that "all men are created equal." The English Declaration of Rights does not agree. It contains no conception of an initial state of no-rule or natural equality and independence. In place of "all men," the Declaration of Rights speaks of "all the estates of the people of the realm," that is, of "the lords spiritual and temporal and commons." The unequal orders or estates of the people of the realm are the ultimate political reality to which the Declaration of Rights refers. Likewise, when it declares William and Mary king and queen, it does not speak of the nation as a sovereign body of naturally equal human beings, but again it speaks of the three estates. The relevant elements of political society are the differentiated and hierarchically ordered existing elements of English society-cum-polity.[9]

The inequality of human beings in the estates pervades the document. One particularly striking example arises in the item affirming the right to bear arms. Unlike the Second Amendment to the United States Constitution, which recognizes a general right to bear arms, the Declaration of Rights carefully limits that right to Protestants, and allows them arms only "suitable to their conditions and as allowed by law." These latter qualifications on the right refer to well-established distinctions governing who could possess arms: no one with an income under 100 pounds a year could own a gun.[10] Just as the Declaration of Rights does not contemplate natural equality, so it does not take for granted equality of rights. Rights vary with one's position in the polity. Again, the Declaration of Independence puts things very differently: the rights it recognizes are possessed by "all men." There is no shadow of an idea that rights derive from or vary according to class membership.

The Declaration of Rights, like most political societies before the American new order, proceeded on the idea that God or nature had selected out "the better sort" to rule; society rested on the acceptance of the propriety of "natural" rulers ruling. The natural condition, or, at least, the relevant condition for politics according to the English Declaration, is the division of the nation into classes—lords, commons, etc., with degree and rank order to which have been attached claims to shares in political power, not the original condition of equality from which all political power must be derived. The Declaration of Rights takes a position rather like the noble lie of Plato's Republic, according to which different persons are born of different metals with individuals of the more precious metals possessing the right to rule over the ones of the less precious metals. The Declaration of Rights was even, in some respects, closer to Sir Robert Filmer's doctrine of divine right of kings, according to which God had selected certain people to rule over other people, than it was to the American Declaration of Independence.

The Declaration of Independence takes up the issue of equality as part of its effort to explore the primeval human condition, the condition prior to the establishment of government and prior to all humanly established laws and rights. The English Declaration of Rights betrays no such eagerness to uncover what preexists the established order. It merely attempts to discern and reassert the principles of that order. The Declaration of Rights thus contains no suggestion whatever that government is a human making. So silent is the Declaration of Rights on this question that even Tory adherents of the divine right of kings doctrine could and did subscribe to the Declaration of Rights.[11]

The Tories could never have endorsed the Declaration of Independence. Here it is very clear that government is an artifact made by human beings for their own purposes. Neither God nor nature makes government—human beings do. Government, like many things that people make, can be better or worse made depending on how well people understand the art of making, on how well they understand what they are doing. Here is one point of Thomas Jefferson's letter to Roger Weightman on the occasion of the fiftieth anniversary of the Declaration of Independence, and indeed a dominant thought for the whole founding generation: people have recently come to understand much better than ever before why and how to make governments, and therefore they can expect great improvements in their political life. Here is one origin of the frequently noted progressive attitude toward politics and society in America. As human constructs, society and polity are open to indefinite improvement. On the other hand, when political life is understood as derived from God or nature, that suggests a limit to what can be done with it; it is what it is, and what it should be; one must accept it with all its limitations.

The idea of government as artifact also leads to the desacralizing of the social life that it interprets. When we recognize society and government as our own making, we recognize nothing sacred in them. This has ambiguous implications for politics. It can be a problem because a feeling of sacred attachment, of reverence for government is, as James Madison pointed out in *Federalist* 49, a way of attaching people to it. Abraham Lincoln returned to the issue in the 1830s when he asked, can a people have reverence for what it knows it has made itself? Can a republican people respect what it has made sufficiently to preserve it? Lincoln saw civil religion as the necessary response to this problem, a cloaking of free government with the sacred aura only religion can supply.[12] Alexis de Tocqueville, on the other hand, brought out how the recognition that government is a human making can be a positive force in securing healthy and free politics. Instead of seeing government as something foreign and imposed, the citizens can see it as something they have made, something they might be attached to for that reason in itself.[13] After all, "we love what we make." Tocqueville's insight finds contemporary echo in the frequently voiced concern that members and clients of organizations come to feel "ownership" of the organizations with which they are involved. Thus we have movements for local control of schools and revitalization of local institutions, for worker involvement in managerial decisions, and for patient involvement in treatment decisions. The Declaration of Rights, not decreeing government to be a human making, promotes neither the loss of legitimacy desacralization threatens, nor the sense of proprietorship it promises. The Declaration of Rights belongs to a universe of traditionalist politics in a way the Declaration of Independence emphatically does not.

Because the American Declaration of Independence presents government as an artifact, and denies the naturalness of political power, it finds the origin of political authority in "the consent of the governed." As we have seen, this does not imply an actual historical process. Rather it refers to a moral, or rational reconstruction of the origin: once one understands nature properly, once one understands that neither nature nor God designates rulers, or makes government, then it is clear humans must do it through consent—voluntarily and purposefully. This is not so much a thesis about the past, however, as one about the present and the future; it presents a way to reconceive the nature of politics and the relationship of citizens to it.

The English Declaration of Rights, on the other hand, does not present government as an artifact, and therefore is not concerned with the means of making it. It contains no language regarding "consent of the governed." The Declaration of Rights does specify that certain powers of government (for example, the tax power) must be exercised with the consent of the governed, or at least of some of them, those represented in Parliament. But it contains nothing of the idea that Parliament derives its powers, is constituted, through consent. The Declaration of Rights does not endorse the doctrine of popular sovereignty as the Declaration of Independence does. The Declaration of Rights neither puts forward a theory of consent in the form of a theory of a social contract, nor does it itself serve as a contract with the new monarchs.[14]

More significant than all the differences we have so far noticed between the two revolutionary documents are those regarding rights. Both documents are concerned with rights, but the nature and function of rights in the two are quite different. To form an idea of the place of rights in the American document, we might reconsider the idea of government as artifact. An artifact is properly made when its making is governed by the end or purpose it is to serve. In the realm of political making described by the Declaration, the dominating end is the securing of rights. Important as other ideas in the Declaration may be—equality, consent, revolution—rights are thus simply central. Government, says the Declaration, is made by human beings, but rights precede and derive from the Creator. Thus, rights are more fundamental than government in the double sense of being more original as well as being the end or purpose of government.

The Americans appeal to rights bestowed by the Creator (God or nature) prior to and independent of any organized political life. On the other hand, the rights declared in the English Declaration of Rights can in no way be described as natural. They are, instead, "ancient rights and liberties" and are defined in the "known laws and statutes and freedoms of this realm." The English rights are very old but they are not natural; they derive from "the laws . . . of this realm," and therefore belong to the subjects of "this realm," not to all human beings. And they belong to those subjects according to their place in the realm, that is, according to their "condition." The rights are restricted, therefore, in a double sense: they are English rather than human rights, and they belong to the English differentially and unequally.

Moreover, the rights in the Declaration of Rights hardly share more than the name with the rights in the Declaration of Independence. For one thing, compared to the sleek economy of the Americans' Declaration, the English list is a veritable hodgepodge. It lacks the compactness and logical interconnectedness of "life, liberty, and the pursuit of happiness." It seems almost a miscellaneous assemblage with no obvious principle of selection or connection. In many cases, it is not even clear what the right being declared is or who is its possessor. Some of the rights are best described as powers (or rejected as nonpowers) of political bodies. One of the "rights," for example, is the king's lack of a right (or power) of "dispensing with laws . . . by regal authority." Another affirms the right of Parliament to "authorize levies of money." Neither these nor many other of the rights affirmed are tied to rights of individuals. Not all the rights in the Declaration of Rights even appear to be rights in the sense in which the Declaration of Independence uses that term. The last of the list, for example, says that "for redress of all grievances and for the amending, strengthening, and preserving of the laws, Parliament ought to be held frequently." This is not so much a statement of a right belonging to anybody, even to Parliament, as much as a declaration of a desirable state of affairs—frequent Parliaments. It is a right in the sense of "a right thing."

By contrast, the natural rights enumerated in the American Declaration are all rights belonging to individuals, and are all rights in a quite specific and different sense; they are not expressions of a right or desirable condition or state of affairs. They are rights which each individual can claim as his or her own, as possessions to be deployed, as options to be exercised at the choice of the rights-holder, rights in a permissive sense, active rights, not a mere condition. Right, according to a classic definition, is "a certain moral power which every man has, either over his own things, or over things due to him," and the Declaration uses the term in that sense.[15] An example: the right of free speech means that the right-holder has the choice to speak or not, to say this or that, as the speaker chooses; it is permissive, but not obligatory. Right in the other sense, however, would imply an obligation, not an option, to speak; it would be a duty more than a right.

Most significantly, the Declaration of Rights fails to affirm the central point in the Declaration of Independence's theory of government: there is no suggestion that government exists for the sake of securing rights, and only for that. Obviously, rights of the sort declared in the 1688 document are important, but they are not the very raison d'être of political life. Since they do not predate, but derive, from political life, there is no question of government's coming to exist for their sake. Rights are conditions or limits or even (as powers) means of rule; they do not stand as the purpose of governance.

Given the centrality of natural rights in the American Declaration, that issue might serve as a good epitome of the entire range of differences between the two documents. In the English Declaration of Rights, the rights and liberties are not tied to God or nature as their source; rather they are "ancient rights and liberties"; they belong not to all human beings but "to the people of this kingdom" as arrayed in their "estates" and "suitable to their conditions." They are limits on the royal power, but their protection is not said to be the very purpose of government. It will thus become very unclear whether these rights limit Parliament as well as the king when Parliment becomes the chief governing institution of the nation in the eighteenth century. The rights mentioned are not the grand human rights of "life, liberty, and the pursuit of happiness," but rather, for the most part, are claims that the king may not take certain actions without the authorization of Parliament. The place of rights in the Declaration of Rights shows it to have been an important document in the rise of constitutional government, but it does not express the same understanding of the nature and purposes of government as the Declaration of Independence does. It could not produce the *Novus Ordo Seclorum* the American Declaration was to do.

The differences respecting rights as well as the other differences point inescapably to the conclusion that the discontinuities between the two declarations are more significant than the continuities. The American Whigs and the English Whigs agree in their opposition to absolutism, but beyond that, disagree heartily. No wonder the English Whigs who ruled in Britain did not understand the American Whigs in their protest against British theory and practice. The American Declaration points forward to an almost entirely different kind of political life than the English document does.

The English Declaration does not point to a *novus ordo seclorum* because, it is now clear, it rests solidly on and affirms almost the very opposite: "the ancient constitution," a constitution whose origin is in the deep past, in "immemorial custom," a constitution that appeals not to nature but to history, a constitution that takes as its main claim to legitimacy its antiquity or its mixed character, its blending and securing the different estates of the nation. The Declaration of Rights, despite its apparently atheoretical character, does rest on a theory, the theory of the ancient constitution, a theory traceable in one form or another back at least as far as Aristotle.[16] "The Declaration of Rights," therefore, "had to be interpreted not as an innovation but as a restoration of the ancient constitution," as Edmund S. Morgan put it.[17]

LOCKE AND THE WHIG TRADITION

We cannot credit the view, therefore, that the Declaration of Independence, in its theoretical section at least, says just the same as did the earlier Whigs of the era of the Glorious Revolution. John Phillip Reid, the author of an impressive series of constitutional histories of the era of the Revolution in America, concedes as much. The theoretical preamble to the Declaration differs from the Declaration of Rights and the Whig theory of rights, but, he argues, the Preamble was "unimportant." The language about natural rights in the Declaration of Independence is mere "rhetoric"; in its operative or nonrhetorical parts, the Declaration of Independence does not contain claims of natural rights. "All rights asserted in the Declaration were English rights," that is, rights traceable to the ancient English constitution. The Declaration of Independence, moreover, does not stand as the most authoritative statement of the colonists' position; that honor belongs instead to the Declaration and Resolves issued by the First Continental Congress in October 1774.[18] Reid concedes that the colonists occasionally appealed to nature as the source or authority for the rights they claimed but, as in the Declaration of Independence, the appeals to nature never were central. The Preamble to the 1776 document was one of the very few places where an appeal to natural rights alone was made; more commonly "claims to natural rights stated alternative authority," alternative to the more authoritative grounding in the Constitution or other forms of positive law. Natural rights were so far from being the core of the colonial position that most often "nature was rejected as the sole authority of rights." So peripheral were natural rights that "rights based on the authority of nature only, and not also said to be positive, were not a factor in the revolutionary debate." They were, in a word, "irrelevant"; those who hold otherwise succumb to "the mythology of natural rights." Although he wavers a bit from time to time, Reid makes a quite precise and circumscribed claim, based on the following distinction: "To say that nature was one of the authorities cited for the validity of rights is quite different from saying that nature defined rights, determined which rights were enjoyed by British subjects." The language of natural rights supplies merely "broad generalities," or "the shared platitudes of mankind"; the real "standards for controlling governmental conduct that can be translated into legal rights" derive from positive, not natural, sources, from the Constitution and the common law.[19]

Despite Reid's erudition, his evidence does not establish his very strong claims about "the irrelevance of natural rights," nor does he manage to capture the function of natural rights and natural law arguments in colonial thinking. These limitations in Reid's study can be seen even if we keep entirely to his own ground, legal or quasi-legal documents like the Declaration of Independence, and the even more authoritative (by his lights) Declaration and Resolves of 1774.[20]

On the basis of the organization of the Declaration of Independence as explicated in Chapter 1 above, we have good reason to question Reid's characterization of the Preamble as "rhetoric," an inspiring (perhaps) prelude to the meat of things in the appeal to constitutional rights in the so-called list of grievances. The Preamble does not serve as a mere rhetorical appendage, a plumed hat for attention and show, but rather forms the crucial part of the syllogistic structure of the document as a whole. The list of grievances finds its place in the Declaration precisely as supplying the minor premises to the Preamble's major premise, both together producing the syllogism's conclusion: "These colonies are and of right ought to be free and independent states."[21]

After having surveyed the English Declaration of Rights, we are in a better position to understand just how important the Preamble's major premise is to the overall argument of the American Declaration. The English and American documents differ most obviously on what is the central issue in the context: is there a right to "alter or abolish" established government? The English appeal to the "abdication" of the king precisely because they lack a theory of revolution; the Americans endorse with no equivocation the right to alter or abolish, and own up to exercising it precisely because they possess the natural rights philosophy of which that right is an integral part.

It is surely true, as Reid emphasizes, that the list of grievances includes references to many rights that appear to have their source in English constitutional law. Many of these, indeed, are strongly reminiscent of rights claimed in the Declaration of Rights of 1688. Yet Reid ignores their function within the American Declaration, and thus misses the way in which the Americans came to understand the relationship between natural rights, to which they laid claim as human beings, and "the rights of Englishmen," to which they also laid claim. The grievances are introduced to establish a quite precise point: to reveal a "design to reduce them under absolute Despotism"; to reveal the "history of repeated injuries and usurpation, all having in direct object the establishment of an absolute tyranny over these states." The point of the grievances is not so much to claim the specific rights implied in the list as to establish the tyrannous intent of the king, through consideration of his "long train of abuses."

Some of the rights appealed to in the list of grievances are natural rights themselves, or direct implications of natural rights. As the Americans learned from Locke, the fact that human beings possess a natural right to property implies that rulers may not "impose taxes on us without our consent." This follows directly from the right to property, for if the king (or his agents) can tax without consent, then it cannot be said that his subjects actually have property, that is, goods over which they have the exclusive right of possession and control. Reid's point, of course, is that the right of legislative assemblies to lay taxes was not a mere natural right but a well-established right under the English constitution. It was a right to which nature was an "alternate claim," but not the sole or important claim. It thus fits, he maintains, the general pattern of rights-claiming he discerns in colonial argumentation. And, to a degree, it does.

But this fit does not make natural rights irrelevant. Two points are especially significant in this context. First, Reid's understanding of the relation between natural and constitutional rights does not even conform to his own observations on the kind of appeal the colonists made to natural rights. "Quite a number of English speaking people in the eighteenth century . . . judged the legitimacy of a constitution by how well it secured those rights." The rights precede or serve as an independent standard for assessing the constitution, and therefore cannot simply derive from the constitution. The echo of the language of the Declaration is not accidental, for the point seems to be the same as that made in that document: the very point of governments is the security of rights and the good ones are the ones that do it well. So many "English speaking people in the eighteenth century" thought this way that Reid regularly ends up quoting such statements in his own text, even though they hurt his case. In one place, for example, he cites a debate in the English journals in which the combatants, despite their other disagreements, concur in the belief that natural rights are "the only foundation of all just Authority; and the sole reason for all Laws." The authors in this debate, just as the Americans, understood the difference between natural and positive rights and held it to be the measure of a good political and legal system that the natural rights "become our *legal* as well as our *natural* rights."[22]

In his *Two Treatises* Locke had attempted to reveal the natural foundation for many contested practices of the English constitution, practices that would necessarily remain contested and insufficiently grounded so long as their foundation remained obscure, so long as they seemed to rest on history, precedent, or custom, all contingent matters of which no definitive version was available.[23] The customary character of the English constitution was indeed one of the reasons why English political history during the seventeenth century was so unstable. Locke attempted, for example, to clarify the status of the traditional rule regarding taxation: the ground was the natural right of property. This validated the constitutional practice against the challenges frequently made by theorists and royalist apologists like Robert Filmer, who argued that the "original" of property was in the king or in the law (reminiscent here of Reid himself), and therefore that either the king or the law could change property relations in the community without any need for traditional consent. Many held that the right of Parliament to consent to tax measures was an act of grace on the part of the king. At the level of the customary constitution itself, it was not so easy to dismiss such claims. Locke's natural rights argument, however, scotched them entirely.[24]

The colonists' acceptance of the natural rights position lay behind their certainty that Parliament, no more than the king, could not tax them without their own consent. At the time of the Stamp Act Crisis the influential Boston preacher Jonathan

Mayhew put the ground of American opposition into the natural rights frame developed by Locke and later expressed in the Declaration of Independence:

> For they . . . are really slaves . . . who are obliged to labour and toil only for the benefit of others; or, which comes to the same thing, the fruit of whose labour and industry may be lawfully taken from them without their consent. . . . Nor are there many American understandings acute enough to distinguish any material difference between this being done by a single person, under the title of an absolute monarch, and done by a far-distant legislature consisting of many persons, in which they are not represented.[25]

The natural rights philosophy gave the Americans a way of resolving an ambiguity in the traditional constitution as affirmed in the Glorious Revolution, an ambiguity that played itself out violently in the American Revolution. According to the British version of the constitution, the requirement was that Parliament lay taxes. The British embodied just this view in the Declaratory Act they passed in 1766 to accompany the repeal of the Stamp Act, and it was this great principle of parliamentary supremacy that they were unwilling to surrender to the Americans.[26] The Americans, on the other hand, denied that Parliament, a body in which they were not and, in the nature of things, could not be represented, could legitimately levy taxes on them under constitutional principles as interpreted and understood in the light of natural rights principles. The natural rights argument, in other words, was neither entirely independent of positive law and constitutional right, nor was it irrelevant. It was decisive in shaping the character and strength of the American attachment to the principle "no taxation without representation." That the Americans were firmly reading the constitution and their rights through the lens of the natural rights philosophy while the British were at least in part reading the constitution through the older lens of the theory of the ancient constitution as expressed in their Declaration of Rights goes far toward accounting for the character and acerbity of the controversy between them.[27]

Many of the colonists' other complaints imply an appeal to established "rights of Englishmen"; the king, they charge, has deprived them "in many cases of Trial by Jury"; he has "transported" them "beyond seas to be tried for pretended offences," thus violating two established rights—to a trial "in the vicinage" and to trial for real offenses. As Reid insists, these are not natural and universal rights, yet they surely have a reasonable connection and find their meaning and import in the context of the natural rights philosophy to which they are attached in the Declaration. The natural rights philosophy affirms a definite view of the character of political authority as held in trust, so to speak, from the people, for the sake of securing them in the enjoyment of their natural rights.[28] To create government is to create an agency possessing rightful coercive power, a necessity in the nature of things, and yet also a danger, for the government created to protect rights can be a formidable threat to rights as well. It is therefore of the first importance to establish the terms and conditions on which governmental coercive authority is to be applied to citizens. Those terms are captured most generally in the phrase "rule of law"; general rules aiming at the welfare of the community, known in advance and impartially enforced, are to be the warrants for the application of governmental coercion to citizens. The ruling authorities must not be free to use coercion merely to serve their own purposes or whims. They must be bound by specific procedures that work toward guaranteeing that conditions for the rule of law are satisfied. In the Anglo-American tradition these conditions came to be called "due process of law," a catchall term for practices ranging from jury trials to the right to examine witnesses, to the right to be apprised of charges lodged against oneself. Many, if not all, of these due process rights are less close to being natural rights in themselves than, say, the natural right based requirement of consent to taxation; while the latter right is a universal right of natural constitutional law and therefore a moral and political requirement in every legitimate regime, there are no doubt valid alternatives to, say, the right to jury trial, or the right to grand jury indictments. Yet, the particular practices that have grown up within English legal history are suitable, if not unique, means for enforcing the implied natural right to rule of law. When the king fails to honor these, it is reasonable to conclude, as the Americans do, that their more fundamental right to protection of their natural rights under rule of law is endangered.[29]

The appeal to natural rights is thus more than an appeal to an alternate source of authority, as Reid would have it, and is far from silent in helping to define the rights the Americans were claiming. Moreover, Reid's theory of the place of natural rights in the colonists' argument runs afoul of a well-known fact about their position, recently restated by Forrest McDonald:

> When the decision for independence was made, all claims to rights that were based upon royal grants, the common law, and the British constitution became theoretically irrelevant. The Americans, thus, "unequivocally justified" themselves in the Declaration "by an appeal to 'the Laws of Nature and Nature's God'."[30]

Reid gives special weight and authority to the Declaration and Resolves of the First Continental Congress, apparently on the basis of his somewhat circular thought that unlike the Declaration of Independence, it does not explicate the natural rights position independently of the British constitution. Granting that (although not the preeminence of the document over the Declaration of Independence), it must also be noted that the Declaration and Resolves does not rest on the British constitution independently of the natural rights philosophy, either. The Congress, in order to "assert and vindicate their rights and liberties" declares those rights they consider to be at risk and states the origin or authority for the rights they claim: "the immutable laws of nature, the principles of the English constitution, and the several charters or compacts." Although some of the rights they assert clearly derive from positive sources like "royal charters," the very first set of rights derive from nature: "they are entitled to life, liberty, and property, and they have never ceded to any sovereign power whatever a right to dispose of either without their consent." Their rights precede their cessions to "sovereign powers" and serve as the basis for their right to "consent," a right confirmed, but not, apparently, originated in the English constitution, a right that the colonists did not forfeit when they emigrated from England. Reid unpersuasively asserts that the colonists meant to trace their rights to "life, liberty and property" to the common law. Yet the language of "cession" speaks much against this attribution, for this language is used of rights possessed by nature which are ceded (or not) to the ruling authorities under the natural rights/social contract theory. It makes no sense to speak of "cessions" of common law rights. As Reid quotes John Dickinson, "A *constitution* is the organization of the *contributed rights* in society."[31] "Contributed [ceded] rights" are just what the colonists in the Declaration and Resolves deny their rights to life, liberty, and property to be. Although they do not use the language, they are thinking of the inalienability of these rights.

Just as in the Declaration of Independence, the Americans find their claims under nature and under the English laws to run in remarkably parallel courses: "the foundation of English liberty, and of all free government, is a right in the people to participate in their legislative council." The English arrangement is validated by the fact that it conforms with the "rights of all free people," rights derived from nature, not from the English law, which surely can say nothing about the rights of all free people. Likewise, it is said to be "indispensably necessary to good government, and rendered essential by the English constitution that the constituent branches of the legislature be independent of each other." Natural principles of "good government" validate and highlight "essential" features of the constitution.[32] Indeed, the pattern in the Declaration and Resolves appears to be much as in the Declaration of Independence: nature not only supplies the standards in the light of which constitutional and legal practices are affirmed and understood, but it supplies guidance as to what practices are to be considered authoritative.[33] The Americans consistently interpret the constitution in the light of the natural rights position, in contrast to the English themselves who interpret it in terms of the very different conception of the ancient constitution and the mixed regime. Thus a doctrine like Thomas Whately's theory of virtual representation could make sense to the British but seems utter sophistry to the Americans.[34] That the Americans did not usually speak of rights with a natural basis alone, or of rights with no rooting in the English laws or constitution proves nothing at all about the role of natural rights thinking.[35] Among other relevant factors is this: the Americans believed that the rights most threatened were those with constitutional recognition as interpreted through their natural rights lens. They were less concerned at first to discern altogether new rights or the full table of natural rights. This is not to say such concerns did not arise. One particularly striking instance involved the issue of slavery. As the Americans more and more thought in terms of natural rights, the institution of slavery seemed to more and more of them to be intolerable and unjust, even if under English colonial law and practice the institution remained acceptable.[36]

Finally, given the very widespread and prominent appeal to the very principles enunciated in the Preamble to the Declaration of Independence at the time of the Revolution, it is difficult to see how one can conclude that these principles were in any sense "irrelevant." We have earlier noticed the parallel language in George Mason's Virginia Declaration of Rights and in John Adam's Massachusetts Constitution of 1780. "Similar wording can be found in the bill of rights adopted in Pennsylvania, Vermont and New Hampshire, and there are provisions in the constitutions of Maryland and of North and South Carolina presupposing much the same point of view," concludes Paul Rahe on the basis of a thorough survey of colonial revolutionary statements. Rahe quite correctly sums up the matter as follows: "From the outset of the Revolution, constitutionalism was conceived of primarily as a formal, legal instrument to safeguard the natural rights of man."[37] The American propensity to assimilate constitutional to natural rights, or to view the former through a lens supplied by the latter, much predates the agitation leading up to the Revolution. A striking example appears in a profoundly Lockean essay by Elisha Williams, an essay written about twenty years before the Stamp Act crisis. "The rights of Magna Charta," pronounces Williams, "depend not on the will of the prince, or legislature, but are the inherent natural rights of Englishmen."[38]

Was America then an offshoot of the Whigs? Yes and no. There was indeed continuity at several levels, a continuity that explains and justifies the Americans' seizure of the name "Whigs." The Americans followed their English predecessors in their hostility to absolutism and their attachment to constitutionalism. Likewise they carried over many of the specific features of the British constitution and common law to which the English Whigs looked in order to realize their constitutionalism. Most obvious are matters like the demand for jury trials and other procedural safeguards that limited the scope of executive discretion and arbitrariness in applying the force of the community against individuals. At the same time the Americans followed the new and reformulated version of the Whig position as developed especially by John Locke and later followers of his like John Trenchard and Thomas Gordon, writing as "Cato" during the first quarter of the eighteenth century. This important reformulation and transformation involved attaching the Whig concern for constitutionalism to an underlying political philosophy, the natural rights/social contract philosophy, quite different from the political philosophy to which Whig constitutionalism had previously been attached, as in the Declaration of Rights, the theory of the ancient constitution, or as in other Whig thinking of the era, a variety of forms of Grotianism.[39] This was not a mere matter of window dressing, however, for the new theoretical grounding had a life and logic all its own, a logic that impelled the Americans into a great controversy with their ancestral homeland, and after that into a new politics. What of the ancient constitution and historic rights that was consistent with the natural rights philosophy, the Americans retained. What was not, they jettisoned or modified.

Chapter Five

NATURAL RIGHTS AND PROTESTANT POLITICS: THE FIRST GENERATION

Dunn, Boorstin, Reid, and the others in effect urge that the beginning is not 1776 in America, but 1688 and earlier in England. Others agree that the beginning was not 1776, but locate it in very different places from the Declaration of Rights or the theory of the ancient constitution. Many, including so distinguished a student of American politics as Alexis de Tocqueville, see the American origins in the religion-inspired immigrants, in those who settled the Massachusetts Bay in the early to mid years of the seventeenth century, well before the Glorious Revolution.[1]

Like much else about the founding eras in America, the early story of Massachusetts had much to do with the accidents of English history. The story is a familiar one. Various groups of settlers came to New England seeking a more Protestantized church and state than was possible for them in England, at least up until the outbreak of the Civil War in 1642. They came both to escape from and to set an example for the Anglican Church they wanted to change and at whose hands they often suffered, but also to realize the new possibilities—religious and political—that Reformation principles seemed to open up for them. In America the Puritans could construct for themselves and all humanity "a city upon a hill." As Edward Johnson, one of the early historians of New England, put it in the 1650s: "this is the place where the Lord will create a new Heaven, and a new Earth in, new Churches and a new Commonwealth together." They saw this city not only as their hope, but as the dread responsibility, a more than human responsibility, they bore: "if we shall deal falsely with our god in this work we have undertaken and so cause him to withdraw his present help from us, we shall be made a story and by-word throughout the world, [and] we shall open the mouth of enemies to speak evil of the ways of God and all professors for God's sake."[2]

Thus we have two sets of American founders, those of the 1620s and those of 1776, both marked by an awareness of the novelty of their enterprise, both confident of the new beginning they were making. Two foundings may be better than one, but they also raise an awkward question: just what is the relation between them? Do they face in the same direction? As with many such questions, the scholars have come up with every logically possible answer, and perhaps a few others besides.

Some, like Leonard Levy and Alfred Young, endorse a view of very strong and pervasive continuity:

> Puritan political theory, like Puritanism itself, left a lasting influence on American development. . . . The social compact theory of government and representative government, . . . natural law and rights, written constitutions and constitutional limitations on the powers of government, religious liberty and separation of church and state, and the exceptional importance of the individual—all may be found in Puritan political ideas.

Levy and Young thus conclude that "anyone studying the origins of American political thought and of American constitutionalism must turn to the Puritan theorists."[3] Charles McLaughlin, a distinguished constitutional historian, sees continuity back beyond American to English Puritanism. "The philosophy underlying the Puritan revolt against Charles I and the philosophy of the American Revolution were essentially identical in character." McLaughlin thinks he can "trace . . . an unbroken line of descent" from the English to the American Puritans and thence to 1776 and beyond. In the same vein, Stanley Gray asserts that "the Revolutionary thinkers were merely drawing through Locke upon the thought of a much earlier time."[4] Susan Power goes even farther. "America's founders . . . did not seek a liberation from Christianity. Rather, they sought a return to the ancient principles of Christianity as found in the inspired word of God." Thus, she concludes, "the colonial Americans were influenced by a series of eminent American covenant theorists rather than by John Locke."[5]

At the other pole from Levy, Young, McLaughlin, and Power are scholars who find only minimal continuity. Thomas Pangle, for one, rejects all attempts to understand "the thought of the founders . . . as a *continuation* of Christian and especially Calvinist thinking." He does not go so far as to deny that the American "leaders were in important respects influenced by Christianity," but he sees this influence as largely extrinsic to their inner thought. The leaders "were compelled to speak and accommodate themselves to a Christian citizenry," but they themselves were "engaged in an attempt to exploit and transform Christianity in the direction of liberal rationalism." Those who find Puritan dimensions in the thought of the founders only do so on the basis of "outlandish characterizations," or discussions "so slippery and ambiguous as to be almost unintelligible."[6]

Pangle goes so far as to concede that "belief in the sanctity of all human beings as such" that we find in the natural rights philosophy "would seem to be a legacy of the biblical social and political tradition rather than the classical one." Nonetheless, he insists that "the sanctity of mankind as the Bible conceives of it is rather different from either rights-oriented or republican conceptions of the sanctity of man and human society." As he points out, "there are not even expressions in the Bible for 'republic,' 'democracy,' 'human rights,' or 'natural rights.'"[7]

Between those who straightforwardly affirm continuity and those who more or less entirely reject it lie two other important positions. One of these, taken by Edmund S. Morgan, the great historian of American Puritanism, affirms continuity, but with a difference: the second American beginning is a secularized version of the first. The later Americans explicitly took their political bearings from John Locke, but "the only novelty in Locke's explanation of the formation of government was the apparent absence of God from the proceedings."[8] Donald Lutz, too, affirms the secularization thesis when he asserts unequivocally that the Declaration of Independence and American constitutionalism more broadly "had [their] roots in the [Puritan] covenant that was secularized into the compact." "From covenant to contract" Lutz concludes, "was a process of secularization." Like Morgan, perhaps even like Levy and Young, Lutz finds that "many of the principles and assumptions of American constitutionalism were operative" before Locke published his *Second Treatise*. "In 1641 [the year of one of the important compacts in America] Locke was only nine years old. Montesquieu, Blackstone and other writers prominent in the late eighteenth century were not yet born." Locke had nothing in particular to do with the Revolution or the Declaration: "The American Revolution was in reality the result of radically extending the logic inherent in the Protestant Reformation, especially as the process occurred in colonial America."[9]

A fourth and sometimes overlapping thesis is the doctrine of eclectic continuity. This last position finds "the political and social theories of New England Puritanism" to be one among several "major sources of the ideas and attitudes of the Revolutionary generation."[10] Some scholars, like Bernard Bailyn, find Puritanism a source of relatively subordinate importance; others find the Puritans preeminent among several sources. Lutz gives a good statement of this version of eclectic continuity when he concludes that

> The American constitutional tradition derives in much of its form and content from . . . the radical Protestant sects to which belonged so many of the original European settlers. . . . That core tradition [was] being modified, [and] enriched, [through] the influence of English Whigs, the European Enlightenment, and English common law.

Lutz thus warns against the "unfortunate habit" among scholars of "seeking a single source that was decisive in the foundation of American political thought. . . . There is no single author, let alone a single text, that can account for even a major part of the core of American constitutionalism."[11] So, four paradigmatic views on the continuity question: strong continuity, secularized continuity, eclectic continuity, and minimal continuity.

The disagreements about the relation between the first and the second foundings, about the character of the American regime more generally persist and produce so much heat, because, in the words of Gordon Wood, "the stakes in these historical arguments about eighteenth century political culture are very high—they are nothing less than the kind of society we have been, or ought to become."[12] Wood has a point. Our conceptions of what we should be as often as not take the form of explications of what we are and have been, of the promises and commitments contained in our ongoing national existence, especially in our origin. Lincoln said as much in his Gettysburg Address; Herbert Croly repeated the theme in the early twentieth century in his *The Promise of American Life;* in more recent times Martin Luther King, Jr., and Ronald Reagan each in his own way made the same appeal to the future through a construal of the American past. When the Republicans regained control of Congress after forty years in 1994, the new House speaker, Newt Gingrich, recommended to all Republican members that they study the documents of the American origins, the Declaration of Independence and the *Federalist.*

Professor Wood has a point, but perhaps he overstates a bit. Knowledge of what we have been can surely help us understand what we are, but it cannot tell us what we "ought to become." History demands much of us, but it does not demand unconditional surrender of all independent standards of judgment. The question of the good society or the good political order, that is, the question of political philosophy remains a more primary question than the question of history. On this proposition, the chief actors in our two foundings, no matter how they turn out to be related to each other, would all agree. What else could it mean, after all, that they were making new beginnings, opting for the good order rather than the traditional or inherited order?

Professor Wood nonetheless remains correct when he emphasizes our stake in this contested issue, for the answer can surely tell us some things relevant to how we have come to where we are and to where we might be going. On this more modest scale we might identify at least three significant issues of our contemporary life where the continuity question has much bearing. As is frequently noted, we are living through a moment when American political principles and practices are exerting an unprecedented attraction around the world, or at least in parts of the world formerly in allegiance to principles antithetical to America's. If the American principles and practices of the second founding derive ultimately and essentially from the principles and practices of the first founding, then does that imply that the American example has little meaning for peoples with very different antecedents?

Indeed, the same question can and has been raised relative to America itself. By Western standards, America remains a religious nation, but it is also now a religiously diverse society; few Americans have a Puritan, and fewer a Protestant, or even a serious Christian background. Can American principles, when probed to their depths, speak to this diverse lot? Or, to raise the even more radical question that Tocqueville raised back in the 1830s: if American institutions are born from the soil of Puritanism, what resources have they to survive and thrive as that soil loses its nutritive power?[13]

This Tocquevillean question may be more than one hundred and fifty years old, but echoes of it are still audible in the "culture wars" we have been fighting in America in the past decade or so. For many, the key issues of American politics now are not issues of political structure or policy, but of "values"—family values, religious values, moral values, and so forth. The battle over these "values" often takes the form of a battle for custody of the founding. So, TV Minister D. James Kennedy asserts that "Christians have a right to reclaim America because the nation was founded by Christians." To that, a liberal columnist responded by arguing that "our constitution [was] written by people—Christian, agnostic, atheist and otherwise—who believed uppermost in protecting the rights of the minority." For both, the questions involved in the continuity thesis have direct and deep bearing on how we answer some of the most troubling questions of our current political life.

Nonetheless, apparently simple judgments about continuity implicate the large issue we might pretentiously call "the metaphysics of identity." What sorts and degrees of similarities and differences justify the conclusion that two historical phenomena are enough alike to be judged continuous? Any two political orders will inevitably share some things, especially when one of those orders is the historical successor to the other. Thus the

France that succeeded the Revolution had much in common with the *ancien régime,* and the Soviet Union with Czarist Russia. But do any of these similarities, do any of the convergences that might be found between any two societies, warrant the conclusion that we are in the presence of essential similarity or continuity?

I propose to finesse these abstruse issues by a simple but, I think, plausible expedient. Both American foundings at their moments of inception produced documents that not only expressed an interpretation of their actions by the participants in them but were themselves more or less constitutive of the political order thus brought into being. Political orders are largely, if not entirely, what they are by virtue of the interpretive understanding with which their participants invest them.[14]

The year 1776 produced a series of documents expressing the self-understanding of the actors, the most perspicuous of which was the Declaration of Independence. The religious dissenters who peopled New England also produced their share of self-interpretative documents. Two are particularly worth comparing to the Declaration: the Mayflower Compact and John Winthrop's sermon on board the Arbella, "A Modell of Christian Charitie."[15]

PILGRIMS

The Mayflower Compact was produced by the Pilgrims on their way to America; Winthrop's sermon was a product of the Puritans on their way to America. These were two closely related but not identical groups at the time of settlement who, over the course of a century in America, easily blended together. Both started out among those Protestants in England who believed the reformation of the English Church had not proceeded far enough. The theology of both groups was very similar—variations on Calvinist themes. The one difference between them concerned the church itself: the Puritans were committed to the further purification of the Church of England while the Pilgrims had concluded that true religion required the establishment of different kinds of churches altogether, voluntary gatherings of believers. The very idea of a national church in which all residents, or at least all who had been baptized as infants, were automatically members, was contrary to what a church, a congregation of the faithful, truly was. Because of their belief in the need for a different kind of church they became known as Separatists, and it was this issue—whether to stay in the Church of England or to form separate voluntary or "gathered" churches—that distinguished them from the Puritans.[16]

Given the nature of the theological-political order in England, the Separatists were required to become Pilgrims in order to form the kinds of churches they sought. In an irony that may be taken to foreshadow the ultimate fate of their movement, they received a patent from the Virginia Company to form a colony in Virginia, but instead landed on the scrubby and rock-hard Massachusetts coast at Plymouth. That mistake bears in important ways on the Mayflower Compact. William Bradford, their governor, tells in his journal of the "combination" the settlers made

> before they came ashore, being the first foundation of their govermente in this place; occasioned partly by the discontented and mutinous speeches that some of the strangers [non-church-communicants] among them had let fall from them in the ship; That when they came ashore they would use their owne libertie; for none had power to command them, the patente they had being for Virginia, and not for New-england, which belonged to an other Government, with which the Virginia Company had nothing to doe.[17]

This seminal political document was in some part the result of navigational errors and jurisdictional fissures. Such is the stuff of which great history is made.

As the "first foundation of their govermente" the Mayflower Compact stands to the Pilgrims much as the Declaration of Independence does to the new American order. The aptness of comparing the two documents has thus not gone unnoticed heretofore. The most common theme in the comparison as commonly made derives from the observation that both documents affirm that government comes to be through a contract, or agreement, or covenant between those subject to it. The first person to make the comparison explicit on contractarian grounds was, apparently, no less a figure than John Quincy Adams. In "An Oration Delivered at Plymouth," he hailed the Mayflower Compact as "perhaps the only instance, in human history, of that positive, original, social compact, which speculative philosophers have imagined as the only legitimate source of government."[18] Because of the agreement on contract, many scholars, like Levy and Young or Morgan, find the two documents identical or nearly identical as political theory.[19] The validity of that easy identification is thrown into question, however, by recent scholarship in the history of political thought. Contract theories can be quite different from each other, deriving their conclusions from different premises and pointing toward different modes of conducting government. The newer scholarship rejects the implicit motto of the older: "a contract is a contract is a contract."[20]

More serious are those like Willmoore Kendall and George Carey, who rest their judgment of identity or continuity on more than the mere presence of contract or covenant in the two documents. They are fierce partisans of the strong continuity thesis. "There was already . . . a very old tradition in America, when the Declaration [of Independence] was written; a tradition, moreover, that we must understand in order to understand the Declaration." That "very old tradition" begins with the Mayflower Compact and exists as a tradition because it consists of the regular "making and remaking [of] the Mayflower Compact."[21] The Declaration, they argue, is such a remaking. They would not read the Declaration through the lenses supplied by "Locke or the philosophers of the so-called age of enlightenment." They insist that to do so, as much of the "official literature" does, "cannot but help to lead to endless confusion and a basic misunderstanding . . . of the American political tradition." The real center of the Declaration lies in its being "the declaration of a religious people, of, more specifically, a *Christian* people, . . . a people who wish to make clear above all else their commitment to work the will of God."[22] Kendall and Carey's claims are important both for what they affirm—that the Mayflower Compact and thus reform Christianity supplies the key to the American political tradition, including especially the Declaration—and for what they deny— that modern political philosophy does not do so. It is this set of claims I wish to contest.

Adapting Kendall and Carey, we may discuss the Mayflower Compact under three heads: what, who, and why, that is, the announcement of what is being done here, the identification of the actors, and the purposes for which it is being done. These categories will allow us to compare it with comparable elements of the Declaration of Independence.

The Mayflower Compact, like the Declaration of Independence, is a performance, a speech-act. But the two do not perform the same act. The Pilgrims act to "covenant and combine [themselves] together into a civil Body Politick." It is not so much a description of a social compact, as the Declaration is, but is itself a compact. This compact begins its act of compacting "In the name of God, amen." As Kendall and Carey observe, "the first words of Western man's traditional Christian invocation." As they do not say, these are more specifically the typical opening words of Separatist church covenants, the agreements fellow believers made when they founded or joined a Separatist church.[23] The whole is an oath, "in the name of God," parallel to a church covenant. From this opening, Kendall and Carey conclude we have here a "nascent society that interprets itself . . . [as] in some sense a religious, more specifically a Christian, society, which calls God in as Witness to its act of founding—nay, even founds itself in His name." They find a close parallel in the Declaration of Independence, which, in its opening sentence, appeals to "the Laws of Nature and Nature's God." Or, as Lutz has it, the reference to "'Nature's God' activates the religious grounding" invoked at the very opening of the Mayflower Compact.[24] Both documents thus appeal to the divine at or near their openings, and this is obviously a central ground for Kendall and Carey's assertions regarding the centrality of the religious or Christian element in the American political tradition.

The Mayflower Compact uses the form of appeal traditional in Christian churches and indeed that form used in the making of churches, themselves congregations of the faithful. The divinity invoked in the Mayflower Compact is beyond doubt the Christian God, the God of the Bible, the God of faith and of the faithful. The appeal to the divine in the Declaration is altogether different, however: here it is "Nature's God" and his "laws"; a God who speaks to humanity through reason and acts in and through nature. His laws are none other than the laws of nature themselves, as understood by human reason. It is thus difficult to see what ground Lutz has for saying the Declaration "simultaneously appeals to reason and revelation." It appeals only to reason.[25] The Christian God is also the God of nature, of course, but *qua* Christian God, *qua* the God of the covenant of grace, he is the God of super-nature. The Christian events, the incarnation, the resurrection, the economy of salvation—these are miraculous, extraordinary events, not events in or of nature.

In accordance with its emphasis on the God of Nature and the truths known in and through nature, the Declaration's crucial theoretical section begins, "We hold these truths to be self-evident." Politics rests on "truths," not on blood, tradition, custom, or habit. It rests on "held truths," implying an element of reflection and thought. They are accessible to human beings as such, not to a charmed circle of true believers, graced with divine grace. The truths concern "all men," not the regenerate, or Protestants, or Christians. The truths are both accessible to and valid for all human beings; the principles of the Declaration are simply universal in character. They point toward a secular society open to the rational as such; they point toward a cosmopolitan, not a closed or sectarian, society. To be an American, therefore, is not to be of a certain descent or religious faith or original human type. To be an American is rather to accept these universal principles.[26]

Given the differences in the appeals made in our two documents, it is no wonder they tell or rest on different narratives of the nature and destiny of humanity, for the Declaration presents a short history of mankind parallel to the history of mankind presented in the Bible but makes significant changes in it. According to the biblical account, human beings are placed by God in a garden, a place where their needs are spontaneously supplied. The beginning is good, even perfect. But what a good, powerful, and caring God provided for humanity, Adam through his own misdeed lost. In disobeying God, humanity brings upon itself death, labor, pain, crime, and ultimately kings, cities, and politics.

According to the Declaration's history, human beings are created free and equal, and endowed with rights. It would seem that according to the Declaration, also, humanity is well provided for by its creator. But, perhaps out of delicacy, Jefferson elided an important fact in his description of the prepolitical situation: in that situation, rights are "insecure," for otherwise there would be no need to institute government "to secure these rights." The Creator supplies human beings with rights, with claims, in the original situation, but not with the security of those rights, or the satisfaction of those claims. The security of these rights—the really valuable thing—is supplied not by God or nature but by human beings themselves when they institute government. Human action is more nearly the foundation for human salvation than the basis for a fall. The Declaration's history reverses the Bible's history.

After the indication of what they are doing, taking an oath as part of making a covenant for their government, the covenanters (as Kendall and Carey put it) "identify themselves, say who they are." This is a necessary part of the Mayflower Compact, for the act of covenanting itself produces the ties that constitute the covenanted community—the church in the ordinary case, the political community in this extra-ordinary extension of the church covenant. The identification of the agents, who also sign the document in order to institute their membership, is thus part of the phenomenon of covenanting itself. The Constitution of 1787, with its opening "We the people of the United States" contains a more obvious parallel, but the Declaration also identifies those who are issuing the document: "We . . . the representatives of the United States of America, in general Congress, Assembled."[27] They speak for the "one people" who here "dissolve the political bands which have connected them with another" people.

This parallel between the two documents is much more significant for the differences it reveals than for any similarities, however. As Kendall and Carey notice, the Compact's signers identify themselves as "the legal subjects of our dread Sovereign Lord King James, by the grace of God . . . King, Defender of the Faith, *etc.*" They are covenanting or compacting to bring themselves under political authority, but there is no suggestion here that they are otherwise free of political allegiance. They are not, that is, moving from a state of nature to a civil society via their covenant; they are already subjects of James. There is, moreover, no hint that their subjection to James derived from some earlier act of covenanting like the one they are performing at that moment. James owes his authority not to their consent but to "the grace of God." On the larger issues of political legitimacy and the origin of political authority, the Mayflower compactors seem closer to the theorists of divine right than to the social contract theory.

If they are already subject, then why are they covenanting for future subjection? Here the story Bradford told of their navigational and jurisdictional mishaps takes on its relevance. They are subject, rightfully subject they insist, to James, who has delegated authority to the Virginia Company, which in turn has delegated authority to the Pilgrims to set up government in Virginia. Unfortunately, they never did arrive in Virginia, but landed instead in a place outside the jurisdiction of the Virginia Company and thus broke the chain of authorization linking them to James. Under these circumstances, the Mayflower Compact represents not so much the embodiment of a general contractarian theory of political authority as the first recorded instance of Yankee ingenuity.[28] They adapted the covenant form they knew from their ecclesiology in order to meet the emergency caused by the gap in the chain of authority. They claim nothing universal here, but seek only to reforge the broken link in order to reconnect themselves to that king who rules "by the grace of God."

The Declaration could hardly be more different. The 1776 document is more concerned to justify the dissolution of already existing political bonds than to forge bonds that do not exist, but it does so in terms of a universal theory of the source of political authority. All legitimate authority derives from covenant or compact, even the authority of George, of whom it is certainly not said that he rules "by the grace of God."[29]

As a universal theory of the source of all political power and not an expedient designed to meet an emergency, the Declaration commits to a set of doctrines which either have no place in the Mayflower Compact or are simply contradicted there. There is no human authority prior to the human making of government, and so the Declaration contemplates a situation prior to government, a situation prior to all authority, a state of nature, or in the language of the Declaration, an original "equality." Since the Mayflower Compact never contemplates human beings outside all authority, it has no room for the doctrine of the state of nature or of equality as the Declaration understands that.[30]

The Declaration affirms equality as part of its mini-human history, from equality as no-authority to the creation of authority, to its abuse and refoundation through "altering or abolishing." This "history" is not, as we have seen, meant as literal history but as rationalist reconstruction of the human situation in nature. One way to see the constructivist character of the Declaration's narrative is to notice that it clearly intends the affirmation of equality in the Lockean sense rather than in the usage of the pre-Lockean Whig contractarian tradition, which looked to the prepolitical situation as a prehistorical condition that human beings left behind at some distant date in the past when they made something called "the original compact." The Declaration insists, however, that *all men* are created equal and must constitute authority through their own consent, not just the consent of those at some past moment. The Mayflower Compact, by contrast, has nothing of the rationalist reconstruction about it. The consent contained here is quite literally that given by those who sign the document. They are much closer to the Whigs than to the Declaration, however, for they do not suggest that later members must consent in some way or other to political authority in order to be subject to it, just as they themselves did not have to consent to the authority of King James.[31]

Because the Mayflower Compact is an actual covenant, its operative element is the oath and consequent adherence to the political community so formed. The actual signers promise obedience; they sign up just as they would for a cable-TV subscription. The Declaration, more insistent on the consent of each and every human being, paradoxically has no such signing-up. Even in the various state and national constitutions, there was nothing of this "sign-up in order to be a member" quality we see in the Compact. Consent is necessary, but it is not expressed in the form of the compact's membership oath. As we will see in Chapter 7, the issue of how consent is properly to be expressed was one of the engines driving American thought and action in the years before and after independence.

A third element shared by both the Mayflower Compact and the Declaration of Independence is a statement of purposes. The Pilgrims "covenant and combine" themselves "into a civil Body Politick" for four purposes: (1) for their "better ordering and preservation," which in turn will allow them to accomplish the three chief ends of their undertaking—(2) the glory of God; (3) the advancement of the Christian faith, and (4) the honor of king and country. It is difficult not to notice the prominence of their religious purposes. Although the compact does not specify how these religious purposes are specifically to be accomplished, it does emphasize the instrumental or secondary character of their "ordering and preservation" as a purpose. In the Mayflower Compact the secular is for the sake of the sacred. This parallels the countermovement which we have already noted in the compact: in order to institute their "civil body politick" they have adapted their church covenant to this secular service.

The Declaration of Independence also contains a statement of the ends for which human beings create civil orders: "in order to secure these rights governments are instituted among men." Government exists to secure rights, period.[32] Rights derive from the creator, it is true, but as we have seen, they neither come from some special relation to the divine nor are they in any necessary way instruments to further service of the divine. Of course, the secured rights to life, to liberty, and to the pursuit of happiness may be used to pursue one's eternal salvation or some other sacred purpose, but this is now entirely in the sphere of the private choice of the rights-holder. The Declaration, in other words, affirms a wholly this-worldly end for political life, and thus points ahead to the First Amendment's separation of church and state as its principled fulfillment.

Rights are a terrible stumbling block for partisans of strong continuity between the first and second American foundings. Rights are prominent, nay central, in the Declaration and all the thinking and acting at the time of the political founding, and have remained at or near the center of American political life ever since. Yet they are totally absent from the Mayflower Compact.

Kendall and Carey concede that the Declaration represents a "most difficult and most controversial" challenge for their account of the nature of the American tradition. They respond to this difficult passage in their journey by arguing, in part, that the Mayflower Compact, saying nothing explicit about rights, implicitly raises some important rights claims according to the following chain of reasoning. The covenanters promise "due obedience" to laws which are "just and equal," from which one can infer a duty in governors "to govern by just and equal laws deemed necessary for the public good." From this duty in governors, Kendall and Carey deduce that "each signer has henceforth an individual right to the performance of that duty by his fellow signers."[33]

Such might be a valid argument for the compact, but it remains a far cry from the rights doctrine of the Declaration. The rights in the Declaration do not derive from some preexisting duty of rulers but predate all rulers because they exist in the state of equality, that is, the state where there are no rulers. The rights are primary, and so far as rulers have duties these derive from the original human rights. The Declaration thus reverses the Kendall and Carey view of the compact's rights theory. Moveover, in the Declaration the securing of these natural or prepolitical rights is the sum and substance of the point of government. This surely is not true of the compact, even in Kendall and Carey's abstruse chain of reasoning.

PURITANS

The Puritans apparently were better navigators than the Pilgrims, for they landed just where they aimed to land, and came armed with their charter from the king. They suffered no gap in the chain of authority binding them to the authority under which they were born. They had no need, therefore, to engage in the performance of constructing wholly new structures of authority— the basic structure with which they began was clearly outlined in their charter—nor of reforging broken links in old chains.[34]

There is no "Arbella Compact" to match the Pilgrims' document, but that is not to say that the Puritans did not attempt to clarify for themselves the meaning and principles of what they were undertaking. In this case, the most striking Puritan statement that we have was a shipboard lay sermon titled "A Modell of Christian Charitie," written and probably delivered by the governor of the colony, John Winthrop.[35] Like the Pilgrims, the Puritans fell back on known religious forms in order to express what they needed to say regarding politics.[36]

Winthrop relies on a religious form, but much of the substance of his sermon reminds one of very traditional, quite secular statements. The eye seeking evidence of continuity between Puritan political thinking and modern thought such as the Declaration of Independence is bound to be disappointed, for Winthrop builds his "modell" of politics from elements far more like those that went into the Declaration of Rights than those that went into the Declaration of Independence. The chief thesis of Winthrop's speech certainly stands in a different quadrant from the American Declaration's first "self-evident truth": "God Almightie in his most holy and wise providence hath soe disposed of the condicion of mankinde, as in all times some must be rich some poore, some highe and eminent in power and dignitie; others meane and in subjeccion."[37] Not "created equal" but ordained to be unequal—that is the first or axiomatic premise from which Winthrop's political thinking proceeds. In this, his view is much more like that of the Whigs in their theory of the ancient constitution—the society cum polity of the estates, with their different and unequal economic, social, and political status, is the *arche* or origin of politics. It is impossible to overemphasize how much Winthrop's political teaching (and practice) turns on this beginning point, a beginning point he brought with him as part of his English inheritance.[38]

Yet Winthrop does not merely restate the theory of the ancient constitution; he adapts it to the Puritans' circumstances and roots it in their theology in a way that the Whigs did not. The implications of Winthrop's Christianization of the theory of the ancient constitution become visible in his hopes for America, hopes far more grandiose than any ever expressed by the Whigs.

Winthrop looks to himself and his colleagues to establish a "city on a hill," that is to say, a new and exemplary kind of political community, going beyond any achievement of the English ancient constitution.[39]

For Winthrop the goodness of the system of orders or estates does not rest simply on its antiquity, as the classical version of the theory of the ancient constitution had it. The goodness of the system of unequal orders rests instead on its connection to the divine order itself. Society, composed of different and unequal parts, reflects the character of the whole of God's creation, marked by "the variety and differrance of the Creatures." The composition of a whole out of very disparate parts shows forth the glory, power, and wisdom of God far more than a homogeneous universe could do. In the complementarity of different parts is also to be found the common good of human society: "that every man might have need of other." Winthrop seems to have partly in mind the social and economic division of labor, but also a moral challenge out of which can arise a deep bond between human beings, a bond going beyond mere mutual service and use: "That every man might have need of other, and from hence that they might be all knitt more nearly together in the Bond of brotherly affeccion." Equality is neither the beginning point nor the end point for politics as Winthrop conceives it. Rather his "modell" is one where the unequal orders of society are held together in harmony by "bonds of brotherly affection."[40] Neither Winthrop nor the other Puritans can be considered democrats, no matter how much in retrospect their institutions might be held to have contributed to the development of democracy. "There is no evidence," Stanley Gray concluded, "that Winthrop ever questioned monarchy as a valid form of government. Winthrop never spoke with any enthusiasm of democracy: "A Democracie is, among most civill nations, accounted the meanest and worst of all formes of government." Winthrop considered the Puritan polity a "mixt Aristocracie," and evidently considered that the best form, warranted both by English inheritance and scripture.[41]

More clearly than the Declaration of Rights or the Declaration of Independence, Winthrop presents a political theology. His authorities are almost exclusively biblical, and, as one interpreter observed, "Winthrop never conceived of a political understanding which did not depend on religious teaching; he relied on scriptural and religious authority rather more, and secular classical writings rather less, than did his clerical contemporaries." This was apparently no mere affectation on his part, for he once blamed another speaker for his reliance on Greek and Roman authority:

> In his sermon he delivered many useful things, but in a moral and political discourse, grounding his propositions much upon the old Roman and Grecian governments, which sure is an error, for if religion makes men wiser than their neighbors, and these times have the advantage of all that have gone before us. . . . It is probable that by all these helps, we may better frame rules of government for ourselves than to receive others upon the bare authority of the wisdom, justice, etc., of those heathen commonwealths.

In place of the authority of "those heathens," Winthrop looks to the Bible.[42] One cannot understand or solve the political problem without the wisdom and help of biblical and specifically Christian materials. One needs to understand, for example, the role of love or charity in politics: the heathen believed politics was a matter of justice or, at best, friendship, but Winthrop insists on the necessity of love. The ground of love can be grasped only by those who understand the creation, the fall, and the new ground of love in the revelation of Christ.[43]

Winthrop's political thought differs from that in the Declaration of Independence in yet another way: not only does he begin with natural, or rather, divinely mandated inequality, including political inequality, but he also understands politics in the mode of political theology. Like the Pilgrims, he appeals to the biblical, the Christian God, and the central points of Christian theology. The Declaration, on the contrary, depends on an appeal to the God known by reason in and through nature. We see in the Declaration, therefore, a kind of appeal to creation, but none to the fall or the coming of Christ.

This is not a merely external dimension of difference, for everything peculiar to Winthrop follows from his appeal to these specifically Christian concepts. In the first place, his Christian understanding supplies him with both an analysis of why the ancient English mixed constitution has not succeeded in its own terms and points him towards a superior and novel solution. The way things were done in England will not suffice: "wee must not content ourselves with usuall ordinary meanes[;] whatsoever wee did or ought to have done when wee lived in England, the same must wee doe and more alsoe where we goe." He has one new or further "means" specially in mind: "That which most in theire Churches maineteine as a truthe in profession onely, wee must bring into familiar and constant practice, as in this duty of love[;] wee must love brotherly and without dissimulation, . . . wee must not look onely on our owne things, but alsoe on the things of our brethren."[44]

The Puritans must go beyond the practices of England because those practices have failed. The expedition to America occurred because life in England was fast decaying; in a widely quoted letter to his wife, Winthrop gave his first hint that he was considering emigration: "God will bring some heavye affliction upon this lande, [but] he will provide a shelter and a hidinge place for us and ours." Winthop's foreboding sense of the evil fate awaiting England was not a bad forecast of developments that came to a head in the outbreak of civil war a decade or so after his emigration. In the years just before his decision to embark for New England, Winthrop had been exposed to much of the disorder of the late 1620s, disorder that could only be taken as an indication of the imperfection of the ancient constitution. Winthrop won an appointment as an attorney in the Court of Wards in 1626, an office that led to his spending long periods of each year in London, where he could witness at first hand the raging contest between king and parliament. The period between 1625, when Charles I became king, and 1629, when Charles dissolved Parliament for what turned out to be eleven years, was marked by harsh conflict, with Parliament asserting its perogatives and the king insisting on his. Parliamentary leaders did not trust the king's commitment to the ancient constitution and in the event had good reason for distrust, as Charles showed by his effort to govern the country for over a decade without Parliament. The intensity of the contention between king and Parliament in those years was perhaps best revealed in 1629, when members of the House of Commons forcibly held the speaker of the House in his chair in order to carry on further business, rather than comply with the king's order to dissolve.[45]

Winthrop's decision to emigrate and his hopes for a *novus ordo seclorum* no doubt grew out of his disillusion with the "old order of the ages" as he observed it during his years in London. He came to see that the breakdown of the ancient mixed constitution was no mere fluke of personality or particular issue but reflected a more fundamental defect in the constitution's very principle of construction. The task set for the ancient constitution, the knitting together of the disparate and unequal elements of the society into a community, was sound, but its typical means were quite incorrect. The only way to knit a society into "one body" is through its possession of the "proper ligamentes": "the ligamentes of this body which knitt together are love." A system of constitutional checks and balances, like the ancient mixed constitution, therefore takes the wrong tack; it is no surprise to Winthrop that the result was the supercharged contention of the 1620s.[46]

Although love is the required ligament, it is not at all easy to produce. Love is, indeed, natural to the human race in its original form: "Adam in his first estate was a perfect modell of mankinde in all their generacions, and in him this love was perfected." This happy original situation was disrupted, however, by the fall: "Adam rent in himselfe from his Creator, rent all his posterity allsoe one from another, whence it comes that every man is borne with this principle in him, to love and seek himselfe only."[47] The human situation thus has something of a tragic character to it; God has created and ordained a differentiated and unequal body of individuals and estates from which a whole akin to God's universe itself, or to an integral human body, must be made. But love, the ligament of this body, is lacking. Love of self monopolizes and drives human beings farther apart, rather than knits them together. The failure of the ancient constitution, and of pagan politics, follows inevitably.

Yet the tragedy is only temporary, and in Winthop's moment, the moment of the revival of the true principles of Christianity, new or newly understood grounds for hope have appeared. "A man continueth" in the self-love to which he is condemned through Adam's fall, "till Christ comes and takes possession of the soule, and infuseth another principle[,] love to God and our brother." This love "cometh of God and every one that loveth is borne of God, soe that this love is the fruite of the new birth, and none can have it but the new Creature." The "new Creature," reborn in the love of Christ, is the only human being who can fulfill the requirements of successful political life. As Winthrop concludes: "This love is absolutely neccesary to the being of the body of Christ, as the sinewes and other ligaments of a natural body are to the being of that body."[48]

The Puritan political community must therefore be a "Company professing ourselves fellow members of Christ." Winthrop thus strongly defends the rights of the community to control its own membership; he supported laws limiting rights of immigration to those who bring "the true doctrine with them," and he generally supported (or led) efforts to expel the heterodox, like Roger Williams and Anne Hutchinson.[49] True doctrine is so important because a proper understanding of divine truth seems to be a necessary if not sufficient condition for Christ's "taking possession of the soul" and "infusing" it with the principle of love of God and of neighbor. Love of neighbor is difficult in the fallen state, for self-love dominates; when individuals look to others, they discover that "the great part of them are most unworthy if they be judged by their own merit" (as John Calvin put it). The pure Protestant faith teaches, however, that human beings do not receive the love of God or deserve the love of others for their merits: love is an act of grace alone, resting on the gracious love of God for humanity and promised through faith in Christ's redemptive act of love. So long as human beings focus on the merits of the other, the necessary love cannot be forthcoming. Love is for "the image of God" in others, "to which we owe all honor and love." Although all have the image of God, "it is among members of the house-hold of faith that this same image is more carefully to be noted, in so far as it has been renewed and restored through the spirit of Christ." The extreme demands of Christian love thus become possible:

> Assuredly there is but one way in which to achieve what is not merely difficult but utterly against human nature: to love those who hate us, to repay their evil deeds with benefits, to return blessings for reproaches. It is that we remember not to consider men's evil intention but to look upon the image of God in them, which cancels and effaces their transgressions, and with its beauty and dignity allures us to love and embrace them.[50]

Winthop echoes these thoughts from Calvin quite precisely when he argues that:

> the ground of love is an apprehension of some resemblance in the things loved to that which affectes it, this is the cause why the Lord loves the Creature, soe farre as it hath any of his Image in it, he loves his elect because they are like himselfe, he beholds them in his beloved sonne. . . . Thus it is between the members of Christ, each discernes by the worke of the spirit his owne Image and resemblance in another, and therfore cannot but love him as he loves himselfe.[51]

Contrary to the image of the Puritans as dour pessimists, Winthrop projects a powerfully optimistic, "idealistic" image of new possibilities for political life, possibilities rooted firmly and exclusively in the Puritan-Protestant grasp of Christianity.[52] The hopes of New England, the original hopes of America as Winthrop voices them here, are simply remarkable, certainly more far-reaching than those of the men who issued the Declaration of Independence and then drafted the Constitution: their *novus ordo seclorum* continued to rest on the system of checks and balances Winthrop eschewed, and to aim at the securing of natural rights, themselves born and always rooted in primeval self-love, in "the selfish passions." Winthrop's statement on behalf of the Puritans thus shares as little, perhaps even less, with the Declaration as does the Mayflower Compact:

Where the Declaration appeals to "nature and nature's God," that is to say, is a form of natural theology, Winthrop appeals quite specifically to the Christian God and revealed Christian theology.

Where the Declaration affirms an original human equality or state of nature, Winthrop sees instead a divine ordination of inequality.

Where the Declaration affirms the ends of government to be the security of the universal and "unalienable rights" of human beings, Winthrop seems to know nothing of such rights, and sees the end of politics in serving God and seeking salvation. Where the Declaration mandates a universal and secular politics, Winthrop mandates a sectarian and religious politics, a good part of which will necessarily be devoted to the contentious and very difficult question of discerning just what God does require by way of service from us. The Declaration, by contrast, affirms the ends of politics in terms of rights—rights to life, liberty, and the pursuit of happiness. The understanding of the ends contained in the Declaration is just that expressed by Locke in his *Letter Concerning Toleration*:

> The commonwealth seems to me to be a society of men constituted only for the processing, preserving, and advancing of their own civil interests. Civil interests I call life, liberty, health, and indolence of body; and the possession of outward things, such as money, lands, houses, furniture, and the like.[53]

One task of statesmanship in a polity devoted to "civil interests" such as these is the encouragement of the increase of wealth "by established laws of liberty to secure protection and encouragement to the honest industry of mankind." Such a vision is alien to Winthrop: "if we . . . shall fall to embrace this present world and prosecute our carnall intencions, seekeing great things for our selves and our posterity, the Lord will surely break out in wrathe against us and be revenged."[54]

Although Winthrop is almost entirely silent on issues relating to the Declaration's natural rights, he does have a very important statement, written about a decade and a half after the Arbella sermon, on the topic of liberty, which helps bring out further the immense difference between the political thought animating the first American founding and that animating the second American founding. According to the natural rights philosophy, human beings possess an original and inherent liberty, which, as inalienable, is preserved even in the process of forming government. This liberty, as Jefferson explains, is a liberty for "innocent actions" only, that is, for actions that do not deprive others of their rights, or that do not interfere with the realization of the community welfare.

Winthrop is, by and large, an enemy of the liberty Jefferson affirms. "There is," he says, "a two-fold liberty, natural (I mean as our nature is now corrupt) and civil or federal." These two forms of liberty do not correspond precisely to Jefferson's discussion, for, according to Winthrop, natural liberty is common to man with beasts and other creatures. "By this, man, as he stands in relation to man singly, hath liberty to do what he lists; it is a liberty to evil as well as to good. This liberty is inconsistent with authority."

The natural rights philosophy embodies quite a different understanding of natural liberty. The liberty right is not, in the first place, shared with beasts and other creatures. Human rights stand on special features of human nature, features that distinguish human beings from all other animals. Winthrop apparently has in mind liberty as a faculty *simpliciter*, a mere power, whereas within the natural rights philosophy liberty is a "moral faculty," that is, a right. As a right-in-the-proper-sense, it is not, and cannot be, a "liberty to evil as well as to good": it is not a liberty to evil or injustice, and it is not limited to being a liberty to good. This natural right to liberty is not "incompatible and inconsistent with authority," but its security is the point of authority.[55]

Winthrop recognizes a form of liberty that is compatible with authority and is moral in character. "It is a liberty to that only which is good, just and honest." This is not "natural liberty," but "civil" or "federal" or "moral," because it derives from or eventuates in the moral law and in "politic covenants and constitutions" between God and man or among men themselves. Winthrop elucidates the compatibility between this liberty and authority or even subjection in the example of marriage: "The woman's own choice makes such a man her husband; yet being so chosen, he is her lord, and she is subject to him." Liberty is the liberty to enter freely into one or another state of subjection. The one who so enters exercises his or her will only so far as to enter that state; the relationship so entered is not in any sense constituted by the wills of the parties, nor is the character of the relationship such as to seek to guarantee and preserve natural liberty. Thus Winthrop can say of magistrates that they are "called by" the people, but "have [their] authority from God, in way of an ordinance, such as hath the image of God eminently stamped upon it."[56]

Given his views of the origin and nature of political authority it is, perhaps, no great surprise that he resisted efforts by others in the community to control the discretionary powers of the magistrates. In a journal entry detailing the grounds for his opposition to a movement for determinate sentencing, this so-called forerunner of natural rights constitutionalism sounds far more like Sir Robert Filmer and the other partisans of divine right governance than like Locke or Jefferson. "Judges are Gods upon earthe: therefore, in their Administrations, they are to holde forthe the wisdome and mercye of God (which are his Attributes) as well as his Justice: as occasion shall require, either in respecte of qualitye of the person, or for a more generall good."[57]

In accord with his conception of liberty, Winthrop presents a semicontractarian or covenantal doctrine that supplies the basis for many who accept the continuity thesis. In fact, however, Winthrop looks to a direct divine ordination as the origin of political (and other) authority, and as the source of the character and degree of authority within human relationships. Winthrop speaks of covenant in several different contexts and in several different ways. In the Arbella sermon, covenant is derivative and subordinate to divine commission: "When God gives a speciall commission he lookes to have it strictly observed in every Article." Winthrop gives the example of Saul, who failed to live up to "one of the least articles" of the commission God gave to him, with the penalty that he "lost . . . the kingdome, which should have beene his reward, if he had observed his Commission." The covenant Winthrop invokes is the acceptance by the people of the commission God lays upon them; it is a covenant because God binds himself to live up to his side—to prosper the people spiritually and otherwise—if they live up to their part. "Wee are entered into a covenant with him for this worke, wee have taken out a commission. . . . Now if the Lord . . . bring us in peace to the place wee desire, then hath he ratified this covenant and sealed our commission [and] will expect a strickt performance of the Articles contained in it, but if we shall neglect the observacion of these Articles. . . . the Lord will surely breake out in wrathe against us . . . and make us know the price of breache of such a covenant."

It should require no extended analysis to notice how far this notion of covenant is from the contractarianism of the Declaration. To mention just two points: Winthrop's covenant is between God and the people; the Declaration's is among the people themselves. Winthrop's covenant is to fulfill a special divine commission, set up for them as a new "chosen people"; the Declaration's is for "all men." The Declaration's compact is to establish rightful political power, dedicated to natural ends; Winthrop's is to dedicate the already established polity to a specific, nonnatural task.[58]

Winthrop also speaks of a covenant between the magistrates and the people in a 1645 speech, defending himself publicly against accusations of arbitrary and extralegal action. "We account him a good servant, who breaks not his covenant. The covenant between you and us is the oath you have taken of us, which is to this purpose, that we shall govern you and judge your causes by the rules of God's laws and our own, according to our best skill."[59] This notion of covenant is no closer to the contractarianism of the Declaration. It is an agreement between the magistrates and the people, not among the people, in order to constitute political society. It sets bounds to the powers of rulers, but these bounds are much qualified by the commission Winthrop affirms to "rule" according to "God's laws"; it is in this very same speech that Winthrop insists, "So it is you yourselves who have called us to this office, and being called by you, we have our authority from God, in way of our ordinance, such as hath the image of God eminently stamped upon it."[60] Winthrop's contractarianism, such as it is, thus remains firmly within the context of a very different approach to the origin and purpose of political authority.[61] No matter how much he moves beyond anything in the Mayflower Compact by way of a general theory, nonetheless, his version of contractarianism remains quite distant from that within the natural rights philosophy, growing out of different soil and producing an entirely different politics.[62] The politics of the Declaration, beginning with the natural rights to liberty and the pursuit of happiness, contains a strong presumption favoring liberty; the politics of the Puritans, beginning with the distrust of natural liberty voiced by Winthrop, contains just as strong a presumption against liberty—thus all the legislation that has earned the censure of mankind as Puritanical. The tension helps to explain one abiding feature of American history and culture: the struggle between the liberal and the Puritan sides of the American inheritance, a struggle that does not make much sense if the continuity thesis is correct.

It is difficult, therefore, to agree with those scholars who see in the seventeenth-century Pilgrims and Puritans the originators of the fundamental American political doctrines of contract, consent, popular sovereignty, and the like. Winthrop and the Pilgrims do not, in a word, articulate "a new vision of political authority derived from agreements, covenants, and promises written into express compacts," at least not as these matters were understood in the second American founding.[63]

Both the natural rights philosophy and the early American Puritanism of Winthrop, Cotton, et al., can be seen to begin with the Whig commitment to the ancient constitution, but the two doctrines move away from the older Whig position in quite opposite directions. The Declaration, following Locke's reformulation of Whiggism, moves toward an egalitarian individualism, an understanding of politics beneath, so to speak, the classes and tradition that constitute the old Whig positions. The Declaration replaces one kind of mythic history (the immemorial constitution of liberty, or the original compact) with another kind of mythic history, although in this case understood as rational reconstruction. Alternatively, the Declaration replaces the appeal to history with an appeal to nature. Winthrop accepts the class base and thus the inequality of the ancient constitution; inequality and difference are God's way, but the pure resources of nature are incapable of realizing the political goals implicit in nature understood as divine ordination. Winthrop thus attempts to ascend from the ancient constitution, to bring to politics the transcendent ends and means of the (Protestant, Puritan) Christian dispensation. Whereas within the natural rights philosophy, politics and religion are intentionally separated more decisively than ever before, within American Puritan politics they are brought much more closely together.

In part, this divergent movement is based on very different historical experiences. The Puritans of their founding generation were in the act of withdrawal from the larger and less committed world. In the flush of their enthusiasm, and in the throes of their hopes, they sought the one true Christian politics, a politics built on the divine truth they embodied. They hoped for the first time, perhaps, to realize the promise of politics. The natural rights philosophy emerged from a later and more melancholy experience. The hopes for the discovery and realization of the one true Protestant politics had resulted in England in unprecedented political conflict and civil war, a regicide, the overthrow of the ancient constitution, the establishment of the Cromwellian regime, almost universally perceived to be oppressive, and then a restoration of the old line of kings and the reinstitution of the ancient constitution, new conflicts, and finally the Glorious Revolution. The natural rights philosophy, hopeful as it was for a *novus ordo seclorum*, nonetheless arose in response to this sobering series of events, and bore the marks of the chastening that an unsuccessful half-century of Puritan politics had produced. The natural rights philosophy bears no marks of the quest for the one true Protestant politics; indeed, it bears many marks of the turn away from the enterprise of a Protestant-grounded politics altogether. While the natural rights philosophy in almost all of its classic formulations contains plentiful reference to the deity, this is not, as we have noticed many times, the contested biblical God of the various Christian sects but a God of nature, in principle available to all and independent of particular sectarian commitments.

On the Continuity Thesis

We are now in a position to draw some tentative conclusions regarding the continuity problem. Of the four positions taken— strong continuity, secularized continuity, eclectic continuity, and minimal continuity—the one that seems easiest to reject is the strong continuity thesis. Whatever echoes and shadows of similarity there may be, our two foundings turn out to be quite different from each other. A contract is not a contract is not a contract—nor is a covenant either. We cannot, it appears, quite accept the Reverend Kennedy's account of America.

The secularized continuity position is more difficult to assess because this thesis is difficult to state in an intellectually satisfying manner. What does it mean to secularize a doctrine, the main point of which is to ground its orientation toward the secular in a particular conception of the sacred? Admittedly, there are philosophically sophisticated versions of the secularization thesis—Hegel, Nietzsche, Weber come to mind—but the systematic differences between the theories embedded in the Declaration and the Puritan and Pilgrim statements are so pervasive that it does not seem helpful or accurate to describe the Declaration as a reformulation of Puritan thought without God. The theory of the Declaration does not, in any case, do without God. It no longer looks to the Christian God or the Protestant story of creation, fall, and redemption, but it does appear fully consistent with a more universal, more rationally accessible God, called in the text, "nature's God."

The eclectic continuity theory is very tempting, especially if we spread our net a bit beyond what I've discussed here. Surely, Tocqueville and others are correct to have seen important institutional carry-overs from the Puritan founding era to the modernist founding, including representative government and democratizing tendencies. Two observations must be made to mute the enthusiasm of those who dwell on these continuities, however. First, many of the most striking institutional developments—the quite parallel structures of colonial government that developed up and down the continent, for example—as often as not owe more to the common British heritage than to specifically Puritan forces.[64] Second, and perhaps more important, the institutions that admittedly carried over into the new era came to be attached to a quite different understanding of the origin, ends, and nature of political authority, to a quite different notion of justice. Just because some of the same wineskin remained in use does not mean the wine was the same.

Chapter Six

NATURAL RIGHTS AND
PROTESTANT POLITICS:
LOCKEAN PURITANS

L et us fast-forward almost one hundred and fifty years from
Winthrop's sermon on the Arbella to Watertown, Massachusetts, at the end of May 1775. The battles at Lexington and Con-
cord had recently occurred, and all the disorder had led the British to shut down the regular legal government of Massachusetts.
An extralegal meeting of a "Congress" is assembled in Watertown,
requiring, as tradition demanded, an election sermon from one
of the colonies' ministerial luminaries. Samuel Langdon, president of Harvard College since 1774, is the eminence selected to
address the political leaders of the colony at this moment of
danger and decision. Representing a tradition from the fathers,
he uses the occasion to berate his listeners for falling short of the
fathers. The evil times on which they have fallen are due in part,
he concedes, to "the present moral state of Great Britain. . . .
There is no truth, nor mercy, or knowledge of God in the land."[1] But, hit-
ting all the chords of the classic Puritan jeremiad, Langdon blames
his countrymen, too:[2]

> But, alas! have not the sins of America and New England, in
> particular, had a hand in bringing down upon us the righteous
> judgments of heaven? . . . However unjustly and cruelly we have
> been treated by man, we certainly deserve, at the hand of God,
> all the calamities in which we are now involved. Have we not
> lost much of that spirit of genuine christianity, which so re-

markably appeared in our ancestors? . . . Have we not departed from their virtues?[3]

Yet, plump in the midst of this appeal to the old Puritan fathers and the old Puritan ways is . . . the natural rights philosophy of Locke and the Declaration of Independence. Although Langdon wishes to recall his audience of patriot leaders back to the "true religion" as present in "the purity and simplicity of the gospel," back to "the gospel of salvation," he nonetheless departs drastically from the example of Winthrop and other early Puritan political thinkers in failing to see in the Bible the indispensable and necessary ground for politics. "Thanks be to God," he says, "that he has given us, as men, natural rights independent on all human laws whatever, and that these rights are recognized by the grand Charter of British Liberties. By the law of nature any body of people, destitute of order and government, may form themselves into a civil society according to their best prudence, and so provide for their common safety and advantage."[4]

In the midst of his traditional appeal to tradition, Langdon imports the very untraditional form and substance of the Declaration's natural rights philosophy. The truths about politics are found in nature, through natural knowledge, the law of nature, and what concerns us "as men." This is no longer political theology, or if it is, it is political theology of the sort that Locke himself in his *Second Treatise* and Jefferson in his various writings practiced—natural political theology.

The deliverances of nature and nature's God according to Langdon are substantially identical to what Jefferson set down in the Declaration—where he did, apparently, speak "the American mind," did articulate a widespread consensus. Although Langdon develops the thought in even less detail than Jefferson's Declaration, nonetheless the chief doctrinal points of the Declaration (and of Locke) are visible: natural rights prior to and independent of all human law, that is, natural rights as the endowment of human beings in a "state of nature"; the contractual or consent-based origin of government, the ends of government as protection of these rights, and, the "right to alter or abolish": "where one form is found by the majority, not to answer the grand purpose in any tolerable degree, they may by common consent put an end to it, and set up another." Just as Jefferson (following Locke) counsels prudence and restraint in the exercise of this formidable right, so does Langdon counsel his no doubt attentive audience to the same: "as all such great changes are attended with difficulty, and danger of confusion, they ought not to be attempted without urgent necessity."[5] Langdon agrees with Jefferson's American mind, not only on the source and substance of the true political teaching, but on its (fortuitous?, providential?) embodiment in Anglo-American history: human laws are not the source of the rights of nature, but "these [natural] rights are recognized by the grand charter of British Liberties." That is, Langdon subscribes to the American Whig synthesis of nature and history we have noticed in chapter 4.

Samuel Langdon, this heir of the Puritans, was by no means unique in combining Christian and Lockean argumentation. Indeed, the best and most thorough surveys of clerical writing and sermonizing of the second two quarters of the eighteenth century show how representative Langdon was, if not of the entire American mind, then at least of the mind of his fellow post-Puritan clerics. These surveys show both that the preachers spoke out regularly and vociferously on politics, and that they, like Langdon, spoke the language of Locke and the natural rights philosophy. Thomas Pangle conveniently summarizes the results of the researches of Alice Baldwin and Claude Newlin into the role of Locke in ministerial political thought:

> Baldwin's detailed study of the sermons and writings of the New England clergy leads her to conclude that Locke's influence, especially as regards the political message of the preachers, was overwhelming: referring especially to Locke and Sidney, she writes, "all through the New England colonies the ministers were helping to spread the theories of the philosophers and to give them religious sanctions." . . . Newlin shows in some detail and with much fuller references how, in the course of the first quarter of the eighteenth century, the "new philosophy" associated with Bacon, Descartes, Boyle, Locke and Newton gradually came to predominate among the New England clergy.

Pangle tellingly summarizes Newlin's important conclusion: "The result was not only a heightened regard for human reason, but a dramatic new openness to 'Natural Religion', which was founded on a philosophical, rather than on a scriptural basis."[6]

A more recent survey by Steven Dworetz, more directly inspired by the questions of current scholarship, arrives at a very similar conclusion. The New England clergy, he finds,

> were demonstrably conversant with Locke's writings, and . . . they openly embraced Locke's political ideas—for example, the justification for revolution . . . and they shared the general philosophical perspective within which those ideas took shape. Moreover, the ministers conveyed the Lockean message, regularly and with great moral authority, to their congregations, by whom they were taken very seriously indeed.[7]

Dworetz finds that the ministers came early to Locke—well before 1763—and their constant preaching of him made his political ideas thoroughly familiar to the American public, regardless of whether the latter had read Locke or not. "Most Americans before and after 1763, and especially in New England, 'absorbed' Lockean political ideas *with* the Gospel."[8] By my rough count, Dworetz finds at least twenty-seven ministers of the revolutionary era deploying recognizably Lockean argumentation in their sermons.[9] He does not indicate what percentage of the total number of preachers he examined this is, but the pervasiveness of Lockean natural rights/social contract ideas in his survey makes very plausible the parallel but differently arrived at conclusion of Donald Lutz. According to a more straightforward citation analysis, Lutz established Locke as the single most cited author (after the Bible) in colonial political writings during the 1760s and 1770s.[10] On the basis of this mass of evidence, Dworetz persuasively concludes that "by the time of the Stamp Act, every churchgoing New Englander took for granted (without having to read) the political theory that would ultimately be used to justify the Revolution itself. . . . The clergy had implanted the Lockean ideological dynamite in the political consciousness of the people long before it had occasion to explode."[11]

As John Winthrop might have said, "whatsoever cometh around, also goeth around." Dworetz's conclusions match to a tee those arrived at forty years earlier by Clinton Rossiter, but supposedly "superseded" in the meanwhile. As Rossiter said,

> Had ministers been the only spokesmen of the American cause, had Jefferson, the Adamses, and Otis never appeared in print, the political thought of the Revolution would have followed almost exactly the same line—with perhaps a little more mention of God, but certainly no less of John Locke. In the sermons of the patriot ministers, who were responsible for fully one-third of the total output of political thought in these years, we find expressed every possible refinement of the reigning secular faith.[12]

In more detail than Dworetz, Rossiter traced out the chief ideas of the American patriot thinkers, including the clerics. A list of the topics for his chapter titles is enough to show the Lockean provenance of colonial thought: state of nature, law of nature, human (natural) rights, the right of resistance, origin of government in consent, the end of government in securing rights or property.[13]

Continuity Revisited

Yet, there is a certain ambiguity in Dworetz, and perhaps in Rossiter, that obscures the import of their arguments for the continuity issue. Dworetz suggests in passages cited above and in many others (e.g., "Locke, then, was the political line of the American Revolution, as it was laid down from the New England pulpit")[14] that the New England clergy learned their politics from Locke, and thus that Locke was in an important respect the source of their views. But on many other occasions he backs away from that conclusion, in part because of uncertainty on how to handle the difficult question of influence and intellectual causation. He frequently retreats to another position:

> Did the ministers learn all this from Locke? No one can say; "influence" is impossible to prove. But the ministers knew of and shared Locke's "theological commitments"; moreover, they

drew essentially the same political inferences from this theistic framework as Locke did. . . . Whether they *learned* . . . from Locke, then, is irrelevant.[15]

If one is attempting to assess the continuity thesis, it is not so "irrelevant" as Dworetz supposes, however. If, on the one hand, the clergy learned their politics, epistemology, and theology from Locke, then that fact is at least very compatible with the discontinuity position. If, on the other hand, we have a convergence based on Locke and the ministers independently sharing fundamental premises ("theism," according to Dworetz) and from these shared premises drawing very similar conclusions, then that at least suggests one or another version of continuity, with the natural rights philosophy best understood as an offshoot of Protestant theism.[16]

Wherever Dworetz stands, the facts he brings forth seem to tilt toward the continuity thesis. What else can explain the overwhelming presence of natural rights/social contract theorizing among the Protestant clergy in eighteenth-century America but the essential continuity or origin of that thinking in the Protestant/Puritan dispensation itself? What else can explain the phenomenon Tocqueville eloquently called to the world's attention—the deep linkage in America of religion and the political commitment to rights, democracy, and so on?

Dworetz pursues the themes of convergence via a detailed examination of four doctrines, in which he finds the ministers endorsing Lockean positions: epistemology, natural political theology, biblical political theology, and individualism. A brief reconsideration of a few pieces of his argument shows that he is too cautious in the way he handles the continuity theme; the evidence favors a stronger inference of Lockean influence than Dworetz himself draws. Most importantly, Dworetz has almost entirely omitted consideration of one element logically necessary to judge anything reliably regarding influence, convergence, and continuity, to wit, the character of Protestant, especially Puritan, political thought in its pre-Lockean phase. One can judge the character and meaning of the clerical assimilation of Lockean politics and philosophy only if one has a proper pre-Lockean base point.

A case in illustration is Dworetz's treatment of the theme of "theistic epistemology." He claims that Locke and the ministers agree on the answer to the question of how "men know the nature of God, or what God intends for or requires of them."[17] Both Locke and the ministers "tended to treat natural and revealed law as two consistent, complementary, and interdependent expressions of a single divine will." Locke did indeed officially argue something very much like this, but his emphasis is slightly different from Dworetz's formulation. Reason and revelation, proceeding from the same source and providing an account of the same world, must agree with one another. According to Locke's official doctrine, however, the deliverances of revelation may extend beyond, but never contradict, those of reason. Thus Locke on more than one occasion says that reason may prove the existence of God but not that of an afterlife. For knowledge of the latter, humanity must rely on revelation.[18] In accord with this view, Locke often emphasizes the harmony between the teachings of reason and revelation. For example, he says at the opening of his important discussion of property in his *Second Treatise*, "Whether we consider natural reason, which tells us that men, being once born, have a right to their preservation, and consequently to meat and drink, and such other things as nature affords for their subsistence; or revelation, which gives an account of those grants God made of the world to Adam, and to Noah, and his sons, it's very clear that God . . . 'has given the earth to the children of men.'"[19]

Dworetz does not bring out so clearly, however, that Locke deploys this doctrine to establish the self-sufficiency or even primacy of reason within the sphere of moral and political philosophy. In the light of Protestant/Puritan political thought, it is jarring to see Locke develop his entire political philosophy in *Two Treatises* with no mention of Romans 13, the decisive text on politics for Luther, Calvin, and the early Puritans. So far as Locke appeals to theistic ideas in *Two Treatises*, he appeals to ideas he claims to be independent of scriptural revelation: the idea of a God, creation, and a natural law deriving therefrom.[20]

Michael Ayers, author of a massive study of Locke's *Essay Concerning Human Understanding*, finds Locke intending even more

than the autonomy of reason in his treatment of the relation between reason and revelation: "His evident purpose . . . was to clip
the wings of revelation by subordinating it to 'reason,' i.e., to the
natural faculties in general."[21] We can see Ayers' point very clearly
in a Lockean journal entry, dated from 1681:

> Religion being that homage and obedience which man pays im-
> mediately to God, it supposes that man is capable of knowing
> that there is a God, and what is required and will be acceptable
> to him. . . . *That there is a God, and what that God is, nothing can
> discover to us, nor judge in us, but natural reason.*

From this principle, Locke draws the very strong conclusion: "Inspiration then . . . cannot be a ground to receive any doctrine
not conformable to reason."[22] Reason must prove the possibility
of revelation in general, the actuality of any revelation in particular, and, furthermore, must assent to the substance of any
purported revelation.

In his political writings Locke applies this principle to supply
him, at the very least, with a scriptural hermeneutic: biblical texts
are to be construed, so far as possible, so as to agree with the
teachings of reason, which, he decrees, is "our only star and compass."[23] So, when Locke does come to speak of Romans 13, in his
Paraphrase and Commentaries on St. Paul, he construes it entirely
differently from the way most Christian exegetes had. According
to Locke, it validates only that conditional obligation to obey
"the higher powers" that he found to be the truth according to
reason in his *Second Treatise.*

Even more revealingly, Locke silently corrects the Bible when
he cannot interpret it so as to cohere with his understanding of
the rational truth. A good example is the passage quoted earlier
from his discussion of property in the *Second Treatise.* Locke implies in this passage that reason and revelation agree in affirming
"that men have a right to their preservation, and consequently to
meat and drink." He cites the "grants God made . . . to Adam,
and to Noah." But in his *First Treatise,* in the context of his
polemic against the Protestant political theology of Sir Robert
Filmer, Locke had emphasized the difference between the grants
to Adam and Noah, and the absence of a right, according to the

Bible, to eat meat in the entire period between Adam and Noah. That is, reason teaches that "once born" there is a right to meat; the Bible denies that there is such a natural right. So far as there is a right, it does not stem from nature but from positive grant, and does not inhere in human beings "once born." Locke plays a complex game here and in related passages: he both calls attention to and blurs the differences between reason and revelation. In any case, Locke's ultimate position is clear: reason is *his* "only star and compass." His official doctrine on reason and revelation covers over how radical his position is. At the very least, Locke's view must be that much hitherto held to be revelation cannot really be so, for real revelations cannot contradict the teachings of reason. Locke's position is thus the same as Jefferson's, who, as will be recalled, rejected the revelatory account of a universal deluge at the time of Noah because that story conflicted with natural possibility as grasped by the rational faculty.

Whether the eighteenth-century divines followed Locke quite so far as Jefferson did is difficult to say without much detailed study and lengthy meditation. But an appreciation for the radicalism of Locke's position helps make more visible how far these clerics departed from seventeenth-century Puritan doctrine. Locke related reason and revelation at four levels, each progressively more challenging to received notions of orthodoxy; to recapitulate our discussion, these levels may be called, (1) the harmony of reason and revelation, (2) the self-sufficiency of reason, (3) the hermeneutical primacy of reason, and finally, (4) the primacy of reason *simpliciter*. Dworetz establishes that many of the divines followed Locke at least to his third level. While the fourth level is obviously the most challenging to traditional doctrines, the other three also represent a significant transformation of Protestant thinking about reason and revelation, especially as applied to the sphere of politics and morality.

Even the first level, the mere claim of harmony, is challenging to many versions of Protestant thought, as is apparent in its opposition to the old formula: *sola scriptura,* i.e., the notion that the truths about religion, including one's religiously underwritten duties in the political sphere, must be garnered from scripture alone. Such was surely Martin Luther's position. Locke's official formula, on the other hand, echoes the understanding put forward by main line Catholic thinkers from Thomas Aquinas to Francisco Suarez and Robert Bellarmine, and part of the initial Reformation impulse was to reject such accommodation—or dilution, as Luther would have it—of the word of God in favor of humanly construed truths. The elevated appreciation for the fall and the loss of human powers through the fall that characterized all forms of early Protestantism contributed to the Protestant distrust of reason and of the ability or rightfulness of raising reason to a level of authority equal to scripture.

The Puritans were perhaps not quite so outspoken as Luther on the subordination of reason to scripture, yet John Calvin, the fountainhead of Puritan theology, was not far from Luther in his treatment of the subject. Calvin concedes natural theological knowledge: "There is within the human mind, and indeed by natural instinct, an awareness of divinity." This natural knowledge or awareness has its definite limits, however: "God has sown a seed of religion in all men, but scarcely one man in a hundred is met with who fosters it, once received, in his heart, and none in whom it ripens." God not only plants this "innate" awareness of divinity in the human bosom, but he has "revealed himself and daily discloses himself in the whole workmanship of the universe." Yet these evidences of God in his creation are of no help: "although the Lord represents both himself and his everlasting Kingdom in the mirror of his works with very great clarity, such is our stupidity that we grow increasingly dull toward so manifest testimonies, and they flow away without profiting us. . . . It is therefore in vain that so many burning lamps shine for us in the workmanship of the universe to show forth the glory of its Author."[24]

Since the natural faculties fail us, another means of coming to knowledge is required: "in order that true religion may shine upon us, we ought to hold that it must take its beginning from heavenly doctrine and that no one can get even the slightest taste of right and sound doctrine unless he be a pupil of Scripture." Even more distinctly, Calvin concludes that the human mind, because of its feebleness, can in no way attain to God unless it be aided and assisted by his Sacred Word." Calvin does not go so far as to deny all value to reason, but he certainly rejects the notion that reason operating on its own comes to an understanding of the world, of God, and of self parallel to or harmonious with what is taught in scripture. Calvin, in effect, calls for a hermeneutic the reverse of that of Locke and the eighteenth-century American theologians: not for reason to guide our interpretation of scripture, but for us to exercise our reason under the tutelage of scripture. The "revelation of God through faith" can serve as "spectacles" to sharpen up our woefully defective natural vision.[25] Calvin looks to scripture for the chief outlines of moral and political matters as much as for the truth about God or redemption through Christ.

The early Puritans for the most part followed Calvin's lead. The New England Puritans, according to Perry Miller, "insist . . . that the natural man, if left to himself, will not read the lessons of nature and reason correctly."[26] The rational faculties since the fall give but "little light." As Charles Norton put it, "The light of nature since the fall, compared with the light of the image of God, before the fall, hath not the proportion of star-light, to the bright sun-light at noon day. This indeed is but darkness."[27] To replenish the light, fallen humanity must have recourse to the Bible, which "must fill the place man made empty through his own folly," on account of which folly man "has thrown away his ability to profit from natural wisdom." Thus, according to Miller, the American Puritans arrived at just the same hermeneutic as did Calvin. "The Bible itself gives us the premises of reason. . . . We do not test the Bible by nature, but nature by the Bible. It is in this sense that the Puritan achieved, or thought he had achieved, the unity of faith and intellect, dogma and reason." In sum: "Reason does not discover fundamental principles in itself. The regenerate intellect does not fetch up truth from its own depths, like water from the well, but is filled with truth from the fountain of scripture."[28]

Early Puritan political thought, as we have seen, quite firmly embraces the position Miller attributes to it more generally; the fundaments of politics can be grasped only on the basis of knowledge supplied by scripture. Winthrop merely said in prosaic form what John Milton was to say several decades later in statelier rhythm. Referring to the wisdom of the heathen ancients (Plato, Aristotle, and so on) in *Paradise Regained,* Christ asks:

> Alas what can they teach, and not mislead,
> Ignorant of themselves, of God much more,
> And how the world began, and how man fell
> Degraded by himself, on grace depending?[29]

So, when the divines of the eighteenth century endorsed the Lockean doctrine of the harmonious relationship between reason and revelation, the self-sufficiency of reason in the political sphere, and the primacy of a rational hermeneutic, they were enacting a substantial break with the reigning political theology of the previous century. Neither Locke nor the eighteenth-century ministers represented a straightforward continuation of traditional Protestant theism. Indeed, in following out the theme of reason and revelation, we see how ambiguous the very category of "theism" is, and how its deployment might stand behind the whole range of ambiguities in Dworetz's presentation. "Theism," in a word, is too vague and ill-defined; Locke, Jefferson, and the eighteenth-century clerics make theistic arguments, to be sure, but these are far different from the theistic appeals made by Luther, Calvin, or the seventeenth-century American Puritans. The God of nature, captured in and through nature by reason, the God to whom Locke, Jefferson, and Langdon appeal, is not the God of supernature to whom Winthrop and the Pilgrims appeal in order to articulate the grounds of their political life. "Theism" has at least as many variants as contractarianism, and no more than contractarianism can it provide in itself a clear thread of continuity from the early reformers to the American revolutionaries.

The Two Kingdoms

In order to understand the Lockeanization of Protestant politics, one must not only understand the political theology of the Puritans, as laid out in chapter 5 above, one must also see Puritan politics as a modification of the original Protestant understanding of politics. The inner meaning of the Puritan experiment lies precisely in this transformation of the original Protestant political teaching. The eighteenth-century Lockeanization in its turn can only be understood against the backdrop of the classic Protestant political theory. We may identify three moments of Protestant (or quasi-Protestant) political thought relevant to our enterprise here: the original Protestant political theology, the seventeenth-century Puritan variant, and the eighteenth-century Lockean version. We can never settle the continuity issue satisfactorily without an adequate grasp of the interrelations among these three.

The original doctrine was developed by Martin Luther himself in his doctrine of the Two Kingdoms, a doctrine confirmed in one way or another by nearly every major mainline Protestant thinker after Luther, including that all-important source for the Puritans, John Calvin.[30] Although Luther's central focus was surely not politics, nonetheless he directed much thinking to that subject and took some pride in his accomplishments there. "I might boast," he once boasted, "that not since the time of the apostles have the temporal sword and the temporal government been so clearly described or so highly praised as by me."[31] Luther's boast reveals several of the most striking features of his political thought: first, he praises the political very highly through establishing its specific dignity, and secondly, he sees himself in this, as in other matters, to be restoring a view held by the apostles, but since their time lost or corrupted.

Luther's central political conception can be readily stated in a few propositions:

1. There are two kingdoms, the Kingdom of God and the Kingdom of the World.

2. Both kingdoms are ordained by God. "God himself," Luther says, "is the founder, lord, master, protector, and rewarder of both [kingdoms]. . . . There is no human ordinance or authority in either, but each is a divine thing entirely."[32]

3. The Kingdom of God consists of those who are "true Christians." These are "all the true believers who are in Christ and under Christ."[33] The Kingdom of the World, on the other hand, consists in the first instance of those who are not true Christians, that is, most human beings.

4. The Kingdom of God is concerned with true or "saving righteousness," which comes only through faith. The Kingdom of the World, on the other hand, is concerned with "external righteousness." It is concerned with external deeds and external goodness, such as comes from conforming to rules or laws and as derives from the imperfect or mixed motives which impel most men most of the time.

5. In the Kingdom of God there is no authority of a political sort, no human authority properly speaking at all. As Luther says: "Whatever belongs to heaven and the eternal kingdom, is exclusively under the Lord of Heaven."[34] While God retains an authority of a certain sort in the Kingdom of the World, here he also authorizes and ordains human authority. God gives this authority directly to the secular rulers and not indirectly through the church or spiritual authorities, or through the people. Luther is no kind of contractarian, and stands much closer to theorists of divine right, like Sir Robert Filmer, than to theorists like Locke or John Milton.

6. God has provided the Kingdom of the World as an "act of Mercy" for the unrighteous. Without it they would suffer from the wicked deeds they would commit. As Luther says, "[God] has subjected them to the sword so that . . . they are unable to practice their wickedness. . . . If this were not so, men would devour one another."[35]

7. The church is the earthly representative of the Kingdom of God; its only instruments are the divine word of scripture and the sacraments. Since it is concerned only with justification, and since justification is by faith alone, the church has no concern with "works"—external deeds—at all. It therefore has no power to regulate or control external acts. Its concerns are purely spiritual. By the same token, since faith must be a "free" act, or is exclusively a gift of God's grace, the church can have no coercive authority in the realm of belief, either. Possessing control over neither deeds nor beliefs, the church has no proper claims to any coercive authority whatever. It certainly has no grounds to claim supremacy or supervisory jurisdiction over the temporal rulers.

8. The temporal rulers are the embodiment of the Kingdom of the World. Since that kingdom is ordained as a response to

human unrighteousness and evil, it must use the sword to do its good work, for the wicked will be tamed only through the threat of the sword. Since temporal rule is concerned only with external righteousness, that is, deeds, life, property, there is no incompatibility between its concerns and the exercise of coercive powers (as there is with the church and its work). Since temporal rule has no proper concern with saving righteousness or faith, it has no authority whatever over those matters. It cannot rightly use its coercive powers in this area to establish articles of faith, modes of worship, or similar matters.

9. While true Christians could, perhaps, live without temporal authorities, they are nonetheless obliged in the strictest terms to obey the secular authorities in all things within the sphere of their competence. Since the powers that be are ordained of God, Christians must obey them; since those powers are beneficial, and since Christians are obliged to do what is beneficial, Christians must support the temporal authorities. Indeed, since the temporal authorities are ordained by God, it is perfectly appropriate, indeed morally obligatory, for Christians to participate in political life.

10. The duty of submission is not unlimited, however. When the secular authorities command something outside their kingdom and its concerns, the Christian is obliged to disobey. If, for example, the emperor demanded that all Christians turn in their copies of the New Testament, all Christians would be justified in disobeying. Likewise, if the rulers command a clearly unjust act, e.g., to participate in an unjust war, the Christian may disobey. If the justice of the case is uncertain, the Christian is obliged to obey. Even where disobedience is permissible or required, resistance to rulers is not allowed. Use of force is never allowable against rulers; neither are attempts to supplant or depose rulers, no matter how tyrannical they may be.

One could summarize Luther's position on the two kingdoms with the now discredited phrase "separate but equal." The kingdoms are equal in the sense that both are ordained independently of each other by God. While the Kingdom of God has greater dignity, it does not stand in a hierarchical relationship to the Kingdom of the World. They are separate in the sense that

they have separate concerns, that is, different kinds of righteousness; they have different means of operation (sword vs. word);
they have separate jurisdictions over which the other must not
step, that is, temporal vs. spiritual matters. Luther emphasizes the
separate, even opposite, character very forcefully:

> God's kingdom is a kingdom of grace and mercy, not of wrath
> and punishment. In it there is only forgiveness, consideration
> for one another, love, service, the doing of good, peace, joy, etc.
> But the kingdom of the world is a kingdom of wrath and sever-
> ity. In it there is only punishment, repression, judgement and
> condemnation in order to restrain the wicked and protect the
> good.[36]

The separate character of the two kingdoms could be stated also
in these terms: the Kingdom of God is the realm of freedom
through Christ while the Kingdom of the World is the realm of
subjection; the Kingdom of God is the realm of equality (the
equality of all believers), while the Kingdom of the World is the
realm of inequality (through the distinction of rulers and ruled,
and the class differences resulting from private property).

Like everything important in his thinking, Luther claimed to
derive his doctrine of the Two Kingdoms from the Bible. The decisive text was Romans 13: "Let every person be subject to the
governing authorities. For there is no authority except from
God, and those that exist have been instituted by God. Therefore
he who resists the authorities resists what God has appointed. . . .
Therefore one must be subject, not only to avoid God's wrath,
but for the sake of conscience also."

But Romans 13, with its clear endorsement of the temporal
power, is not the only text relevant to politics in the New Testament, and some of the others seem much less supportive of
the political. For example, in Romans 12, Paul says "Repay no one
evil for evil . . . never avenge yourselves, but leave it to the wrath
of God, for it is written, 'Vengeance is mine, I will repay, says the
Lord.' . . . Do not be overcome by evil, but overcome evil with
good." Temporal power is constituted above all by the execution
of the very retributive justice which seems here to be forbidden.
It would thus seem that the New Testament both underwrites and

undercuts the temporal authority at once. Luther's doctrine of the Two Kingdoms emerges from the attempt to reconcile these two thrusts of the biblical teaching. The prohibition of all retribution applies to the subjects of the Kingdom of God. For themselves, they are forbidden to take vengeance, or to oppose evil with evil. So obliged, they would seem unable to participate in political life.

But the faith that justifies a Christian also produces "good works" as its fruit. These good works are not strictly speaking part of the economy of salvation; they do not earn salvation, but they follow from the right kind of faith. Luther describes these good works as "works of love," which means the Christian is impelled and therefore obligated to "love his neighbor" and to do that towards his neighbor that expresses that love. Given the wickedness of the world, love for the neighbor requires that the Christian support the secular authority for the sake of the neighbor. It requires not a grudging and unwilling subjection to the authorities, but an enthusiastic and loving submission. It requires not only submission but positive cooperation and aid. It is not only permissible but even obligatory for a Christian to be an obedient and enthusiastic citizen, or even ruler, of his polity.

The Christian is thus both obliged to the higher authorities, as in Luther's interpretation of Romans 13, and obliged not to seek retribution, as in Romans 12. That means that Christians are to be active and enthusiastic citizens—veritable scourges of justice—on behalf of everyone but themselves. So far is Luther from the point of view of modern politics, which sees the assertion and protection of one's own rights, liberties, and interests as the foundation of politics, that he even forbids the Christian from going to law for his own sake. A Christian may, on the other hand, do an act of love and become a soldier and kill with a good conscience on behalf of his ruler.

Luther adumbrates his doctrine of the two kingdoms in the first instance for the sake of the church and of faith. The temporal authorities are the beneficiaries of the analysis Luther arrives at of the causes for the deep and vicious corruption in the Roman church. Luther differs from many of the other critics of abuses in the church of his time in that he links these abuses to a full-scale theologico-political analysis, an analysis which relates the abuses to the entire structure of the medieval church, including its theology. According to Luther, the church has gone wrong in confusing the two kingdoms. It is no accident that the first abuse Luther lists in his great list of abuses in his "Open Letter to the Christian Nobility" is that the pope, "who claims the title of 'most holy' and 'most spiritual', is more worldly than the world itself."[37] The church forgets its own office and intrudes into the Kingdom of the World to the detriment of both. This intrusion in turn is made possible by the church's having forgotten, or having failed to hold sufficiently tightly to the chief doctrinal claim of Christianity—justification by faith alone—for only through trapping men in the belief in works has the church come to mix itself so perniciously in the Kingdom of the World.

Luther sees a very substantial reordering of the ecclesiastical-political structure following from his doctrine of the Two Kingdoms. The church must give up all claims to temporal authority in its own right, and it must also give up all claims to supremacy over the secular authorities. It must give up its claimed right to legislate rules and prohibitions on external deeds as required for salvation. Luther treats these rules and practices as part of the church's political or economic apparatus—the church forbids or requires certain acts only or mainly for the sake of then selling believers the right to do or not to do the thing in question. As Luther says: "It looks as though all the laws of the Church were made for one purpose only—to be nothing but so many money-snares from which a man must extricate himself, if he would be a Christian."[38] Moreover, the church must give up its claimed immunities to civil law and its separate canon law and ecclesiastical courts; regarding temporal things all are subject to the temporal authorities. There are no exceptions for the church or for ecclesiastics.

The separation of the two kingdoms both follows from and enforces the doctrine of justification by faith alone, and thus is the precondition for the church's playing its part in the all-important and highest human task of seeking God. For example, if the church no longer offers opportunities for those who really belong to the Kingdom of the World to satisfy their desires for wealth and power within it, it will cease attracting those men and will instead attract and have its tone set by men who are interested in sowing the seeds of faith. It will stop being an agency with a product, salvation, for sale. The church, which should be the agency for preaching the free gift of grace, instead sells its wares. This is especially vicious, for the church so constituted leads farther and farther from what is truly needful for salvation—saving faith.

Luther's separation of the two kingdoms is not intended to benefit and purify only the church, but to improve the condition of the Kingdom of the World as well. This kingdom suffers as much from the confusion of the two kingdoms as does the church. Many, if not all, of the major political disputes of Luther's time and before stemmed from the conflicts and tensions between the church and the secular authorities, and derived, Luther believes, either from the efforts of the church to assert its supremacy over secular authorities, or to claim immunities for its persons and property, or to extract various resources from the secular authorities. Medieval history was punctuated by a series of dramatic conflicts between the ecclesiastical and secular authorities. In addition, Luther sees the church's claims as contributing to the difficulties the secular rulers have in governing their kingdoms well. The separate canon law and ecclesiastical immunity from ordinary civil law mean there is a "state within a state" in every Christian polity, that there are large areas where the secular rulers are unable to extend the rule of their law. Luther is especially distressed over the amount of wealth the church extracts from Germany in the form of indulgences and other devices that amount to taxation. This leaves the people poor and siphons off a source of revenue from the secular rulers. So Luther sees his doctrine of separation redounding to the benefit of the secular authorities as well, by curbing those and other practices which harm civil peace and derogate from civil authority.

Despite his confidence in it, Luther's political doctrine did not prove an unmitigated success, even within Protestantism. Because it failed to establish itself as particularly authoritative, we find later and other versions of Protestant political theology, like Winthrop's. The story of Protestant political thought in the century between Luther and Winthrop is sufficiently elaborate that I can mention here only a few manifestations of Luther's failure to settle the theologico-political issue.[39]

Luther's own doctrine was itself unstable. He preached almost unlimited submission until 1530, when he changed his position somewhat in the light of threats to his followers from the emperor. He preached the illegitimacy of intrusion by the Kingdom of the World in the Kingdom of God, as in, for example, matters of heresy, but he shortly authorized a most brutal suppression of various "left-wing" Protestant groups that arose in the wake of his reformation. Luther, moreover, was unable to establish authoritatively the content of his political doctrine from the principles on which he based it. For example, Paul says "Be subject to the higher powers"—but who are the higher powers? Are all who claim political power equally ordained of God? What does it take to become so? In one direction, this question led to the adumbration of doctrines of divine right of kings, extreme doctrines indeed in the hands of men like Robert Filmer, who implied that kings were so absolute that they might eat their subjects if they so desired. In the other direction, this question led to the doctrines of a John Milton, in whose hands the Reformation principles became warrant for regicide.[40]

Luther rested his doctrine on the duty to works of love. But this doctrine had two very serious problems. First, how could Luther dictate the substance of works of love as support of the political and social status quo and only that? The peasants during the Peasants' Revolt raised that question and it was a good one. On the other hand, if definite prescribed duties followed from the "works of love," then why not God's laws themselves as outlined in the Old Testament? Calvin and the Puritans pressed this interpretation of Protestant politics. Moreover, was not the doctrine of "works of love," as developed by Luther into obligatory duties, verging on incompatibility with his own doctrine of justification by faith alone? Such questions were raised by the various so-called "antinomian" groups that arose on the left wing of the Reformation, and which caused so much trouble to John Winthrop in Massachusetts.

I mention only a few of the difficulties. These did not remain merely theoretical; they produced the tremendous fragmentation not only of Protestant sects but of Protestant politics. The liberal solution probably arose in England before it arose elsewhere because in England the failure of the Reformation to find an authoritative or definitive political embodiment produced not only the mass migration to America of the Puritans but also a civil war of major magnitude between two Protestant parties, a war which was only the most violent event in a century's long intramural struggle within Protestantism. Luther believed he had arrived at the true and in principle final political teaching. That belief proved false, and the political thought of the American Puritans, although showing many of the marks of Luther's stamp, was one of the versions of Protestant political thought that strayed significantly from Luther's formulations.

The remarkable character of the Puritan experiment shows up extraordinarily well when compared to Luther's doctrine of the Two Kingdoms. Although Winthrop and the Puritans pay more than lip service to the central Lutheran thesis of the separation of the two kingdoms, they modify the Lutheran position in several places, the overall effect of which is to consistently threaten to overcome the separation that was the very hallmark of Protestant (as opposed to Catholic) Christian political theology. In Winthrop's sermon we can see this tendency in two particularly prominent places—with regard to the end of politics, and with regard to the necessary means of politics. The "work" he and his fellows have in hand, he asserts, is "to seeke out a place of habitation and consorteshipp under a due form of goverrnment both civile and ecclesiasticall"; that is, to establish Luther's two kingdoms in America. But unlike Luther, he does not attribute different ends to the two kingdoms; both have one comprehensive set of ends: "The end is to improve our lives to doe more service to the Lord[,] the comforte and encrease of the body of Christe wherof wee are members that our selves and posterity may be the better preserved from the Common corrupcions of this evil world to serve the Lord and worke out our Salvacion under the power and purity of his holy Ordinances." As Susan Power concludes, Winthrop "thought the major purpose of a government was to protect, aid, and advance religion and the church. The sword was under the control of the state, but . . . government existed to serve religious ends and purposes, as these ends and purposes were defined by the Church."[41] Exactly like the Pilgrims, and quite differently from Luther, the Puritans conceive their end nondualistically, "to serve the Lord and worke out our Salvacion." This is not merely the end of the Kingdom of God, but of the Kingdom of the World, as well. "Serving the Lord" apparently does not mean only working out salvation; it includes, at a minimum, achieving that communal harmony and integrity in the human social world that imitates the divinely ordained harmony in the universe as a whole. The Puritans have a strong political and social dimension to their sense of religious mission. Unlike many other Protestant sects, they are not politically quietistic because oriented solely toward individual salvation.

The means by which Winthrop envisions his flock achieving this "extraordinary" end is that equally extraordinary practice of love, grounded in genuine Christian spirit, that we have already noticed.[42] The Kingdom of the World in both its end and its means must draw very near to the Kingdom of God. Luther's Kingdom of the World thus loses its autonomy, self-sufficiency, and specific difference from the Kingdom of God. Although the Puritans retain a commitment to the formal separation of the institutions of church and state, there nonetheless exist right in the heart of Puritan aspiration and conception forces drawing the two kingdoms together.

The Pilgrims and the Puritans reveal the same underlying tendency of thought and practice. More striking, perhaps, because done so briefly and unselfconsciously, the Pilgrims in their Mayflower Compact display the quality that will return to plague the entire Puritan experiment in America. In the Mayflower Compact the form of covenant migrates—in a very limited context and with a narrow meaning, to be sure—from the sphere of the sacred to the sphere of the secular. At the same time, the ends or purposes of the secular are set in a relatively straightforward and unproblematical way as means to sacred purposes. In these movements are presaged the ironic fate of the Puritan polity—theocracy. Protestantism began with the rejection of what were taken to be the theocratic aspirations of Roman Christianity and then ended up reinstating a version of that very order. This happened, of course not only in America but also in Calvin's Geneva, and the battle for the soul of the Puritan revolution in England was in part a battle over whether the victory of Parliament in the Civil War would mean the institution of a theocracy there.[43] But it could certainly be argued that theocracy was nowhere more firmly established than in seventeenth-century New England, for it was there that the connection between political power and the church was most tightly drawn through two crucial practices. On the one hand, political rights were limited to those who were full members of the churches—a relatively democratic standard according to the practices of the time, but nonetheless one that premised one's status in the secular society on one's status in the ecclesiastical society.[44] On the other hand, church membership was limited to those who could give persuasive testimony to the experience of saving grace, a criterion that both tended to limit the numbers who could become members and to put the judgment over who would be admitted to membership in the hands of the powers in the church, the ministers and the church elders. This was not, to be sure, a normal or formal theocracy in which the priests ruled; the Puritans maintained formal separation of the instruments of church and state by forbidding, for example, the holding of formal office in both institutions by the same person at the same time. Nonetheless, at a more informal level, the principle of the separateness of the two spheres was constantly overcome. This was reinforced when a law was passed requiring approval by the authorities for the formation of any new church congregations in the 1640s. That is, "rogue churches" would not be allowed to create new members and thus new citizens.[45]

As we have seen, eligibility for membership in the political community, to say nothing of citizenship, was defined in terms of the spiritual purposes of the community. Although the Puritans found it difficult to live up to the standards of Christian love Winthrop so hopefully outlined in his sermon, yet the process of governance, too, reflected a consistent tendency to break down the border between the spheres. Winthrop's *Journals* reveal how frequently "informal" conclaves of the ministers were called on to resolve difficult issues facing the community. Formal institutions do not always express the totality of political reality. Finally, the interpenetration of the secular kingdom with spiritual purpose guaranteed that the secular sphere would be constantly pressed into service for spiritual ends—establishments of religion, requirements of church attendance, adumbration of moral rules and regulations inspired by religious conceptions.[46] Even so great an admirer of the Puritans as Tocqueville commented on the character of their legislation:

> The framers of these penal codes were especially concerned with the maintenance of good behavior and sound mores in society, so they constantly invaded the sphere of conscience, and there was hardly a sin not subject to the magistrate's censure. . . . The lawgivers, completely forgetting the great principle of religious liberty . . . enforced attendance at divine service by threat of fines and went so far as to impose severe penalties, and often the death penalty, on Christians who chose to worship God with a ritual other than their own. Finally, sometimes the passion for regulation which possessed them led them to interfere in matters completely unworthy of such attention. . . . We must not forget that these ridiculous and tyrannical laws were not imposed from outside . . . and that their mores were even more austere than their laws. . . . Such deviations undoubtedly bring shame on the spirit of man; they attest the inferiority of our nature.[47]

Tocqueville's judgment is probably just, but he fails to recognize how much this legislation flows not from mere flaws of human nature but from the specific character of Puritan principles and aspirations.

Lockean Puritans

Just as the American Puritans represented a modification of the original Protestant political theology, so the eighteenth-century theorists represent a further modification, a modification involving the Lockeanization of the earlier Puritan politics, but ironically perhaps, this Lockeanization was a process made possible by a partial reversion to the older doctrine of the Two Kingdoms.

To put the issue bluntly and perhaps too starkly, in place of Dworetz's view of fortuitous convergence, I am arguing for a Lockean conquest, or at least assimilation, of Puritan political thought. Even though influence is extremely difficult to prove conclusively, I think the evidence strongly supports the view that Locke did indeed influence the Protestant divines of the revolutionary era. Before Locke, the Puritans said one sort of thing about politics; after Locke, they said quite different sorts of things, which turn out to be the same things Locke said, in more or less the language of Locke. As I mean to demonstrate in a moment, this is more than a *post hoc, propter hoc* connection.

Because Dworetz, Rossiter, and others have argued at length for the Lockean character of eighteenth-century clerical thought, there is no need to duplicate the broad kind of survey they undertook. But a return to the theme in a slightly different way is warranted in order to establish beyond a reasonable doubt that the transformation of clerical thought represents a Lockeanization of the Puritan tradition. Dworetz himself unearthed a great deal of evidence that points in this direction, but he hesitates to credit the force of the remarkable parallels of doctrine and language he uncovered. Not merely do the ministers agree with Locke and each other and Jefferson and . . . in the general way people sharing a larger set of commitments might do, but they share very specific formulations. Merely opening at random in Dworetz's discussion, one finds a statement like this: "the clerical teaching [on religious toleration] reads, on the whole, like a paraphrase of Locke and actually contains quite a few citations to what one commentator called Locke's 'unanswerable *Letter of Toleration*'."[48] Doesn't this sort of thing, especially when conjoined with the observation that the Puritan forebears were committed to no doctrine of religious toleration at all, impel a strong conclusion of Lockean influence? Surely the appeal to common theism will not do, for Calvin's theism, for example, led him to insist on religious homogeneity in Geneva, and Winthrop's theism led him to expel Roger Williams and Anne Hutchinson, and to favor banning all who lacked the true faith from entering Massachusetts Bay.

The Lockean provenance of the transformation of Puritan thought appears particularly clearly in an election sermon by

Abraham Williams, a pastor at the outlying church at Sandwich, Massachusetts. According to Edmund Morgan, Williams was not one of the real luminaries of the era; he is memorable chiefly because of his "illustrativeness," which is to say, his representation of "the transformation that had taken place in Puritan ideas."[49]

Despite his lack of distinction, Williams preached the election sermon before the General Court of Massachusetts in 1762, and gave the assembled legislators a remarkably nuanced version of Lockean political philosophy. All the Lockean theses familiar from the Declaration of Independence are there. He treats in succession the topics of the origin, the end, the nature, and the structures of government. He understands the origin in an entirely Lockean manner as a "state of nature" or a state of equality, and explains that equality with a direct paraphrase of a passage in the *Second Treatise*, although neither here nor elsewhere in his sermon does he mention Locke by name.[50] Natural equality does not suffice because the "idle and impudent" are constantly tempted "to seize what they had not labored for; which must put the industrious and honest upon methods of self-defense, and dispose them to unite in societies for natural security, against the assaults of rapacious men." Williams thus not only picks up the Lockean emphasis on the economic causes of discontent—nature requires hard and painful labor and without government the fruits of labor are most insecure—but he almost exactly paraphrases Locke's presentation in the *Letter Concerning Toleration*: "the pravity of mankind being such that they had rather injuriously prey upon the fruits of other men's labours than take pains to provide for themselves, the necessity of preserving men in the possession of what honest industry has already acquired, and also of preserving their liberty and strength, whereby they may acquire what they farther want, obliges men to enter into society with one another."[51]

Government is formed through "combinations and compacts," says Williams, following Locke very closely in identifying the source of political authority in a power "every man, prior to government is authorized" to use, a power "to vindicate his own right, and inflict adequate punishment on the invader, . . . as will probably prevent future injuries, and render men's right and properties . . . secure." Locke calls this the "executive power of the law of nature" and describes it as a power "put into every man's hands [in the state of original equality], whereby everyone has a right to punish for transgressions of that law to such a degree as may hinder its violation."[52] Government is formed when, as Williams puts it, "men reasonably surrender to society the right they before had of judging in their own case, and of executing those righteous judgements." Locke's point is precisely the same: "Wherever, therefore, any number of men are so united into one society as to quit every one his executive power of the law of nature, and to resign it to the public, there and there only is a political or civil society."[53]

According to Williams, the making reveals the purpose: "the end and design of civil society and government, from this view of it's [sic] origin, must be to secure the rights and properties of its members." Locke, and later, Jefferson, of course make the identical claim: "the great and chief end . . . of men's uniting into commonwealths, and putting themselves under government, is the preservation of their property [or rights]."[54]

In his treatment of "the nature of civil society or government," Williams again closely paraphrases a passage from Locke's *Letter Concerning Toleration.* "The nature of civil society or government, is a temporal worldly constitution, founded upon worldly motives to answer valuable worldly purposes." Government is interested only in "men's outward behavior," and then only as it may "injure the properties and enjoyments of others." Since "the rights of conscience are inalienable," they "cannot possibly be given up to society."[55] Locke's version is again very close to this:

> *The commonwealth* seems to me to be a society of men constituted only for the procuring, preserving, and advancing of their civil interests.
> Civil interests I call life, liberty, health, and indolence of body; and the possession of outward things, such as money, lands, houses, furniture and the like.

Furthermore, Williams again echoes Locke in his discussion of "the various orders and ranks necessary to answer the purposes of civil society." His treatment here is especially instructive because at first he seems to be harkening back to Winthrop's older notion of political society as a knitting together of different orders on the model of the ancient constitution, but Williams moves off in a Lockean direction instead. The "orders" that he has in mind are the functional elements of the separation of powers that Locke had described in the second half of his *Second Treatise*—the legislative, executive, and federative powers.[56]

Finally, Williams roots his political theory in the divine order in exactly the way Jefferson does. "The Law of Nature (or those Rules of Behavior, which the Nature God had given Men . . .) is the Law and Will of the *God of Nature*, which all then are obliged to obey."[57] Williams is emphatic that the core of politics derives from the "Nature God," not the God of Abraham, much less the God who so loved the world that he gave his only begotten son. The obligations inherent in political life derive from nature, not from positive divine command, not, for example, from Romans 13. Williams not only agrees in substance with Locke and Jefferson, but his entire style of argument is theirs. Gone is the scriptural politics of Luther and Calvin, Winthrop and Cotton.

Williams and Locke converge in their political theories, to be sure, and it strains credulity to imagine they are merely drawing parallel conclusions from similar premises: Locke influenced Williams, and by extension, those other Puritan divines of whom Williams is so representative. Puritan thought has been transformed, it has assimilated or been assimilated by Locke. The relation of Lockean politics to Puritan politics parallels the relation between the natural rights philosophy and the older Whig tradition of constitutional right. The ability of the natural rights philosophy to forge such alliances is a singularly noteworthy fact about it and about the American founding era. It appears to account for the revolution in opinion that made possible both the Revolution and the American political tradition.[58]

Recognition of the Lockeanization of Puritan politics is necessary, for it is only on that basis that the truly interesting questions emerge. These are two: (1) Was the convergence of Lockean political philosophy and Puritan political thought all in one direction, or did Protestantism contribute something of its own, so that Lockeanism was also transformed in the process of constructing the amalgam? (2) What made possible this remarkable assimilation of Puritan thought by Locke?

Dependent as the ministers are on Locke, their political statements do often add elements to Locke of a loosely Christian character. In his momentous election sermon, for example, Samuel Langdon combined Lockean doctrine with the more traditional Puritan jeremiad, blaming the ills of the times on religious decline and the displeasure of God. Although Langdon went further in deploying the jeremiad format than most of the Lockean clerics did, he was not atypical in giving firmer religious overtones to Lockean political philosophy than did more secular Lockeans such as Trenchard and Gordon, writing as Cato in England earlier in the eighteenth century. The ministers gave greater weight to three themes in particular than did Locke himself or Cato: (1) they attended much more to scriptural passages and argumentation; (2) they gave greater emphasis to divine providence and divine judgment; and (3) they dwelt far more on the practical requirements of sound religious practice in producing healthy politics. Much less often a deeper effort at doctrinal synthesis was attempted, such as Charles Chauncey's gesture toward assimilating Lockean politics and the doctrine of the fall. What is most remarkable, however, about the clerical modifications is how shallow they are, how little they really change or add. It would not be correct to say they are merely rhetorical, but it would be incorrect to say that Lockean doctrine is substantially Christianized by their patronage of it.

The clerical appeal to scripture is most revealing. All the clerics use scripture far more than Locke had done, and probably all of them appeal to and discuss at greater or lesser length the crucial text, Romans 13, a text which Locke had mentioned not even once in his presentation of his political philosophy. In part, the conventions of clerical discourse account for their greater use of scripture: most of the writings we have from them are sermons, and sermons are typically built around a scripture text.

The conventions only begin to account for the clerical use of scripture, however. As Christians and men of faith, as Protestants devoted to *scriptura,* if not *sola scriptura,* they needed to give some acount to themselves and their congregations of how the political and moral principles they were taking over from Locke cohered with the touchstone of their faith. But what they say about biblical texts reveals how much has changed with their adherence to Locke. In a text which Luther had seen as the unanswerable basis for a duty of passive obedience and the divine ordination of "the powers that be," American preachers like Jonathan Mayhew found a right, or even a duty, to resist rulers.[59] Samuel West of Dartmouth, close friend to many Massachusetts revolutionary leaders, and later selected to attend the Constitutional Convention, delivered an election sermon in 1776 in which he illustrates very clearly the Lockeanized version of Romans.

He opens with a statement of "the nature and design of civil government" in order to "discover the foundation of the magistrate's authority to command, and the duty of subjects to obey"; to do that, he insists, "we must consider what 'state all men are naturally in,' and that is (as Mr. Locke observes) a state of perfect freedom." After outlining, mostly in Lockean language, the Lockean doctrines of equality, liberty, state of nature, natural rights, right to enforce the law of nature, the breakdown of the state of nature, the creation of government through consent, the limitations on the rightful power of rulers, and the resulting limitations on the duty of obedience in subjects, he observes, "This account of the nature and design of civil government, which is so clearly suggested to us by the plain principles of common sense and reason, is abundantly confirmed by the sacred scriptures." Notice, it is the commonsensical and reasonable (i.e., Lockean) explanation that comes first and guides the interpretation of biblical texts, "which have often been brought by men of slavish principles to establish the absurd doctrine of unlimited passive obedience and non-resistance." Romans 13, of course, is the chief of these texts, and his thoroughly Lockean version of it reverses the old "slavish" reading.

> If the apostle, then, asserts that rulers are ordained of God only because they are a terror to evil works and a praise to them that do well; . . . if the sole reason why they have a right to tribute is because they devote themselves wholly to the business of securing to men their just rights, and to the punishing of evil-doers—it follows, by undeniable consequence [even though Paul himself says no such thing] that when they become pests of human society . . . they then cease being the ordinance of

> God; . . . and it is so far from being a crime to resist them, that in many cases it may be highly criminal in the sight of Heaven to refuse resisting and opposing them to the utmost of our power.[60]

Dworetz observes that West and the other ministers "frequently fortified their 'liberal' interpretation of *Romans* 13 with citations of 'Locke on Government' as they sought to establish beyond dispute the right and duty of resistance." Moreover, Dworetz points out that Locke himself supplied an interpretation of Paul on the duty to obey "the powers," which was very much along the same lines as the one adopted by Mayhew, West, and the other American preachers. As Dworetz comments, "though his exegesis was not directly tied to his explicitly political work, his 'liberal' interpretation of *Romans* 13 complemented the arguments of the *Two Treatises*."[61]

Scriptural materials not only receive a very different substantive interpretation in the sermons of the post-Lockean divines from their earlier readings by Luther, Calvin, and the others, they also serve a very different function in the argument. Not the primary source of insight, they are discussed in order to confirm the teachings of (Lockean) reason, and to clear any imputation of inconsistency between Lockean theory and biblical teaching. Once this has been accomplished, the biblical texts are then free to fulfill yet another, and politically very significant, function: the higher or more intense authority of religion now stands behind the cool rationalism of Locke. There can be little doubt that the enlistment of St. Paul in Locke's army had much to do with the fervor Americans of the revolutionary era brought to the political conflicts of the day.

One also sees in the ministerial writers a stronger sense of divine presence than in Locke or his secular followers. In the entire *Second Treatise*, Locke never once speaks of divine providence; likewise he does not speak of divine punishment, either in this life or the next. The closest he comes to a notion of providence is the famous "appeal to Heaven," which can certainly be interpreted as an affirmation that God guides the outcomes of important political conflicts into the just path, but little else in *Two Treatises* resonates with this reading.

The American minsters are much quicker to appeal both to providence and divine judgment. Charles Chauncey, for example, backs up his Lockean notions of the duties of rulers with a direct appeal to divine judgment: "it should be a constraining argument with rulers to be just, that they are accountable to that Jesus, whom God hath ordained to be judge of the world. . . . And if . . . they have . . . misused their power, sad will be their account another day." Likewise the ministers are apt to collapse the mandates of nature, as understood by Locke, with the designs of providence. Abraham Williams, for example, says that "when men enter into civil societies, and agree upon rational forms of government, they act right, conformable to the Will of God, by the concurrence of whose Providence, rulers are appointed."[62] As with the use of scripture texts, the ministers evoke divine action to give support and greater weight to the normative positions posited within the Lockean philosophy: God supports the natural norms Locke has articulated. The appeal to the divine has little or no independent force beyond that, although the practical import of the appeal is no doubt significant.

It is also an import Locke himself endorsed in an indirect way. Locke's argument in *Two Treatises* is a complex one, operating at least at two levels—a level of natural theology and a level of pure naturalism.[63] These two levels in Locke correspond largely to Jefferson's two views of the natural bridge. Within his natural theological argument, the so-called workmanship argument, Locke does not deploy arguments for direct divine action in this or the next world, because he appears to believe that even if reason can establish the central truths of natural religion (the existence of a God, for example), it cannot establish these other propositions. Thus these sorts of propositions are no part of his political philosophy proper. Positive religion or faith can, of course, supplement the deliverances of reason with hopes such as Chauncey voices, and Locke believes that such is healthy and perhaps necessary in political life. Locke, in other words, provides warrant for the divines' claims about divine action as politically desirable if not as philosophically provable.[64] On the whole, the clerics have done the same with providence and divine punishment as they did with scripture: they have pressed these ideas into the service of the Lockean moral and political system, and therewith have added a great deal to the efficacy of Lockean theory.

The ministers were especially sensitive to the practical contribution religion could make to sound politics, and they frequently pressed for public recognition and support of religion beyond what Locke himself or his secular followers usually did. Charles Chauncey, for example, finds it "easy to distinguish between government in it's [*sic*] abstracted notion, and the faithful advantageous administration of it. And religion in rulers is necessary to the latter, tho' not to the former." Although the abstract theory of government does not depend on religion, the reliably effective practice of it does. Locke never goes this far, apparently putting more weight on proper institutions, practices, and the threat of rebellion to keep rulers in their proper courses. Chauncey here draws nearer to Winthrop, who, it will be recalled, saw the Christian (Calvinist) commitments of rulers and people as essential to the successful realization of the political task facing humankind. Yet here, where they draw closest to each other, the great difference between Chauncey and his forebears remains pronounced. Chauncey, in the first place, hedges a great deal on the necessity of religion: "Not but that [rulers] may be considerably useful in their places, if the religions fear of God does not reign in their hearts. From a natural benevolence of temper, accompanied with an honest turn of mind, they may be instrumental in doing good service to the public."[65] Religion adds at the margins: "if destitute of religion, they are possessed of no principle that will stimulate a care in them to act up to their character steadily and universally."[66] This is surely a far cry from Winthrop's notion of a community thoroughly Christian, both in ends and means. Chauncey's understanding of the ends is no longer Christian at all—religion has nothing whatever to do with that. And his treatment of means deviates just as much; where Winthrop saw specifically Christian (Protestant, Puritan) qualities to be necessary in both people and rulers, Chauncey sees the much vaguer "religion," that is, a generic "fear of God" to be useful. Winthrop, moreover, looks to the specifically Christian quality of love or charity to make possible the well-knit or harmonious exemplary community; Chauncey, like the later American founders, aims much lower. He relies on fear of God to prevent people and rulers from being unjust and oppressive, respectively; he does not anticipate the more heroic positive consequences Winthrop expects love to accomplish.

Abraham Williams is another who looks to religion as a necessary support for civic life. Even though "the rights of conscience are unalienable" and religion "can be regulated only by God himself," nonetheless, "civil societies have a right, it is their duty to encourage and maintain social public worship of the Deity, and instructions in righteousness; for without *social vertues, societies can't subsist*; and *these vertues can't be expected, or depended on*, without a belief in, and regard to, the supreme Being, and a future world: consequently, a religious *fear* and regard to God, ought to be encouraged in every society, and with this view, publick social worship and instructions in social virtues, maintained."[67] Williams believes that such established religion "is consistent with an entire *liberty of conscience*," a view with which not all would concur. Locke himself had reservations about such practices, as he made clear in his *Letter Concerning Toleration*; the civil authorities have no jurisdiction to establish religious practices or articles of belief.[68] Nonetheless, it must be noted that Williams is carrying through a Lockean theme here (although surely not one exclusive to Locke): he is concerned to establish religion not for truly religious purposes but for the civil virtues it fosters. Locke concurred with the judgment that religion, properly constrained and confined, can indeed be a force for civil good. In this respect, Williams and quite a few of the other clerics kept touch with the Puritan past—Massachusetts retained a religious establishment longer than any other state. Yet even so, the emphasis has shifted a great deal from the old Puritan emphasis; the purpose of public religious practice is wholly secular and, for Chauncey, much more modest than for the Puritan settlers.

Many explanations have been offered over the years for the remarkable affinity the New England clergy showed for Locke, most of which do not seem very plausible in the light of the above analysis. The suggestion that the descendants of the Puritans found Locke so congenial because he and they were all theists fails to convince, not only because Locke's theism, such as it is, is far different from Puritan theism, but also because theism as such coheres with many different kinds of political commitments. Thomas Aquinas, Luther, Calvin, Winthrop, and the Thomas Jefferson of the "below the bridge" view of nature all qualify as "theists" of some sort, but all combine that with systems of political thought quite different from the others. Even "theists" like Luther and Calvin, who stand relatively close to each other in their theism, differ significantly in their politics. This is not to say that Locke's "theism" was simply irrelevant. I have argued elsewhere that Locke could have presented his political philosophy in a simply nontheistic manner, grounding rights not in the relationship to the "creator," whose "workmanship" all human beings are, but in the self-grounding character of human selfhood. Instead, Locke presented his political philosophy as the point of convergence of two alternative and in a sense complementary lines of argument—the theistic and the nontheistic. The theistic version of Locke's political philosophy served as an intermediate term between the more traditional Christian theism of his audience, especially of the Protestant clergy, and his more strictly philosophic, but nontheistic reasoning. Locke's natural theology served as a bridge across which many of his more traditional or more orthodox contemporaries and successors came at least halfway (more I think) to his more secular position. Without that bridge, this would probably never have happened. Thus Locke's "theism" must be accounted a necessary but not a sufficient condition for his success with the ministers and their congregations.[69]

The suggestion that the ministers had a special openness to Locke because their traditional covenantal theology resonated with Locke's contractarianism is only slightly more plausible than the argument about theism. The Puritans were not, it turns out, so "covenantal" in their political theory as often claimed—I suspect that scholars often read back from the eighteenth century to the earlier period—and so far as covenant or contract did play a role in their political understanding, it was really quite different from the natural rights/social contract position of Locke and the Declaration of Independence, of the Massachusetts constitution and the writings of Jonathan Mayhew or Abraham Williams or Samuel West. This is not to say that contractarian motifs in earlier

Puritan thought were entirely irrelevant. At the very least there was a familiar sound to the idea of contract, even if the natural rights philosophy appealed to a very different sort of contract. The covenant tradition in Puritanism was probably neither necessary nor sufficient, but it did perhaps contribute to developing the special links between Locke and the descendants of the Puritans.

It is often speculated, further, that the historical experiences of the American settlers made them particularly open to Lockean motifs—the idea of a state of nature, of an identifiable and deliberate beginning to political life resonating with their experience of the wilderness and the founding of new communities in a way it never could in stable, well-established, long-settled communities which seemed to "grow" and not to have been founded. Perhaps features of the natural rights philosophy which were meant to be essentially rational reconstructions or moral histories were more readily or easily imagined or taken seriously in the condition of early settlement in America, but on the whole this suggestion also fails to persuade. After all, the Puritans were closest to their "state of nature" experience in the seventeenth century, when their system of thought was most distant from the natural rights philosophy. Only as their communities came to be longer settled and more historical did the natural rights position come to be established.

Of all the proffered explanations, the least satisfactory is the "strong continuity" view, that is, the view that Locke and the Puritans share not only some vague "theism" but that Locke's political philosophy is only a variant of Calvinism itself, and its affinities for other variants of Calvinism easy enough to explain. The proponents of this view have never rendered it plausible, and I believe the account of both Protestant thought and the natural rights philosophy presented here shows why not.

Paradoxically, however, I want to suggest in a somewhat tentative way that it is precisely the way Locke's political philosophy relates to the tradition of Protestant political thought that does account for his remarkable triumph among the Americans. The most revealing text is an extraordinary pamphlet by Massachusetts-turned-Connecticut clergy-man-turned-politician, Elisha

Williams. Williams was great-grandson of the leading Puritan minister of the founding generation, John Cotton, and, judging by his "The Essential Rights and Liberties of Protestants," a formidable thinker in his own right. He published his pamphlet in 1744 in direct response to a 1742 Connecticut statute aiming to curb the itinerant preaching of revivalist preachers during the Great Awakening. The law set limitations on who could lawfully preach where, and thus in effect, maintained the monopolies of ministers in their own parishes. Williams wrote against this law in the strongest terms, deploying arguments for the most part from two quite different sources: Locke and Luther. The power of his argument derives from the way he fits those two sources together, and produces a real synthesis of them.

The question posed to him by the Connecticut law concerns "the extent of the civil magistrate's power respecting religion." There are, of course, many strategies open to one seeking to answer such a question, but Williams thinks it "needful to look back to the end, and therefore to the original" of the magistrate's power. For the treatment of "the origin and end of civil government," for an understanding of what these things "be in their own nature," and of "what reason teaches concerning them," Williams admits that he has but "given a short sketch of what the celebrated Mr. Lock [*sic*] in his *Treatise of Government* has largely demonstrated." Locke is a great authority, it appears, for Williams thinks "it is justly to be presumed all are agreed [in Locke's philosophy] who understand the natural rights of mankind." Locke is thus for Williams "the great Mr. Lock."[70] Williams implies that Locke's political philosophy already stands high in the minds of his countrymen. There is other evidence to support his view, but after Williams's pamphlet we begin to see the real dominance of Lockean theory, with Lockean argumentation appearing in important places like Mayhew's 1750 "Discourse on Unlimited Submission."[71] Williams's testimony to the contrary notwithstanding, there is room for the hypothesis that his (Williams') pamphlet was itself a great contributor to the power Lockean theory came to hold.

Williams not only appeals to Locke's authority, he shows an unusually fine grasp of Locke's theory. His presentation is more richly detailed, more nuanced, and more insightful than that of any other of Locke's clerical admirers in the eighteenth century. He not only picks up fine points in the *Two Treatises*, like the ambivalence between divine ownership and self-ownership as the ground of rights, but he also shows an impressive knowledge of many other parts of the Lockean corpus—the *Letter Concerning Toleration*, the *Reasonableness of Christianity* and the *Essay Concerning Human Understanding.*

Williams counters the Connecticut law with a two-pronged argument, the first clearly deriving from the *Two Treatises*, the second to some degree from the *Letter Concerning Toleration*, but also drawing on Luther's doctrine of the Two Kingdoms. The first prong approaches the question of the magistrate's authority in religious matters with a straightforward Lockean argument beginning with the natural equality of the state of nature and proceeding through the social contract to the issue of what powers rational actors would or could rightly give to the political authorities they establish. Control over religious beliefs or practices being no part of the purpose for which human beings can be conceived to construct government, they would not empower the civil authorities to control religion. "So much of liberty and no more is departed from, as is necessary to secure . . . the ends for which men enter into a state of government." Williams correctly follows Locke in noting that the so-called executive power of the law of nature must be wholly given up, and "the power that every one has in a state of nature *to do whatever he judgeth fit*, for the preservation of his power and property . . . he gives up to be regulated by laws made by the society, so far forth as the preservation of himself (his person and property) and the rest of that society shall require." In sum, he concludes, "*no more natural liberty or power is given up than is necessary to the preservation of person and property.*"[72]

The rights of conscience are among those that human beings have no reason to surrender when they form government. "The members of a civil state *do retain their natural liberty or right of judging for themselves in matters of religion.*" The surrender of this right cannot be justified by the supposed need "to have unity of faith and uniformity of practice in religion" in order to have "peace and good order in the state." The latter is certainly a (or the) valid end of the entire process of governmental authorization, but enforced unity of religion is not a means to its achievement. Uniformity in religion cannot "be effected . . . by any such legal establishment of religion." Human beings differ too much "with respect to their understandings, tempers and advantages . . . for improvement in knowledge" for there to be genuine "uniformity of opinion and practice of religion." The best that can occur is "artificial conformity," and this can be won only at potentially great cost in oppression.[73]

Rational actors in the state of nature will notice the cost of this artificial, imposed conformity, and will recognize further that "such unity, or uniformity in religion is not necessary to the peace of a civil state." Rational actors will accept as "natural and un-avoidable" differences in matters of religion and will conclude from this fact that "the civil authority's protecting all in their just rights, and particularly this inestimable and unalienable one, *the right of private judgment* in matters of religion" is the best way to civil peace.[74] The uniform platform of rights can supply a suffi-cient basis for civil unity and peace, and the mutual acceptance and toleration of difference can further, not hinder, that peace. Indeed, the attempt to impose uniformity threatens civil peace far more than it ever contributes to its achievement. "Civil punish-ments have no tendency to convince the conscience, but only to inflame the passions against the advisers and inflicters of them."[75]

Rational actors in the state of nature not only would be entirely unwilling to authorize civil control over religion, they would be morally incapable of doing so even if they did want to. The "natural liberty or right of judging" for oneself "in matters of reli-gion . . . is an original right of the humane nature, and so far from being given up by the individuals of a community that it cannot be given up by them." It is, he says, "an unalienable right." To defend that point he makes a far-reaching argument, reminiscent both of Locke's most important statements on rights and Jeffer-son's reasoning on human nature.

> Man by his constitution as he is a reasonable being capable of the knowledge of his Maker, is a moral and accountable being:

and therefore, as everyone is accountable for himself, he must reason, judge and determine for himself. . . . No action is a religious action without understanding and choice in the agent. Whence it follows, the rights of conscience are sacred and equal in all, and strictly speaking, unalienable. This *right of judging everyone for himself in matters of religion* results from the nature of man, and is so inseparably connected therewith, that a man can no more part with it than he can with his power of thinking. . . . A man . . . cannot transfer the rights of conscience, unless he could destroy his rational and moral powers.[76]

In short compass we thus have the main outlines of the first prong, the Lockean prong, of Williams's argument. It is clear in his presentation that this argument is meant to be purely rationalist in character and perfectly universalist in scope. That is, it makes no appeal to specifically Christian or Protestant doctrines, nor is it limited in application to Christians or Protestants. The "unalienable rights of conscience" belong to all human beings, of whatever religious profession.

Williams's second prong supplements the first with an argument of a quite different character; it is based on the principles of Protestant Christianity; it appeals to the Bible, the authoritative text of Protestant Christianity, and it establishes religious freedom in the first instance for Protestants, although by extension for others as well. It proceeds in the opposite direction from the first argument, establishing not the limits of the civil authority, but the necessity that the true Christian religion be entirely free from civil control. Williams captures the complexity of his own position exceedingly well when he objects that a "religious establishment" at all "binding to the subjects," or carrying "any penalties whatsoever" is "oppressive of Christianity" and "breaks in upon the sacred right of conscience, and the common rights and priviledges of all good subjects."[77]

That he has two prongs, and that these are the two prongs, represents another respect in which Williams parallels Locke's discussion in the *Letter Concerning Toleration*. In that text Locke had first explicated the "jurisdiction of the civil magistrate," showing that it does not extend to religious matters, and then "what a church is," showing both its immunities from civil authorities and the limits of its powers.[78] Despite this parallel, Williams's development has a rather different tone and spirit about it, deriving from the much heavier and more explicit reliance on particular themes of Protestant theology for the development of the second prong of the argument. He begins his examination of religion by affirming a traditional Reformation principle, harking back at least to Luther: "the sacred scriptures are the alone rule of faith and practice to every individual christian."[79] This contrasts strongly with the sway of rational principles in the political sphere.[80]

Williams draws this Protestant principle in an extremely individualistic and libertarian direction.

> Now inasmuch as the scriptures are the only rule of faith and practice to a Christian; hence every one has an unalienable right to read, enquire into, and impartially judge of the sense and meaning of it for himself. For if he is to be governed and determined therein by the opinions and determinations of any others, the scriptures cease to be a rule to him, and those opinions or determinations of others are substituted in the room thereof.[81]

From this follows for Williams a strongly separationist conclusion: "the civil authority hath no power to make or ordain articles of faith, creeds, forms of worship or church government." Nor do "the civil authorities have [any] authority to determine for Christians the *form of church government*, and that for the reasons before given, *viz.* Because this would be going beside the end of civil government, and because this is already done by Christ." By the same token, churches exercise no authority approaching the coercive powers characteristic of the civil rulers. "As to ecclesiastical rulers, Christ has precisely bounded their authority. . . . Christ's officers have nothing to do but to teach Christ's laws." Church structure, articles of faith, and forms of worship thus remain voluntarist and pluralistic. There is no power in civil or ecclesiastical authorities to definitively "determine this or the other ceremony or mode of attending them." Each "worshipping assembly" is to decide for itself how it interprets Christ's word with respect to worship.[82]

Williams, far more than the Puritans, and even more than Locke, moves toward a reinstatement of Luther's doctrine of the Two Kingdoms, separate, autonomous, and moved by entirely different principles of action. Williams calls attention to this side of his thought when he reminds that "Christ is the head of his church, a king in his owne kingdom." More than most other American Puritan writers, Williams makes explicit reference to Luther as well.[83]

As much as Williams reminds of Locke, Luther, and his Puritan forebears, his achievement can only be appreciated by comparing his position more systematically with each of the other three. This reveals, I think, the nature of the transformation that occurred in American Puritan thought when it assimilated or was assimilated by Lockean thought. The comparison with Locke can be quickly restated: Williams makes a clearer and stronger appeal to specifically Protestant principles to articulate the character of the religious sphere. Locke's *Toleration* is not entirely lacking such appeals, but the whole has a more secular and universalistic tone. Locke does not endorse Williams's claim that the only rule in faith and religious practice is scripture; in his *Reasonableness of Christianity*, he argues, in effect, that reason is as good (or perhaps a better) "rule" whereby to understand the principles of Christianity. He does say that scripture, properly understood, will harmonize with the teaching of reason, but given the ambiguities of scripture, reason turns out to be at least as authoritative as scripture.

Williams thus seems even closer to Luther than to Locke. That is not quite correct, however, for he makes three important changes in the Lutheran doctrine of the Two Kingdoms. To repeat a point we have already noticed: Williams derives the principles of the secular or political sphere from reason (as delivered by that oracle, "the great Mr. Lock"); Luther derives the principles for the understanding and governance of the secular sphere, the Kingdom of the World, from scripture. Luther and Williams (and Locke) agree in the principle of the separateness of the spheres, but Luther derives the principles for both spheres from the Bible. Thus his political thought is a form of political theology, whereas Williams's is a form of political philosophy.

Luther's depends decisively on texts like Romans 13, from which he derives a conscientious duty of nearly absolute obedience. Williams subordinates Romans 13 and other biblical texts on politics to the Lockean rationalist account. Williams, no more than Locke, relies on Romans (or any biblical text) to develop the main outlines of the civil sphere. When he turns to the biblical texts, it is long after he has established his main points.

> Romans 13.1 No doubt relates to civil powers: A text often wrecked and tortured by such wits as were disposed to serve the designs of arbitrary power, by erecting a civil tyranny over a free people and as often wrested out of their hands by the force of truth.[84]

Williams will oppose "truth" to this "wrecked and tortured" interpretation, but it is Luther himself who stands at the head of those "wreckers and torturers."

Williams's revisionist reading of Romans is very much along the same lines Mayhew will later make so famous in America, and which Locke had already presented in his *Commentary on Paul.*

> Let me distinguish between two things, which as they really are different, must be kept so in our minds, if we would understand the Apostle; *viz.* between the powers which are, and the powers which are not. . . . Now the higher powers in the text are the powers which are.

The text enjoins submission to the "higher powers," but this applies only to those "which are," i.e., truly are.

> On the other hand—the powers that are not, are not the powers that be; and so not the powers in the text, not the powers that are of God, not his ordinance, and so no subjection to them is required in this text.[85]

But which powers "are" and which "are not"? To which is subjection due and to which not? "The truth of the case is plainly this; that this text shows obedience is due to civil rulers in those cases wherein they have power to command, and does not call for it any farther." But how to determine "wherein they have power to command"? Williams's answer is to refer to his earlier argument:

"we have seen before that civil authority relates to the civil interests of a people (their persons and properties), and is bounded by the same."[86] Thus, as he argued earlier, civil authority never extends to matters of religion. Romans 13 does not call for unlimited subjection to rulers, only for subjection to them within their proper sphere, precisely the argument Mayhew, West, and a whole string of clergy in the revolutionary era will make.

Williams has not only turned the teaching of Romans 13 almost about-face from where Luther had it, he has used it to support his practice of deriving the principles of politics from rational (Lockean) argumentation rather than from scripture. This move by Williams proves to be decisive for the Lockeanization of Protestant political thought, for it renders the political sphere, the Kingdom of the World, not merely institutionally autonomous, but theoretically autonomous as well, open to rational adumbration in its own terms, subject only to the loosest supervision from scripturally and theologically grounded argument.

Williams departs from Luther not only in finding the principles of the secular sphere in wholly secular reasoning, but also in his description of the ruling principles governing the Kingdom of Christ. He endorses Luther's notion of *sola scriptura*, but he notably holds back from accepting Luther's even more central claim—*sola fide*—salvation by faith alone. Luther had derived the principles to govern the religious sphere from this very principle; and in Luther, this emphasis on faith alone had two rather important results for the fate of the separateness of the Two Kingdoms. On the one hand, Luther's Kingdom of God was much more monistic than Williams's—for Luther there is but one true Christianity. Each believer must have his or her own faith, but what each believer must do is have faith. And Luther knows perfectly well what faith that is. Because the one saving faith is all that is necessary, many other matters become more or less indifferent from the point of view of salvation and absolute religious duty—the whole sphere of works, to say nothing of matters of ecclesiology and ceremony. The complete immunity and freedom required in the Kingdom of God does not, it turns out, require complete immunity of the entire institutional sphere of religion from the civil authorities. Luther's doctrine of the separateness of the Two Kingdoms thus culminates, paradoxically, in an established church, largely under the civil authorities.

Williams's version of the doctrine of the Two Kingdoms resists this breakdown of the separateness and autonomy of the two spheres. Each Christian must judge for him or herself what scripture requires of a Christian, but Williams leaves it perfectly open what that may be, either as to belief or practice. Nothing can be rightly mandated, except the freedom for each to judge for him or herself and to act on the basis of that judgment. Nobody can decree what must be believed, and nobody can decree that all matters like church organization or ceremonial practices are essentially indifferent. The institutions and practices of Christianity must have complete autonomy from all authority, civil or ecclesiastical.

Although Williams defends his doctrine of ecclesiastical autonomy in language that reminds more of Luther than of Locke, his conclusions are far more parallel to Locke's. His third modification of Luther, which stands somewhere behind his second modification, also seems to derive mainly from Locke. Williams affirms confidently that "the rule" for religion must be scripture, but that each Christian must be free to determine what that rule requires. Williams is far less confident than Luther that the one true scriptural teaching can be identified with any certainty. "Since God has formed the understandings of men so different, with respect to clearness, strength, and compass, and placed them in such very different circumstances; a difference of sentiments in some things in religion, seems natural and unavoidable." Nobody has a sufficiently privileged position to justify imposing a uniformity to overcome this diversity, especially since the one perfectly clear principle is that each person is required to take scripture as a rule for him or herself. Locke had also emphasized this inevitable disagreement and the toleration for the opinions of others that ought to follow.[87] Since disagreement about religion is both inevitable and highly charged when it occurs, the only solution for both Williams and Locke is to leave religious opinion and practice per se entirely in the sphere of the private and voluntary and to base public coerced life on rational principles presumably more open to agreement, or at least less explosive.

Williams's differences from his orthodox Puritan ancestors are at least as significant as his differences from Luther. The Calvinists accepted the doctrine of the Two Kingdoms in principle, but in practice they were even more emphatic in overcoming the institutional separateness of the two spheres. As we have seen, the original American Puritans blurred the lines between secular and sacred spheres to such a degree that their regime constantly faced the threat of falling into theocracy; the secular sphere was with little ado made subordinate to the sacred both with regard to ends and means. Rather than the purely autonomous missions Luther and Williams identified for the authorities in the Kingdom of the World, the Puritans saw the purpose of this world in terms of its service to the needs and goods of the next world.[88]

A particularly helpful source for understanding the way in which the Puritans moved toward bridging the chasm between the Two Kingdoms is the major work of Protestant theology called *The Decades*, published by Henry Bullinger of Zurich in the 1570s. Bullinger was a Calvinist who had much contact with the Marian exiles who became the inspiration of the English Puritan movement in the seventeenth century. There is, thus, a known chain of transmission from Bullinger to the American Puritans.

Bullinger considers the regime that Luther appears to, and Williams actually does, opt for: "many are of opinion, that the care and ordering of religion doth belong to bishops [or churches] alone, and that kings, princes, and senators ought not to meddle therewith." He quite decisively rejects this separationist position, however: "the care of religion doth especially belong to the magistrate; and that it is not in his power only, but his office and duty also, to dispose and advance religion." This involves, at the least, what Williams would consider an establishment of religion. The secular ruler must "provide to have the word of God preached to his people, and cause them to be taught the true worship of God, by that means making himself, as it were, the minister of true religion." More than that, the ruler is not to respect liberty of religion, either. "The magistrate [is] to make trial of doctrines, and to kill those that do stubbornly teach against the scriptures, and draw the people from the true God," a principle that justified Calvin, for example, in executing Michael Servetus for heresy in Geneva.[89]

For Bullinger, the magistrate's duties with regard to religion ultimately root in the scripturally imposed prohibition of idolatry and the consequent "command to advance true religion." As he concludes in the most general terms, "the care of religion belongeth to the magistrate."[90] Bullinger has in turn merely echoed the views of Calvin, who asserts unambiguously that the duty of magistrates "extends to both Tables of the Law," that is, to religious as well as moral duties. "No government," Calvin insists, "can be happily established unless piety is the first concern; . . . those laws are preposterous which neglect God's right and provide only for men." Calvin agrees with Bullinger that "those who would neglect the concern for God and would give attention only to rendering justice among men" are guilty of great "folly."[91]

If anything, the American Puritans take the religious duties of the civil rulers even more seriously than Calvin and Bullinger, but clearly they conceive the issue along the same lines as the two Swiss reformers. The Cambridge Platform of 1648, a document epitomizing first-generation American Puritan views, not only presented the doctrines but in many cases spoke the very language of Calvin and Bullinger. "It is the duty of the Magistrate," pronounced the sixth article of the Platform, "to take care of matters of religion and to impose his civil authority for the observing of the duties commanded in the first, as well as for observing of the duties commanded in the second table." The Puritans retain the form of the distinction between the inner and the outer, but the magistrate's authority extends to religious matters the moment they have an external manifestation. "The objects of the powr of the Magistrate, are not things merely inward, and so not subject to his cognizance and view, as in unbeliefe, hardness of heart, erroneous opinions not vented; but only such things as are acted by the outward man." The magistrate's brief includes a broad array of evils afflicting the religious sphere. "Idolatry, Blasphemy, Heresy, venting corrupt and pernicious opinions, that destroy the foundation, open contempt of the word preached, prophanation of the Lords day, disturbing the peaceable administration and exercise of the worship and holy things of God, and the like, are to be restrayned, and punished by civil authority." In sum, "the Magistrate is to put forth his coercive power, as the matter shall require."[92]

Elisha Williams, partly following Locke and partly returning to themes present from the outset in reformed Christianity, makes an extremely strong case for the incorrectness of the Calvinist-Puritan version of the relation between the two spheres, and along with that for the insertion of Locke as the most adequate account of the principles governing the secular sphere. That is, Williams makes a case for the convergence of Locke and a certain version of Protestantism; or, to use the language of John Rawls, he shows how Lockean political philosophy can be a "module" within a version of Luther's doctrine of the Two Kingdoms, or, perhaps more accurately, how Luther can be a module within the Lockean argument.[93] Williams especially reminds of Luther in his dissociation from the Puritan affirmation of the sacred as the end of the secular. Yet even here, it must be reiterated, his thinking is much more Lockean than Lutheran: neither Romans 13 nor the Lutheran doctrine of works of love shapes the political sphere.

Williams helps to engineer a convergence between Locke and Protestantism; Lockean principles are no mere continuation of Protestant principles, either in their Lutheran or their Calvinist variant. The historical reasons that may have favored Williams in his enterprise will require our attention in a moment, but Williams does bring out a deep-lying contribution that Protestantism made to the ultimate emergence of liberal modernity of the Lockean sort. In the context of discussing the biblical text (Hebrews 13:17) regarding the duty of officials to "watch for the souls" of their subjects, Williams insists that this must relate to ecclesiastical officers, and not civil officers, for "care of the soul" is not within the ambit of the latter. It is not part of the authority of secular rulers because within Protestantism the true "good of the soul" is understood entirely in terms of the soul's ultimate fate in the eyes of God. The "good of the soul" is salvation, and salvation cannot be effected by civil authorities. Some versions of Protestantism may assign religious duties to magistrates, but no version of Protestantism claims that the magistrate can serve "the good of the soul." Protestantism has effected a more or less complete disassociation of the "good of the soul" from political life. This is, of course, a major shift from the perspective of ancient political philosophy, or of the Christian Aristotelianism, which dominated Christendom on the eve of the Reformation. Although the

Protestant doctrines remain quite different, they may be said to prepare the way for the liberal focus on rights as the central category of politics; a rights emphasis effects the same dissociation of the fundamental norms governing political life from the good of the soul. Protestantism was perhaps a necessary prerequisite for the emergence of liberal modernity, even though the two do not stand to each other as the continuity thesis says.

By any measure, the success of Lockean doctrine in conquering Puritan political theology was quite remarkable and suggests the presence of historical conditions that made eighteenth-century Americans in New England ripe for assimilating Locke. While a good deal more research than has yet been done is required to speak with anything approaching certainty on such a complex and elusive matter, several trends in the long-term sweep of developments within American Puritanism are certainly suggestive. The Puritan project began in a combination of confidence and hope—confidence that the one true ecclesiastical-political order was readily visible in the holy documents of the Christian revelation if only those documents were read in the right spirit and without the wrong presuppositions or by-interests; hope that churches and states founded on these principles, inhabited by godly men and women, could accomplish unheard of things, could build a "city upon a hill."

The confidence was soon challenged by the rapid emergence within the community of disagreements over the presumably plainest of matters, as well as over sophisticated complexities of theology and the principles of social, political, and ecclesiastical ordering. Roger Williams did not accept the community's way of constituting churches, or its conception of the relation between political power and religious life. Anne Hutchinson and her many supporters questioned the entire delicate adjustment the Calvinist community had achieved among its various theological and moral commitments, frighteningly holding open to momentary view the possibility that the Puritan ordering was internally incoherent, the worldly and heavenly spheres hopelessly out of harmony with one another. They and other dissenters and heretics were banished, expelled, or denied admission. Others voluntarily departed to found new settlements revolving around other readings of the "plain meaning" of these plain doctrines, Connecticut and New Haven joining Massachusetts Bay and Rhode Island as independent centers of settlement.

So long as the hope remained strong, these challenges to confidence did not, apparently, lead to widespread loss of confidence. Hope in the form of enthusiasm led to redoubled assertion of the orthodox way: the Cambridge Platform of 1648, a product of the closing moments of the founding generation of New England, confirmed in strong and uncompromising terms all the important features of the ordering and norms worked out by the first generation. Part of that confirmation was a reaffirmation of the founding confidence: the magistrate's duties to foster the true religion extend to "such acts, as are commanded and forbidden in the word; yea, such as the word doth clearly determine, though not always clearly the judgement of the Magistrate or others, yet clearly in it selfe."[94] Those acts "clearly determined" extend, it will be recalled, to the full gamut of issues the civil authorities are to apply coercion to deal with: idolatry, heresy, blasphemy, corrupt and pernicious opinion, and so on. Yet, perhaps most remarkable about this provision of the Platform is the oddly tense notion that although neither the magistrates nor others may recognize these matters as the plain meaning of "the word," they are "yet clearly in it selfe." This represents, on the one hand, continuing institutional ascendancy of the clergy—the operational meaning of "clearly in it selfe" must be "found to be so by the experts"; it represents, on the other hand, the community's efforts to hold on to its confidence in the wake of the confidence-challenging events of the decade and a half before. Even though not everyone sees the clarity of what is "clear in it selfe," it is clear nonetheless. So long as the hope remained strong, the confidence could withstand challenge.

Over time, however, enthusiasm, and with it, hope for extraordinary things waned. The most universal and cosmic forces combined to undermine Puritan hope and Puritan enthusiasm. Perry Miller has emphasized the irony of the Puritan experience in space: these settlers came to America as an offshoot of international Calvinism; they saw themselves as a model for the Christian church and state at home; they were not initially a provincial backwater but a vanguard. With the coming of the Civil War and the triumph of Puritan forces in England, their hopes seemed to be nearing fulfillment: the way was open or opening to the installation of the models of church and state they had pioneered in England itself. Yet developments at home went in quite another direction: Cromwell instituted a regime of toleration and backed away from the hopes for a Calvinist commonwealth that inspired the Americans.[95] The American Puritans were convinced their English peers had taken a wrong turn, but it had to become apparent to them that the fracturing of their own order, which they had resolved through sending dissidents out into the wilderness, was a yet more severe problem in England, where the variety of sects and alternatives was much greater, and where the wilderness solution was not so readily available. The godly commonwealth proved unattainable in England, and since the hopes of the Americans were never merely for themselves as an isolated people, the possibilities they had been pursuing appeared to recede from grasp just when they seemed closest to realization. The complete and utter failure of the Puritan Commonwealth achieved official and public recognition in the restoration of the old order in England in 1660, the restoration of the Stuart monarchy, and the Church of England as it had been, complete with bishops. With the Restoration, the American Puritans were more isolated than before—if not physically, then in terms of aspiration. No set of hopes or enthusiasm could withstand the disappointments the parallel history of England inflicted in those years.

Simultaneously, time buffeted the New Englanders as well. Many historians, Perry Miller and Edmund Morgan in particular, have detailed the generational changing of the guard in New England. The original settlers were certainly classic cases of an "intentional community," men and women with a mission, with a belief in, a hope for, an enthusiasm about, and a commitment to a task for which they would and did suffer nearly any hardship, tolerate nearly any deprivation. That commitment made their settlements successful beyond any European settlements yet planted in the New World. The hopes and commitments of the first generation were born of the enthusiasms of the early seventeenth century in Europe: the international Calvinist movement, the unleashing of reform zeal in England in those years, the strength added by opposition, conflict, the arousal of spirited resistance.

The younger generation lacked these formative experiences and, the evidence shows, cooled in their enthusiasm. A striking instance is the so-called "Half-Way Covenant" of 1662, a facing up by the community to the fact that the children of the original settlers were not demonstrating the same intense religious enthusiasm, the same testimonials of personal faith and conversion that had been the basis at first for church membership. Church membership, and along with that, eligibility for political privileges, became a far more external matter; descendants of members became eligible for membership in a compromised or lesser, yet real, way.[96] With the waning of enthusiasm went the waning of the extraordinary hopes of the Winthrops and Cottons of the first generation. With the waning of hope went the resistance to challenges to confidence. The Puritan mission was no longer so clear cut, and the biblical warrant no longer so visible for all—or perhaps any—to see.

In the later years of the seventeenth century Puritan thinkers, if they can still be rightly called such, turned increasingly toward natural religion as a supplement, if not a replacement, for the older scriptural theology. With that turn, came a turn away from some of the more stringent doctrines of the old Puritanism—predestination, the strict line between faith and works, the stringency of politically enforced discipline.[97] According to Newlin and to Miller, it was apparently in this context that Locke first began to make inroads on "the New England Mind," as the philosopher who knew the map of the human mind and outlined both the limitations and possibilities of human knowledge, and as the purveyor of a "rational Christianity" related to the Bible, yet deploying reason all along the way to guide the interpretation of that ambiguous book.[98] That Locke had become the most celebrated philosopher in Europe surely did not hurt; it also did not hurt that Locke had been allied with the Whigs and had defended the Glorious Revolution against the Stuarts, traditional enemies to the Puritans in England, and new enemies now because of James II's efforts to reorganize and thus reduce the autonomy of the New England colonies.[99]

It would be misleading to draw the history of New England as a one-directional ebbing of religious enthusiasm. That was not so, as the very occasion for Elisha Williams's treatise serves to remind. In the 1740s, the largest of a series of religious revivals, the Great Awakening, occurred. New England was swept with a renewed enthusiasm for "New Light" preaching, an enthusiasm seen as a threat and, perhaps, an embarrassment by main-line churchmen, who attempted to control the new preaching through the law Williams was protesting. The revivalism of the 1740s, like latter-day revivalism in general, was not the community-oriented, even political thing the old Puritanism was, however. It was personal, it was pietistic, and it concerned the individual and his or her faith and relationship to God. The revived religious enthusiasm of the eighteenth century, in other words, was concerned exclusively with Luther's Kingdom of God. It did not renew Puritan social and political commitment to remake the public sphere in the image of Calvinism.

Williams's version of Christian Lockeanism was an ideal response to this situation. The secular sphere was affirmed to have its own autonomous principles, rooted in reason, and consistent with the Kingdom of Christ largely through keeping a strict line of separation from it. Room had been made for each to be a module in the other. Americans were able to bring their still lively religious sensibilities to the sphere of politics, but in the service of a substantive politics very different from the traditional political teachings of Christianity. The natural rights philosophy, while not itself a Christian philosophy, or even particularly descended from Christian positions, was able to win the support of American Christians and Christianity. Thus began that potent alliance Tocqueville noticed and all American politics has attested to for two centuries in what Robert Bellah and others have spoken of as the American civil religion. The result has been remarkable: a society in which religion has been supportive of an essentially secular political orientation and in which private and public morality both have derived salutary aid from deep-flowing religious impulses. Religion has been supportive of the secular sphere, and the secular sphere respectful and mildly supportive of the sacred, all within a context of a real separation of church and state and a very wide protection for freedom of religion.

Although the history of political religion in America is more complex than can reasonably be surveyed here, nevertheless Tocqueville's general view seems largely correct—America has worked best when the convergence between liberal modern (Lockean) politics and religion has held most tensionlessly. American politics seems beset by its gravest moments of self-doubt and sense of crisis when the two fall into disharmony and tension, as is the case in the late twentieth century. However, this is surely not the first time such tensions have existed, and American culture has in the past shown the capacity to reforge the ties between religion and liberal politics, and such may be possible once again.

The alliance between religion and liberal philosophy in America was not at all an unwelcome development to the main sponsors of the modern liberal orientation. Both Locke and Jefferson, to take two particularly important examples, insisted that modernist liberal politics required the support of religion. As Locke put it, since "the greatest part cannot *know*, . . . they must believe." They cannot know the full ground of morality and rights. Most human beings lack the time and, perhaps, the ability to follow demonstrations such as might supply the philosophic ground for rights. "You may as soon hope to have all the day-labourers and tradesmen, the spinsters and dairy maids, perfect mathematicians, as to have them perfect in ethics this way." The only effective form of popular ethics is an authoritative, i.e., religious ethics.[100] Jefferson made the point in his suggestive treatment of the issue of self-evidence in the Declaration of Independence, and even more directly in his *Notes on Virginia:* "And can the liberties of a nation be thought secure when we have removed their only firm basis, a conviction in the minds of the people that these liberties are the gift of God? That they are not to be violated but with his wrath?"[101]

Chapter Seven

THE NATURAL RIGHTS
REPUBLIC

Abraham Lincoln directs us to 1776 and the Declaration of Independence as the origin of the American political tradition, but some of our most influential students of the tradition disagree. They not only deny that the Declaration is the origin; they do not find it to be any significant part of the tradition at all. Instead of natural rights liberalism, they see classical republicanism or civic humanism as the defining feature of America, at least during the founding era.

The Declaration of Independence and the natural rights philosophy more generally are almost literally absent from the accounts of American political origins in the so-called republican synthesis. Bernard Bailyn, usually considered to be the originator of the synthesis, began the trend when, in a survey of *The Ideological Origins of the American Revolution*, he barely mentioned the Declaration. Indeed, his only discussion of it centered on the rather peripheral issue of the notion of conspiracy it contained.[1] Bailyn, however, did not entirely slight the natural rights philosophy. He emphasized, for example, that as the constitutional arguments between Britain and the colonists heated up, the Americans came to the conclusion that "the entire legitimacy of positive law and legal rights must be understood to rest on the degree to which they conformed to the abstract universals of natural rights."[2] Bailyn admitted the role of Locke, of Enlightenment theory, and of natural rights philosophy in the mix of ideas animating the Americans at the time of the Revolution. He differed from earlier students of the era like Carl Becker or Clinton Rossiter merely in downplaying these elements somewhat and elevating instead another stream of thought, identified by him as a "tradition of opposition thought." This tradition had its origin in the Commonwealth period following the English Civil War and was carried forward into the eighteenth century mostly by the Whig opposition, that is, by Whigs who remained in opposition to the Whigs who held power after the Glorious Revolution. Although there were a great many thinkers identified by Bailyn as part of this tradition, the leading lights were John Trenchard and Thomas Gordon, writing as "Cato" in the 1720s. These opposition thinkers, according to Bailyn, "dominated the colonists' miscellaneous learning and shaped it into a coherent whole."[3] Bailyn concedes that these opposition writers "overlapped" in their commitments with Enlightenment thinkers like Locke, and that the natural rights/social contract philosophy did indeed play a part in their thinking about politics.[4] Nonetheless, the dominant opposition tradition had a content and temper quite different from Enlightenment thought. The one produced "glittering generalities" and proceeded on a sophisticated intellectual and emotional level; the other contained a quite specific political analysis and prescription for action, and was crude, simplistic, vulgar, and emotionally charged. Those elements of opposition writings that were most different from the writings of philosophers like Locke contributed the power that made the whole attractive to a mass public and made it suitable to serve as an ideology for a mass movement.[5] The substantive core of the opposition tradition, according to Bailyn, was an interrelated set of concepts revolving around the dangers of power. Bailyn would see Lord Acton's famous dictum—"power tends to corrupt, absolute power tends to corrupt absolutely"—to be typical of his group of writers. Where Locke and the liberal philosophers put natural rights, the opposition tradition put power, but the emphasis on power gave the whole theory a rather negative cast. It was easier to say what they were against and what they feared than what they favored. Like Cecilia Kenyon's Anti-federalists, Bailyn's opposition tradition was composed of "men of little faith."[6]

Bailyn's version of the republicanism thesis left Locke, natural rights, and so forth on stage but in the wings; surely he did not understand the Revolution as the unfolding of a Lockean narrative, delivered in a series of dramatic monologues culminating in a triumphant rendition by the entire company of the *Second Treatise*. It was not until subsequent elements of the "republican synthesis" were put in place that the natural rights position was ushered more or less completely out of the theater. The most decisive event, probably, was the redescription of the opposition tradition by J. G. A. Pocock. Far more than Bailyn, he was interested in this tradition itself, and only secondarily in its impact on the Americans; accordingly, he inquired far more strenuously into its character and pedigree. His reconstruction of the tradition is extraordinarily complex and most impressive in its sweep and scope, but for present purposes it may be summarized simply as follows: the opposition tradition Bailyn identified was an Anglicized version of a much older republican tradition, originating with the Greeks, especially Aristotle, and revived by the Italian Renaissance humanists, especially Machiavelli. Thus, Pocock locates the American founding within a very old tradition: it was no *novus ordo seclorum*. On the contrary, Pocock decrees, "The American Revolution, [was] less the first act of revolutionary enlightenment than . . . the last great act of the Renaissance." America was founded in a "dread of modernity."[7]

Pocock, like Bailyn, also notes the negative cast to the political thought of his civic humanists; they feared change, they looked to the past for their norms, and as a result they produced an orientation toward political power that Pocock pronounced "barren."[8] He also discerns a more positive content, however, a content tracing back ultimately to the original Aristotelian impulse of the tradition. As one scholar has summarized Pocock's position, "Part Aristotle, part Cicero, part Machiavelli, civic humanism conceives of man as a political being whose realization of self occurs only through participation in public life, through active citizenship in a republic."[9] Aristotle expressed the core of civic humanism thus understood when he pronounced human beings to be, by nature, political animals. The mature theory of civic humanism as Pocock sketches it thus concerns the meaningfulness of and conditions for political participation. Its preference for republican regimes derives from their embodiment of "participatory ideals"; the constitutional and other developments that eighteenth-century forms of civic humanism opposed were those elements of modernity seen to be threatening to the active sort of citizenship favored by the humanists. The humanists as described by Pocock, then, are not at bottom as sympathetic to Lord Acton's dictum as Bailyn's opposition Whigs: they do not oppose politics and political power per se—quite the contrary—but they do oppose concentration and uses of power that threaten the independence of citizens whose liberty for participation stands as their highest human potentiality.

Gordon Wood, the third member of the triumvirate of writers who constructed the edifice of the "republican synthesis," applied the republicanism idea more specifically to the Americans. He modified Bailyn's view of the tradition to which the American founders belonged more along the lines of Pocock's analysis. He finds the source of the tradition where Pocock had, in antiquity; and thus Wood calls the theory he sketched "classical republicanism." Also like Pocock, he emphasizes the positive republican aspect of this tradition: "republicanism was the basic premise of American thinking—the central presupposition behind all other ideas."[10] The emphasis in Wood's presentation differs slightly from that in Pocock's, however. Wood understands the classical dimension of his republicanism as an expression of the naturalness or organic character of the political community. As Aristotle said, the *polis* is by nature and is prior to the individual, as the whole human individual is prior to a part like a hand. Wood's republicanism demanded not Pocock's participative ideal of citizenship or Bailyn's suspicion of all power, but rather the recognition of a supervening common or public good, the good of the whole, superior to and in principle demanding the submergence of individual private goods. Virtue is the habitual pursuit of the public over the private good, liberty the corporate involvement of the people in ruling, and not (as it was for Bailyn) the individual security of natural rights.[11] For Wood, the republican ideal is one more of duty than of self-fulfillment. Wood's republicans seem to share some important commitments with Christians, as well as with classical republican heroes like Brutus or Cato.

Where Bailyn made a place for Lockean liberalism in his version of the "synthesis," Pocock and Wood develop the republican ideal as a full-scale alternative to the natural rights/social contract liberalism of Locke. As Isaac Kramnick explains, Pocock is quite explicit about his displacement of Lockean liberalism:

> Pocock has seen the history of political thought "dominated by a fiction of Locke," whose importance "has been wildly distorted." . . . To understand the debates of eighteenth century politics does "not necessitate reference to Locke at all." Pocock has applied this revisionist verdict about Locke to an alternative reading of America and its founding. . . . The proper interpretation "stresses Machiavelli at the expense of Locke."[12]

The distance of the republican conception from the theory of the Declaration should be apparent from even this brief sketch. According to the republicanism thesis, human beings are intensely political (Pocock) and/or communal (Wood); according to the Declaration, human beings are not originally or naturally political—the origin is a state of nature understood as an apolitical condition. Although polity is essential, it is not natural; it is made by human beings. Politics, according to the Declaration is for the sake of natural rights, and natural rights are emphatically prepolitical. The Declaration nowhere intimates that in political participation lies human fulfillment; in place of human fulfillment is the right to the pursuit of happiness. Nor does the Declaration endorse the notion that political life requires as duty or virtue the submersion of one's private and particular interests in the common good. The common good, on the contrary, is precisely the coordinated satisfaction of those fundamental individual interests called rights, and the conditions necessary for the broad security of these rights. Within the Declaration's conception of politics, tension between the interests of the individual and the common good are certainly possible, but they are not necessary, inevitable, and defining, as in the "republican synthesis."[13]

Within the natural rights philosophy politics and political participation are instrumental; accordingly the Declaration shows a remarkable openness on form of government—whatever form seems most conducive to rights-securing is fine. The Declaration reveals no inherent antipathy to monarchy. The republicanism thesis is defined by a commitment to a particular form, however, which is either for the sake of expressing the moral demand to seek the common good over one's particular good (Wood) or for the sake of humanly fulfilling participation in republican rule (Pocock).

The understanding of property likewise differs almost entirely between the two political theories. For Pocock's republicans, property is for the sake of gentlemanly or citizenly independence, a precondition for the citizen's participation and public-spiritedness. Property is, above all, a political, not an economic, phenomenon. Within natural rights liberalism, property is a natural right and, therefore, not particularly tied to its political function. The emphasis is not on static "estate," which can equip one for citizenship, but on dynamic wealth production. Various limitations on the terms and nature of ownership are perfectly compatible with property understood in Pocock's republican way; entail and primogeniture, for example, two practices that keep property concentrated and in the same family line, are suitable to a system aiming to support an independent political class. Such practices are much less compatible with liberal republicanism, however, for, among other things, they deny the inherent character of the property right—the near sovereignty one has over one's property—and they interfere with the dynamics of wealth production.

Few scholarly theories have been subjected to so many sustained bombardments as the "republican synthesis." Nearly every petal in its bouquet has been picked or at least picked over. The picture of Greek and Roman republicanism used by the synthesizers has been challenged;[14] the interpretation of Machiavelli, who supposedly carries forward while partially transforming the Aristotelian political philosophy, has been rejected;[15] the accuracy of the portrayal of James Harrington, who allegedly "anglicized" the Aristotelian-Machiavellian tradition, has been impugned;[16] the vision of "neo-Harringtonianism," which supposedly transformed Harrington in ways that put the tradition into its newfound form as the Whig opposition, has been said to be blurred, at best;[17] the validity of the application to the Americans has been denied.[18] Moreover, some of the most important early participants in the creation of the "republican synthesis" have reformulated their own positions in a way that is friendlier to the natural rights liberalism that the synthesis in its classical form is thought to have turned against. For example, Lance Banning, the author of the importantly republican *The Jeffersonian Persuasion* in the early 1970s, describes his more current writing as an effort "to incorporate some schooling [he has] gotten from the critics of the republican interpretation." The criticism has led Banning to conclude that Pocock and Wood "suggest . . . that early Revolutionary thought was more completely classical or more decidedly pre-modern than was actually the case." Indeed, he now believes, "early revolutionary thinking was by no means truly classical . . . in its image of the good republic."[19]

The Declaration of Independence and related statements by the Americans during the founding era have proved a major stumbling block for the proponents of the republican synthesis. All sides seem to admit what we have just argued, that the theory of the Declaration and the themes of the republican synthesis are quite different and often quite contrary to each other. The chief architects of the synthesis dealt with this largely by ignoring the Declaration and related statements. After the first flush of enthusiasm for the new insights brought by the republican revisionists, the profession is now experiencing the return of the suppressed. It just will not do to ignore so much of the most prominent and prominently placed literature of the founding era. As Scott Gerber rightly points out, "the neglect of the Declaration . . . is certainly curious," for "after all, it was through the Declaration of Independence . . . that the Founders were expressing to the 'opinions of mankind' the *official* political philosophy of the newly independent United States of America."[20] The founding generation itself obviously took all this Lockean-type philosophy seriously, placing it not only in the Declaration but in their new state constitutions, in their various official representations to the British, in their sermons, in their histories. They saw no line of division between their commitment to republicanism and to the natural rights/social contract account of the issues of political philosophy.

The counterrevolution against the republican revisionists has thus gone very far, and has been almost altogether successful in trimming the exclusivist claims of the synthesizers; the unquestioned dominance of the revisionist account is now merely a matter for textbooks and other venues that lag behind current scholarship. Having passed out of the "either/or" phase of the discussion, scholars now seem to have entered into a "both/and" mode; somehow both liberalism and republicanism are present at the founding and subsequently. Thus Garrett Ward Sheldon speaks of Jefferson beginning with a Lockean period, moving on to a republican period, and then, late in life, returning to a Lockean period—the statesman as Picasso. Banning now wishes to speak of something he calls "liberal republicanism"; Michael Leinisch of a "hybrid" of the two traditions. Wood wants to deny he ever saw republicanism and liberalism as contraries.[21]

In some respects this movement toward a more inclusive approach is appropriate. To say nothing of any other considerations, the founding generation and the entire subsequent American political tradition have shown commitments to *both* natural rights liberalism and to republicanism (or its descendant, democracy). The most astute of the founders understood there to be some tension between these various commitments. For example, the greatest work of political science produced during the founding era, *The Federalist*, proceeded on the basis of a clear understanding that popular republican government is not inevitably or effortlessly compatible with rights-securing government. The authors of *The Federalist* believed that a "new political science" was required in order to render these two harmonious. Nonetheless, even at the height of their perception of tension between liberty and republicanism, the founding generation never conceived that these were contrary or, in principle, incompatible elements. Thus the current scholarly movement beyond "either/or" is not only welcome but indispensable for recapturing the frame of mind prevailing at the origins of the American political tradition.

Nonetheless, the current efforts have not been entirely successful, because they too much bear the marks of the scholarly dispensation immediately preceding them. For anybody other than Hegel, the combination of elements as contrary to each other as liberalism and republicanism as conceived in the current literature is simply impossible. One needs to see how these two elements fit together for the founding generation, but one can never do that so long as one takes as a point of departure the conceptualization of these matters prevalent in the literature. They must be rethought in a more original way, that is, by a more strenuous effort to recapture the perspective of the eighteenth century. This can be done only if we set aside our reified notion of "traditions" or "paradigms" and listen to the way the founding generation framed the issues for themselves.

The artificiality of the received manner of conceiving the natural rights liberalism/republicanism nexus stands forth with great clarity if we think of Thomas Jefferson. He gave America's most authoritative version of the natural rights philosophy in the Declaration of Independence, he showed how it governed the American constitutional position prior to the Revolution in his "Summary View of the Rights of British America," and he engaged in the deepest reflections of any American of the founding era on the nature and ground of rights. Yet, at the same time, Jefferson was a thoroughgoing and deeply committed republican; he founded a political party devoted to republicanism and he turned his thoughts to the requirements and possibilities of republicanism from his earliest to his last days. Indeed, it is in his thought that one of America's most remarkable—and ambiguous—gifts to the world took shape. Jefferson not only developed the most clearly democratic variant of republicanism among the founders, he also formulated a principle that has become nearly orthodox throughout most of the world: this very democratic form of polity is the only legitimate form of polity, the only one consistent with natural or human rights, the one to which human beings have a right. Jefferson is the thinker who meditated most deeply and most revealingly on the relations between natural rights liberalism and republicanism. Jefferson can thus not merely help us overcome the stale and unfruitful ways in which the origins of the traditions are now discussed; he can also help us understand the remarkable emergence in America of a new and unique political orientation, an orientation both natural-rights liberal and republican.

The Foundation of Republicanism

Jefferson pondered republicanism more seriously than any other American of his age. He began with the prevailing understanding of it but moved on to a novel and independent theory. He came to his unique theory of republicanism in the context of three alternative or competing views: the classical or ancient form of republicanism, represented most eminently by Rome and defended most eloquently by Machiavelli and a series of successors including men like Algernon Sidney; a modern form of republicanism, which Jefferson saw as an oligarchic republicanism, defended by many of his fellow planters in Virginia, and embodied in the revolutionary-era Virginia Constitution; and finally, a modern American form of republicanism, modeled on the British constitution, developed by his friend, James Madison, among others, and embodied more or less in the Constitution of the federal union. Jefferson rejected all three as insufficient embodiments of the authentic republican principles.

No American was more committed to republicanism than Jefferson, but Jefferson's primary political commitment was not to republicanism. In the epitaph he prepared for himself shortly before his death, he identified those "testimonials" by which he "most wished to be remembered": "Here was buried Thomas Jefferson, Author of the Declaration for American Independence, of the Statute of Virginia for religious freedom, and the Father of the University of Virginia."[22] Disparate as the three are, a common thread runs throughout—all express or derive from the natural rights philosophy. The Declaration succinctly states that philosophy and justifies the colonists' move toward independence in its terms. The long-run meaning of the Declaration, Jefferson believed, is to be "the signal of arousing men to burst the chains under which monkish ignorance and superstition had persuaded them to bind themselves." In place of this legacy of chains is the new order heralded by the Declaration: "All eyes are opened, or opening, to the rights of man."[23] The Virginia Statute for Religious Freedom bears on the transition from the old "monkish" order in a particularly close way: religious freedom, the very freedom "monkish ignorance" was most apt to reject, the right established in Jefferson's bill, is itself a "natural right," perhaps the chief right to which the "eyes of mankind were opening."[24]

The last of his "testimonials" proves to be most revelatory of the relationship between his concern for natural rights and his dedication to republicanism. The project of founding the University of Virginia was but a part of a much broader scheme of educational reform that Jefferson put forward soon after the Revolution. His plan for "the more general diffusion of knowledge" sets the need for a system of public education, including a public university, in the context of the following thought: "certain forms of government are better calculated than others to protect individuals in the free exercise of their natural rights."[25] Protection of natural rights is the standard in terms of which forms of government are judged. According to this standard, if republicanism is good, it is good because it secures rights better than other forms do. The understanding of government contained in the Declaration's natural rights philosophy points toward republicanism and, indeed toward one particular version of republicanism above all.

CLASSICAL REPUBLICANISM

The version of republicanism to which the natural rights philosophy pointed was emphatically not classical republicanism. Neither the theory nor the practice, neither the ideal nor the exemplifications of the ancient republic held much allure for Jefferson. He spoke fairly often, for example, of Plato, who stands in the background of most later classical republican theory, including that of Aristotle, Polybius, and Cicero. Without exception, Jefferson was hostile to Plato, more violent in his opinions on the Greek philosopher than even his cranky friend John Adams. To the latter, he wrote in 1814:

> Having [some] leisure . . . for reading, I amused myself with reading seriously Plato's *Republic*. I am wrong, however, in calling it amusement, for it was the heaviest task-work I ever went through. . . . While wading through the whimsies, the puerilities, and unintelligible jargon of this work, I laid it down

often to ask myself how it could have been that the world should have so long consented to give reputation to such non-sense as this?[26]

Moreover, he once admitted that he considered the very imperfect condition of Aristotle's *Politics* no great loss, because such great progress had been made over the ancients in the science of politics.[27] Classical politics fell short because the ancients did not understand the true foundational principles of politics, natural rights, the social contract, or their implications. It is again not surprising, therefore, that although Jefferson frequently read and recommended ancient "ethical writings," which he held to be "highly and justly esteemed," nonetheless he gave it as his "own opinion" that "the moderns are far advanced beyond them in this line of science."[28]

Jefferson paid more explicit attention to ancient republican practice than to ancient republican theory. He was as little impressed with the one as the other, although he did recognize that the example of ancient Rome had a certain attraction for many of his fellow Virginians. He himself found the Romans a valuable model, up to a point. The Roman republic provides the first and last instance before America itself of an "experiment in government . . . founded on principles of honesty, not of mere force."[29] Nonetheless, Jefferson on the whole had a negative view of Rome.

It was a "seductive example," one which lured otherwise well-meaning men into false, even dangerous political experiments.[30] On the authority of Rome, twice during the difficult years of the Revolution, distinguished Virginians had proposed in the legislature that a dictator be created, "a *dictator*, invested with every power legislative, executive and judiciary, civil and military, of life and death, over our persons and over our properties!"[31]

Jefferson did not merely use his discussion of this proposal as an occasion to denounce the dictatorship, but more interestingly, to reject the entire model of classical republicanism from which it was adapted. It is just not possible to understand Jefferson as Professor Pocock would have us do, as a partisan of some form of classical politics, Aristotelian, Polybian, or (as he would have it), Machiavellian. Jefferson saw that the vaunted Roman constitution was self-defeating. It "allowed a temporary tyrant to be erected, under the name of a Dictator; and that temporary tyrant, after a few examples, became perpetual." The dictatorship "proved fatal" to the republic, yet it was also indispensable to it. Rome was marked by "tumults which could not be allayed under the most trying circumstances, but by the omnipotent hand of a single despot."[32] If the Roman republic required an institution inevitably fatal to republican government, then Rome can be no sort of model for a republic.[33] In drawing that conclusion, Jefferson broke not only with those fellow Virginians who admired Rome but with much seventeenth- and eighteenth-century thinking about republics, going back to Machiavelli, who had set Rome as the very model of what a republic should be.[34]

The tumults in Rome that required the intermittent but fatal experiments with the dictatorship in turn flowed from the most characteristic features of its constitution. The rulers of Rome were "a heavy-handed unfeeling aristocracy." They governed "a people ferocious, and rendered desperate by poverty and wretchedness."[35] Jefferson sees basically the same Rome that Machiavelli saw—the Rome of a conflict between classes, which, Machiavelli believed, produced salutary results.[36] For Jefferson, however, that class structure produced a system "rent by the most bitter factions and tumults," the ultimate result of which was an even more heavy-handed and unfeeling tyranny.

So far as Rome was willing to countenance a dictator it did not qualify as a real republic, for a dictator is entirely antithetical to republicanism's "fundamental principle . . . that the state shall be governed as a commonwealth," that there be majority rule, and no prerogative, no "exercise of [any] powers undefined by the laws."[37] "Powers of governing . . . in a plurality of hands" and rule of law—these are the minimum requirements of a legitimate republic as Jefferson understands republicanism in the period between the Revolution and the framing of the Constitution.

Moreover, as an aristocracy, Rome fails to satisfy the principles of legitimacy expressed in the Declaration of Independence and inspiring all the new American constitutions. "The foundation on which all these [constitutions] are built is the natural equality of man, the denial of every preeminence but that annexed to legal office, and particularly the denial of a preeminence by birth."[38] The principles embodied in the Declaration establish the highest

principles of legitimacy for American politics. Jefferson's principles of good or legitimate government exclude from that category perhaps every historical republic of note, for all the well-
thought-of classical ones had hereditary elements. They were all,
from Jefferson's point of view, aristocratic, and therefore unacceptable, republics.

Jefferson's hostility to aristocratic republics reveals quite clearly
the way in which natural rights liberalism had primacy for the
Americans and how it conduced to an American transformation
of the old republicanism. Hereditary elements were not only
prevalent in earlier practice but had been emphasized in earlier
theory as well: prior to the American founding it was not understood that the republican principle, or, more broadly, the criteria
of good or legitimate government, excluded in principle the possession of some share of political power by a hereditary class.
Jefferson not only found all hereditary power illegitimate because
it contradicted the true foundation of political power in the natural equality of human beings; he also thought it prevented the
accomplishment of the true end or purpose of political power,
the security of natural rights: "Experience has shown that the
hereditary branches of modern governments are the patrons of
privilege and prerogative, and not of the natural rights of the
people whose oppressors they generally are."[39] Jefferson's interpretation of the natural rights principles excludes not merely the
chief classical examples—Sparta, Rome, Carthage—but the chief
"approved" regimes of modern times as well—Venice and especially Britain. In this respect, Jefferson shows himself to be far less
tolerant in his politics than most of the important natural rights
thinkers who laid the groundwork for the political tradition in
which he was operating. Locke, Montesquieu, and the English
Cato, to name but a few of these earlier thinkers, had eagerly endorsed the English mixed constitution, with its two hereditary
branches, as the very model of a good government compatible
with the underlying natural rights philosophy. Jefferson thus goes
substantially beyond the opposition tradition the republican revisionists invoke.[40]

Rome, the paradigmatic classical republic, not only failed to
satisfy the most elementary requirements of liberal republican
legitimacy, it was also a society so different from Virginia as to

supply no shadow of a precedent for the latter. Since Virginia was nothing like Rome, there was even less reason for Virginians to chase after the dangerous institution of a dictatorship necessary only in a place like Rome. The people in Virginia are "mild in their dispositions, patient under their trial, [and] united for the public liberty." The rulers in Virginia are not an aristocracy, but are all elected. The result is that Virginians are "affectionate to their leaders."[41] Virginia stands as a very different kind of polity from Rome—not faction and tumult but real affection between leaders and people.

Jefferson took as his chief task in the wake of the Revolution the maintenance and reinforcement of Virginia's differences from Rome. Those efforts reveal the main outlines of his early alternative to classical republicanism, whether as portrayed by classical philosophers or historians, or by Machiavelli. They also reveal how deeply Jefferson saw the requirements of proper republicanism to cut into the substance of the polity.

Rome, the classical form of the classical republic, was ruled by a "heavy-handed aristocracy." But since hereditary power counters the first principles of legitimate government, Jefferson's natural rights republic, as sketched in his 1776 Draft of a Constitution for Virginia, would contain no hint of hereditary power, or of any source of political power other than the people. The "authority of the people," says Jefferson's draft, deposes George from his hitherto royal power, and the same "authority aforesaid" establishes "the following fundamental law and principles of government."[42] Likewise, "none of these fundamental laws and principles of government shall be repealed or altered, but by the personal consent of the people."[43] His draft constitution, like the Virginia Constitution actually adopted, makes all offices elective, or appointive by officers either themselves elected or accountable to elected officials.

In 1776 when Jefferson drew up his constitution he was especially moved by the antihereditary principles he proclaimed; he was not, for example, opposed to long terms of office per se. Senators in his scheme would serve for nine years, but he was willing to accept much more. "I could submit, tho' not so willingly to an appointment for life."[44] Neither electoral accountability nor ultimate return by the rulers into the population at large was as much a matter of principle for Jefferson as was the avoidance of any hereditary power.

In Rome, the heavy-handed, because hereditary, aristocrats ruled over "a people rendered desperate by poverty and wretchedness."[45] Heavy-handedness, on the one side, and wretchedness, on the other, conspired to produce the tumult and disorder that necessitated the institution of the dictatorship. Just as Jefferson rejects the aristocratic rulers, so he aims at a very different kind of populace, in order that real affection rather than distrust and hatred can prevail between leaders and people. Jefferson proposes a variety of measures to keep the people of Virginia different from the people of Rome. He sought, for instance, to prevent the future emergence of a desperately poor populace. In his "Draft Constitution for Virginia," therefore, he established as a fundamental right of all persons an entitlement to "an appropriation of [50] acres or to so much as shall make up what he owns or has owned [50] acres in full and absolute dominion."[46] No person who already owned fifty acres would be eligible for such an appropriation. The land is to come from unappropriated public lands only; Jefferson was not advocating expropriating land from those already possessing more than fifty acres, among whom he himself was numbered. Likewise, he was not suggesting a limit of fifty acres on land ownership. He was seeking not equality of possession, but rather to avoid the "desperate poverty" which had characterized the Roman people.

Jefferson would moderate the property holdings of the wealthy not through any violation of their rights to property but through a reformation of the laws of inheritance. "Legislators cannot invent too many devices for subdividing property, only taking care to let their subdivisions go hand in hand with the natural affections of the human mind." Jefferson himself had, of course, acted the part of such a legislator, for he sponsored legislation abolishing entail and primogeniture. "The repeal of the laws of entail would prevent the accumulation and perpetuation of wealth in select families, and preserve the soil of the country from being daily more and more absorbed in mortmain."[47] Just as laws of entail were the prerequisite for the accumulation over time of great concentrations of land in the hands of certain families, so the abolition of those laws would permit the breakup of land into smaller, and therefore more widely distributed, parcels. Jefferson saw his reforms as especially valuable because they would produce their good effect through the operation of the "natural affections" with no violation of the natural right to property, for most parents would prefer to distribute their property equally among their children.[48] Jefferson also saw his reforms as valuable because they would free land to circulate, allow it its dynamism. Jefferson was not a friend to the static pattern of landownership characteristic, according to Pocock, of the Harringtonian republicans. So essential did Jefferson consider the law of descents that he included a provision on this subject in his draft constitution of 1776. When that was not adopted, he put these reforms at the top of his agenda for the "revisal" of laws on which the Virginia legislature, under his leadership, embarked after the Revolution.[49]

Jefferson's policies on landownership were meant to prevent the emergence of a "desperately poor" populace, but the Roman people were "ferocious" as well as poor. Their ferocity, both a cause and a consequence of Rome's martial existence, contributed to Rome's factious, tumultuous political life. By contrast, the people of Virginia are "mild." The "ferocious" Romans lived by and for war; the "mild" Americans live by and for agriculture, and to a lesser degree, commerce. Agriculture does not make human beings ferocious; it rather disposes them to all manner of virtues. The "husbandmen . . . look to their own soil and industry."[50] They are not predators on the labor of others, as were the bellicose ancient republicans who sought wealth through conquest, nor are they dependent on others, as are those who devote themselves to manufacturing. The farmer stands at the right mean—neither seeking dominion over others, nor subservient to others as are those who need customers.[51] Their temper is thus mild but not pusillanimous. Jefferson's nonfactious republic requires a people of such temper, and his land policy is intended not merely to save the bulk of the people from Roman poverty but also from Roman ferocity, for it makes available to all a way of life productive of industriousness and rationality, and, therefore, of virtue.

The classical republic, not founded on the principle of the natural equality of human beings, produced republics of the factious and tumultuous sort that inevitably failed to maintain their republican character. Jefferson's view of ancient republicanism seems not so far distant, in fact, from that of his later arch-rival Alexander Hamilton:

> It is impossible to read the history of the petty republics of Greece and Italy without feeling sensations of horror and disgust at the distractions with which they were continually agitated, and at the rapid succession of revolutions by which they were kept in a state of perpetual vibration between the extremes of tyranny and anarchy.[52]

No less than Hamilton, Jefferson relies on "advances" in the science of politics to salvage republicanism from its sorry history; no more for Jefferson than for Hamilton can Rome or any ancient republic serve as a model for America.

Oligarchic Republicanism

Jefferson appealed to the letter and spirit of the Virginia constitution against both the Roman dictatorship and the Roman republic. Virginia was committed in principle to republican forms and the rule of law, commitments which Rome either did not make or could not maintain. Yet Jefferson finds the Virginia constitution to be very defective also. "This constitution," he generously says in *Notes on Virginia*, "was formed when we were new and inexperienced in the science of government. . . . No wonder then that time and trial have discerned very capital defects in it."[53]

Rome was unacceptable because it was an aristocratic republic; Virginia falls far short because it is an oligarchic republic. Although Virginia's constitution does not commit the error-in-chief of ancient republicanism, the acceptance of hereditary rule in any part of the constitution, nonetheless it contains echoes of the aristocratic leanings of the classical republics. The Virginians did not create a separate and overbearing hereditary ruling class, but they did keep rule in the hands of a very small group, quite separate from the people. The constitutive principle of the Virginia constitution was a simple one: "confine the right of suffrage to a few of the wealthier of the people."[54]

Virginia aimed at being a true commonwealth, through commitment to "republican forms" and rule of law, but, Jefferson demonstrates, its oligarchic foundations prevent it from achieving either goal. One result of the arrangement of the suffrage in Virginia was very like the result in Rome: "the majority of the men in the state . . . are unrepresented in the legislature"[55] The malapportionment of the legislature, favoring the wealthier and better established eastern strip of the state, increased the oligarchic, nonmajoritarian character of the regime.[56] As in Rome, the governors therefore were a quite distinct and different body from the people they governed. Jefferson, by contrast, is seeking a form of republicanism which minimizes the distance between rulers and ruled, so that "real affection" prevails between them. The alternative, in Virginia as in Rome, is heavy-handedness, ultimately productive of distrust, faction, and tumult.

Harmony cannot persist between the people and their rulers if government is "trusted to the rulers of the people alone," for every such government "degenerates." "In every government on earth is some trace of human weakness, some germ of corruption and degeneracy, which cunning will discover, and wickedness insensibly open, cultivate and improve."[57] This tendency to degeneracy, a tendency for rulers to govern in their own interests and not in that of the ruled, is, Jefferson insists, a universal tendency. But "certain forms of government are better calculated than others to protect individuals in the free exercise of their natural rights." To protect the people in their rights, therefore, "the people themselves . . . are [government's] only safe depositories."[58] Oligarchic rule secures rights no better than does aristocratic rule.

The republican form, properly understood, or as consistent with the principles of government articulated in the Declaration of Independence, requires not only nonhereditary and multiple offices, but a far more democratic representation of the majority. Therefore Jefferson's draft constitution takes an altogether different approach to representation than the Virginia Constitution does: "All male persons of full age and sane minds" who pay local taxes are decreed electors, and also eligible to stand for office.[59] Likewise his draft provides for the apportionment of legislative seats proportionate to qualified voters, in order to prevent the kind of drastic malapportionment the adopted constitution embodies.

Even though Jefferson suggests in *Notes on Virginia* that the defects of the Virginia constitution stemmed from "inexperience in the science of government," the differences between him and the drafters of the constitution go much deeper than that. Jefferson's draft constitution was drawn up at precisely the same time as the Virginia constitution he decried; he had no more "experience" of the science of government than they; as a younger man, perhaps less. The differences are not mere adventitious differences such as flow from different experiences, but are to some degree matters of principle.

Jefferson explains his desire for nearly universal male suffrage in a letter to the more oligarchic-minded Edmund Pendleton: "Whoever intends to live in a country must wish that country well, and has a natural right of assisting in the preservation of it."[60] The principles of legitimacy in the Declaration not only deny the validity of hereditary power but demand a democratic republic. Universal manhood suffrage is required not only as a means to bring about a non-factious, harmonious politics of "real affection" but as an implication of the primary natural rights: government exists to secure the rights of all, and all therefore possess a right to secure the instrument of their security.

Jefferson's principled differences with the drafters of the Virginia constitution emerge also in his discussion of the failure of that document to secure the rule of law, a failure deriving from a failure to establish a proper system of separation of powers. That failure in turn derived from Virginia's commitment to, not accidental fall into, oligarchical republicanism. "All the powers of government, legislative, executive, and judiciary, result to the legislative body," Jefferson charged, and that is unacceptable, because "concentrating these in the same hands is precisely the definition of despotic power."[61] Jefferson, like Madison later in *The Federalist*,[62] follows Montesquieu on the function of separation of powers in guaranteeing nondespotic or lawful government.[63]

Jefferson insists there be a genuine separation of powers where the Virginia constitution does not. The drafters of the constitution, Jefferson implies, thought it was enough "that these powers will be exercised by a plurality of hands": what is not monarchic is not despotic. But Jefferson disagrees: "173 despots would surely be as oppressive as one. Let those who doubt it turn their eyes on the republic of Venice."[64] (Venice, that other famous example of a republic, the "serene republic," fares no better in Jefferson's eyes than Rome, the dynamic republic.) But the Virginians had another principle in mind as well as "plurality of hands." The legislators "are chosen by ourselves." The drafters apparently believe that the "electoral connection" makes the legislature a safe depository for these concentrated powers. But, retorts Jefferson, "an *elective despotism* was not the government we fought for."[65] The despotic potential results not only from the restricted suffrage in Virginia, but electoral responsibility is never sufficient. Government "founded on free principles," i.e., electorally responsible government, is a necessary but not a sufficient condition for a nondespotic regime. A proper government is one "in which the powers . . . should be so divided and balanced among several bodies of magistracy, as that no one could transcend their legal limits, without being effectually checked and restrained by others."[66]

Admittedly, the Virginians did partially recognize the necessity of a separation of powers, but they left it at a mere declaration and, in fact, proceeded to establish practices according to which "the judiciary and executive members were left dependent on the legislature." The Virginians do not take the problem of concentrated powers seriously because they are "deluded by the integrity of their own purposes, and conclude that these unlimited powers will never be abused, because themselves are not disposed to abuse them."[67] Behind the inadequacy of the provisions for separation of powers lies the Virginians' confidence in their own integrity or virtue. That appears to be connected with the provisions for representation and suffrage in their constitution. These qualifications guarantee that only the "better sort," the "respectable" members of the community, can hold office and take part in the selection of officeholders; one can rely, the Virginia drafters seem to believe, on the virtue of such men. Those features of the constitution to which Jefferson objects, in other words, are commonly inspired by a commitment to placing political power in the hands of "a few of the wealthier people," from whose good qualities—virtue, integrity, incorruptibility, wisdom—good government is to spring.

The Virginians were committed by design and conviction, not by mere inadvertence, to their oligarchic system. Jefferson rejects almost every element of their analysis. Not only does he insist on the fuller involvement of the people, he challenges the so-called virtues of the wealthy. "My observations," Jefferson observes in 1776, "do not enable me to say I think integrity the characteristic of wealth. In general I believe the decisions of the people, in a body, will be more honest and more disinterested than those of wealthy men."[68] If the virtue of any class is to be relied on, it is the virtue of the people. But, as Jefferson says in a slightly different context, "the fantastical idea of virtue and [commitment to] the public good being a sufficient security . . . I assure you was never mine."[69]

Jefferson surely does not mean to substitute a simple reliance on the people for the Virginians' oligarchy. In the very same place where he praises the people as "more honest and disinterested," he indicates he was under few illusions as to popular political capacities. "I have ever observed that a choice by the people themselves is not generally distinguished for it's [*sic*] wisdom. This first secretion from them is usually crude and heterogeneous."[70] A proper constitution must rest on the people but must supplement them in a number of ways. That is one reason a proper bicameralism is required—not merely for the added checking and balancing a second legislative chamber provides, but perhaps more importantly for the sake of adding wisdom to popular honesty. Thus Jefferson at this period in his career favors an upper house selected not by the people but by the lower house. "Give to those so chosen by the people a second choice themselves, and they generally will choose wise men."[71] Jefferson seeks to supplement the people, not with the wealthy as such, but with the wise, or with "the aristocracy of virtue and talent," or "the natural aristocracy."[72]

Jefferson seeks to secure something like the old mixed constitution as in Britain:

> The purpose of establishing different houses of legislation is to introduce the influence of different interests or different principles. Thus in Great Britain it is said their constitution relies on the house of commons for honesty, and the lords for wisdom; which would be a rational reliance if honesty were to be bought with money and wisdom were hereditary.[73]

Jefferson seeks a more effective means to achieve the ends he attributes to the British constitution. Those means are not only more effective but also in accord with the principled requirement that political power derive from the people. He aims to accomplish much the same thing that Madison identified as the goal of the new political science animating the federal constitution: to find a democratic, i.e., nonmixed, remedy for the evils of democracy.[74] Jefferson, no less than Madison, recognizes the need to supplement democracy, in his case with wisdom, or with talent, but to do so without recourse to nondemocratic practices.

Jefferson's democratic republic requires an ambitious scheme of education. The people may be "the only safe depository" of political power, but "even they must be rendered safe," and to that end "their minds must be improved to a certain degree."[75] Thus he proposes a daring plan of universal education, every child, male or female, to be provided three years of free education. As opposed to most earlier proposals for widespread education, Jefferson's inspiration was political and not religious. Indeed, "instead . . . of putting the Bible and Testament into the hands of the children, at an age when their judgments are not sufficiently matured for religious enquiries, their memories may here be stored with the most useful facts from Grecian, Roman, European and American history."[76]

The people are to receive an education "directed" not to their salvation but "to their freedom and happiness" in this world. History will serve as the center of this education, for "by apprising them of the past [it] will enable them to judge of the future; it will avail them of the experience of other times and other nations; it will qualify them as judges of the actions and designs of men; it will enable them to know ambition under any disguise it may assume; and knowing it, to defeat its views."[77] Education is to fit the people for a certain kind of citizenship—to act the sentinels over their "freedom and happiness." Education will make the people's honesty more effective by arming it with a modicum of defensive wisdom.[78]

Jefferson's educational system would also reinforce or help form the people's honesty itself. "The first elements of morality too may be instilled into their minds; such as, when further developed as their judgments advance in strength, may teach them how to work out their own greatest happiness, by showing them that it does not depend on the condition of life in which chance has placed them, but is always the result of a good conscience, good health, occupation, and freedom in all just pursuits."[79] Jefferson's commitment to natural equality and to democratic republicanism does not extend to a commitment to social or economic equality. The people's education will help make them fit citizens of a free republic dedicated to the security of rights, including the right to property, by leading them to see that plundering the wealthy is no necessary part of their own happiness. With such schemes, Jefferson hopes to reassure his fellow wealthy Virginians that their oligarchic system is not necessary in order to protect their own rights. Of course such a system of moral education can succeed only if the people do not live in desperate poverty. That is, education "indeed is not all that is necessary, though it be essentially necessary."[80] Nonetheless, Jefferson could go very far in his hopes for education: "Enlighten the people generally, and tyranny and oppressions of body and mind will vanish like evil spirits at the dawn of day."[81]

The educational scheme helps provide not only a fit people for Jefferson's natural rights republic but the wise and naturally talented rulers who must supplement the people. "It [is] expedient for promoting the publick happiness that those persons, whom nature both endowed with genius and virtue, should be rendered by liberal education worthy to receive, and able to guard the sacred deposit of the rights and liberties of their fellow citizens."[82] Education helps both to identify and to form the "natural aristocracy" who will take the lead in Jefferson's democratic republic. The educational system will be the expected entree to the public sphere for the young men of Virginia. There they will prove themselves in company with their peers; there they will be exposed to what Jefferson considered the undeniably salutary effects—moral and intellectual—of "liberal education." Since "nature has sown talents as liberally among the poor as the rich," the educational system will also be the avenue for finding and raising up the natural aristocrats among the poorer elements of society.[83] Through a complicated system of screening and evaluation, the very best of the poorer youths will be advanced to higher levels of free education. Jefferson's system of education is to be, then, a limited vehicle for social mobility, but that is neither its purpose nor justification. Its purpose is political—to find and form the talented among the poor and put them into a position from which they may "be called to the charge" of "guarding the sacred deposit of the rights and liberties of their fellow citizens."[84] "Worth and genius" are thus to be "sought out from every condition of life and completely prepared by education for defeating the competition of wealth and birth for public trusts."[85]

Education is a necessary but not sufficient supplement to the resting of politics securely on the great body of the people; Jefferson insists that the constitution of his democratic republic contain a proper system of separated powers and checks and balances. He would not make the mistake of the oligarchic republicans who thought virtue in the holders of power a sufficient safeguard. (He does not share the theories of our republican synthesizers, either.) However virtuous the Virginia rulers may feel themselves to be—Jefferson diplomatically does not challenge their self-assessment—nonetheless the future holds for America what the past has revealed elsewhere. "Human nature is the same on every side of the Atlantic, and will be alike influenced by the same causes. The time to guard against corruption and tyranny, is before they shall have gotten hold on us."[86]

The Virginia constitution, with its failure to establish a proper separation of powers, illustrates the danger Jefferson fears. All powers, legislative, executive, and judicial, rest in the hands of the legislature. Concentration of power is in itself very bad, for the legislature is thus free to substitute its will for the rule of law that the separation of powers fosters. Not only can the legislature make the general rules which govern society, it can control the application of them to individuals; it can override all efforts by other officials to resist its self-interested acts of will.

In Virginia the problem is exacerbated, for the constitution itself has no higher status than an act of the legislature. It can itself be changed by the legislature. The legislature, moreover, has the power to establish its own quorum, a power which can be used to empower successively an ever smaller number with the full legislative authority "till [the legislature] loses its fundamental character of being a representative body."[87] Given the status of the constitution itself, what is to prevent this unrepresentative body from declaring itself, or some individual, the sovereign? Without a system of separation of powers Virginia may progress under purely legal forms from a reasonably republican system to a clearly despotic one. Although he does not mention it explicitly, Jefferson appears to base this vision of a spiral into tyranny on the historical example of Parliament in the period after the abolition of the monarchy and the House of Lords; the result was just as Jefferson says, first the ever-decreasing Parliament and then the Protectorate, all accomplished more or less legally, and without the resistance separated powers could provide.

The corruption and degeneracy Jefferson particularly fears is that the rulers, numerous as they may be, electorally responsible as they may be, liberally educated as they may be, will forget their trust—the rights and liberties of their fellow citizens—and pursue their own interests to the extent of destroying the republic and setting up themselves or some of their number as absolute and irresponsible rulers. This is a fate to which Virginia's extraordinarily defective oligarchic republic is especially prone, but it is one that Jefferson fears lies in the future of any republic that is not very well constructed.

AMER-ANGLO REPUBLICANISM

Within a few years after he left the presidency, Jefferson reconceived the entire problem of republicanism. He comes now to judge his own earlier draft constitution to have been nearly as inadequate as the Virginia constitution itself, and for much the same reason. "At the birth of our republic," Jefferson writes in 1816, "I committed [my] opinion . . . to the world, in the draught of a constitution annexed to the *Notes on Virginia*." But that draft contained "gross departures . . . from genuine republican canons." He attributed his errors and those of his fellows to the same erroneous opinion. "The abuses of monarchy had so much filled all the space of political contemplation, that we imagined everything republican which was not monarchy."[88] In Jefferson's new light, the Virginia constitution and his own alternative to it are more alike than different.

By 1816, Jefferson came to see the early American experiments in republicanism, including his own projections, as overly mild adaptations of European, especially British, models. "It must be agreed," he writes in 1816, "that our governments have much less of republicanism than ought to have been expected."[89] The Revolution, after all, "commenced on [very] favorable ground. It presented us an album on which we were free to write what we pleased. We had no occasion to search into musty records, to hunt up royal parchments, or to investigate the laws and institutions of a semi-barbarous ancestry." Even though the Americans were not engaged in the Whig enterprise of a restoration of an antecedent order, even though they made their "appeal to the laws of nature" and not to the ancient law or constitution, "yet we did not avail ourselves of all the advantages of our position."[90] The Americans' failure to exploit to the full the opportunity presented by their *tabula rasa* was not due to "any want of republican disposition in those who framed these constitutions, but to a submission of true principle to European authorities, to speculators on government."[91]

European practice and European theory deterred the Americans from following their own better instincts. Instead of striding forward into fully republican systems, they remained in thrall to the authority of the Europeans. Some of the Federalist Party, Jefferson thought, were aiming at an actual restoration of the British constitution—complete with hereditary monarch and House of Lords—but even the sounder heads who forbore from that remained too much within the orbit of European models. They dismantled the obviously unacceptable elements—monarchy and trailing nobles—but put in their place substitutes too much like the originals and failed to appreciate the immense difference natural rights republicanism made for a proper constitutional order.

Jefferson's critique of the oligarchic republicanism of the Virginia constitution can easily be recast in terms of these later complaints. The Virginians essentially did away with monarchy and the hereditary principle, but placed power in the hands of an oligarchic class, considering this sufficiently republican because nonmonarchic and nonhereditary. This was deficient because insufficiently popular, and also because in practice the hereditary principle maintains more hold than it ought to have, since the "leading families," largely hereditary elements, tend to acquire a natural call on political power in such a system.

Another example, a particularly striking one, of the hypnotic hold of English models, are the provisions made in most American constitutions for judicial independence.

> In the Judiciary, the judges of the highest Courts are dependent on none but themselves. In England, where judges were named and removable at the will of an hereditary executive, from which branch most misrule was feared, and has flowed, it was a great point gained by fixing them for life, to make them independent of the executive.[92]

But a suitable arrangement in the context of a monarchy is not necessarily suitable in the context of a popular republic. "In a government founded on the public will," judicial independence is no longer a virtue, for it "operates in an opposite direction, and against that will."[93] Thus by 1816 Jefferson favored popular election and accountability of judges—all the way up to the highest courts. This represents a truly major shift from his own earlier position. The draft constitution for Virginia of 1776 provided for "good behavior" tenure for judges. Likewise in 1787, judicial independence in the proposed U.S. constitution appears to have been one of the features that Jefferson especially approved, and he had no objection at that time to "good behavior" tenure for judges, nor to their appointment by the executive.[94]

Jefferson's own 1776 constitutional provisions for the Senate in Virginia betray how much the Americans were inclined to substitute for the old British institutions new American versions much like what they were replacing. Jefferson incorporated long terms of office and was even willing to contemplate life tenure. Moreover, he sought an indirect election for the upper house— not the popular electorate directly, but the lower house was to select the upper. By 1816, Jefferson shifted ground substantially. He now favored a shorter term of office, four years, and he now favored direct election of the Senate by a much expanded electorate.[95] Likewise, in 1787, Jefferson had found nothing to blame about the Senate in the proposed U.S. constitution, but in 1816 he pronounced it "scarcely republican at all, as not elected by the people directly, and so long secured even against those who do elect them."[96]

Jefferson in 1776–87 had favored a different mode of selection for the Senate because he sought to bring different qualities into the two houses of the legislature, honesty reflecting the people as such in the lower house, and wisdom in the upper house. At the time he was quite explicit about the model for his plan—the theory of the British constitution.

It is especially at this level that Jefferson's later judgment on his own earlier constitutional scheme makes good sense: his draft constitution was deeply indebted to the British model as to its aims, the combination of the many and the few, and as to its means, popular dependence in some places and exclusion of the people (more or less) elsewhere. In this light, Jefferson's draft constitution did remain close (perhaps not as close as he said, however) to its European precedents, sans the hereditary monarchy and nobles, of course.

Even in his later thought, Jefferson did not entirely renounce ways of thought associated with the British constitution. Early and late he considered "the few" to be an indispensable element of a healthy republic. "The natural aristocracy I consider as the most precious gift of nature, for the instruction, the trusts, and government of society."[97] The "natural aristoi" are those distinguished by "virtue and talents," but certainly not those marked by "wealth and birth." The later Jefferson went so far as to conclude that "that form of government is the best which provides the most effectively for a pure selection of these natural *aristoi* into the offices of government."[98]

These later musings on the natural aristocracy certainly continue themes from Jefferson's earlier writings on constitutions and education, but they contain two emphases which distinguish them from his earlier positions. First, he no longer thinks of one particular place in the government as the specific home of wisdom, talent, and virtue. So far as possible, these men of ability ought to fill the whole government. Although Jefferson continued to see politics as involving some sort of interplay between the few and the many, he no longer saw it on the pattern of the British constitution's division of two houses with affirmative "set asides" for members of each class. His second major shift is implicit in his new thinking on the Senate. No special techniques of selection are necessary or desirable to bring these men of talent and virtue into leadership positions. "I think the best [method] is . . . to leave to the citizen the free election and separation of the aristoi from the pseudo-aristoi, of the wheat from the chaff." The people, Jefferson believes, will "in general . . . elect the real good and wise,"[99] a substantial change of view from his earlier days. The cooperation of the few and the many is to take place on an entirely different basis from any version or adaptation of the English constitution; it is to be truly popular, thoroughly dependent on the people.

The English constitution, thought Jefferson as early as 1791, was but a "kind of half-way house"; it was nonetheless one with a lingering attraction: the Americans persist in "taking . . . English precedents . . . for our guide, . . . the habit of which fetters us, with all the political herecies [*sic*] of a nation, equally remarkable for it's [*sic*] encitement from some errors, as slumbering under others."[100] Perhaps therein lies the great danger of the mother-country as model: she has freed herself sufficiently from some inherited errors so as to appear the very home of progressive and rational politics, but in fact America has both the obligation and the opportunity to move forward more decisively.

Jefferson clearly had come to see British models as seductions which needed to be resisted by his countrymen, as he had earlier seen classical models as dangers to American political health. His period of party leadership was devoted, therefore, to rallying the country against what he saw to be the Federalists' concealed but real reversion to the British constitution, either in the corrupted form patronized by Hamilton or in the purified form patronized by John Adams.[101] The postpresidency phase of his career was devoted to the development and promulgation of his more radical new republicanism. The enemy now was not the more or less unvarnished Anglicism of Hamilton and Adams and their like but the subtle Amer-Anglo republicanism of the likes of the early Thomas Jefferson and the James Madison who drafted the U.S. Constitution.

The Americans fell short of real republicanism in their earlier efforts at political construction because, dazzled by European authorities, they failed to "penetrate to the mother principle, that 'governments are republican only in proportion as they embody the will of their people and execute it.'"[102] While Jefferson had earlier been a partisan of a popular or democratic republicanism, his emphasis here is rather different. Earlier, the core of his concern was defensive, so to speak. He had contemplated a checking and controlling role for the people but nothing so active and positive as the notion that the popular will as such ought to rule.

In other statements, Jefferson went even further: "Were I to assign to this term [republicanism] a precise and definite idea, I would say, purely and simply, it means a government by its citizens in mass, acting directly and personally."[103] The standard of republicanism is what we would now call direct democracy. All forms which retreat from that (and Jefferson knows most will require some retreat) are only republican to a degree; "the further the departure from direct and constant control by the citizens, the less has the government of the ingredient of republicanism."[104]

The contrast to Madison's Anglified republicanism (as Jefferson would describe it) could not be clearer. Like Jefferson, Madison was unwilling to accept the traditional catalogue of republics. Holland, Venice, Poland, England—all nations sometimes called republics but containing little popular control and some hereditary parts—are thrown off the republican team by Madison.[105] According to Madison, a republic is "a government which derives all its powers directly or indirectly from the great body of the people, and is administered by persons holding their offices during pleasure for a limited period, or during good behavior."[106] The tone of this is surely different from Jefferson's late republicanism. Nothing here of that activist popular role, that insistence on rule by the will of the people. Thus, Madison considers his life-tenure judiciary, his indirectly elected Senate and president, his distant and rather independent representatives to be perfectly adequate embodiments of the republican principle.

In his postpresidency years, in other words, Jefferson's conception of republicanism has shifted substantially from where his own views had been earlier, to say nothing of from where his contemporaries were. It would be a mistake, however, to conclude, as some do, that this shift signifies an equally significant metamorphosis in Jefferson's understanding of the grounds and purposes of government, that it implies, for example, a shift away from the natural rights philosophy and towards a conception of politics according to which "no one could be called happy without his share in public happiness, that no one could be called free without his experience in public freedom, and that no one could be called either happy or free without participating, and having a share, in public power."[107]

Contrary to such speculation, Jefferson in 1816 continued to express the criteria of political legitimacy in terms of rights. "Believing, as I do, that the mass of the citizens is the safest depository of their own rights. . . . I am a friend to that composition of government which has in it the most . . . popular election and control."[108]

"The true foundation of republican government," then, lies not in novel ideas of public (as opposed to private) happiness, nor in a sudden appreciation for the classical idea that "man is a political animal," but rather "in the equal rights of every citizen, in his person and property, and in their management."[109] The ground of republicanism, in other words, is in the private and individual rights each has as his or her own. Jefferson's later republicanism represents an attempt to take these rights extremely seriously. They are, as he had affirmed in the Declaration of Independence, "unalienable." As he restates the point almost fifty years later: "Nothing . . . is unchangeable but the inherent and unalienable rights of man."[110] The European models, and the Americanized versions of these do not take the ground in natural rights seriously enough. They proceed as though the rights to the management of one's self and one's own are alienable, as though they are merely theoretical postulates which have little abiding significance for the construction of political society.

Jefferson thinks quite otherwise:

> Society [is] one of the natural wants with which man has been created; . . . when . . . he has procured a state of society, it is one of his acquisitions which he has a right to regulate and control, jointly indeed with all those who have concurred in the procurement.[111]

That is, the democratic republic is not merely conducive to rights-protecting, not merely expressive of the status of all citizens as rights-bearers, but is itself a right. The flexible and prudential standards Jefferson, following Locke and Montesquieu, had articulated in the Declaration of Independence are gone; democracy is now understood to be a right, a matter of principle, and simply the only legitimate form of government.

Jefferson derives this right by drawing the implications from the conclusions of natural rights philosophy about the nature of government: It is not merely an instrumental thing but is itself "an acquisition," that is, a property as well as an instrument for the securing of property (in the broad Lockean sense). The whole system rests on the underlying principle that human beings are rights-possessors with the inalienable right to "manage" themselves, "their person and property." Public institutions, the joint making of the citizenry, must be "managed" consistently with their purpose as rights-securers and their nature as "acquisitions." As property in this sense, government must be made and operated so that it really belongs to, that is, proceeds via the actual and active consent, or better, will of the governed. Jefferson's most republican or political moment thus arises in a line of thought more or less the reverse of the picture of republican politics in the republican synthesis. Jefferson formulates this extraordinary right to democracy when he assimilates the public sphere entirely to the theory of private property, that is, when he comes to see the state more completely through the lens of the Lockean theory of property and property rights.

From these axioms, Jefferson in his postpresidential years derives a quite novel principle for constituting and organizing public authority. "We think experience has proved it safer, for the mass of individuals composing the society, to reserve to themselves personally the exercise of all rightful powers to which they are competent, and to delegate those to which they are not competent to deputies named, and removable for unfaithful conduct, by themselves immediately."[112] Applying that principle, Jefferson develops a new kind of complex system of government to replace, more or less, the complex models based on the British constitution. He replaces one kind of complexity, the largely horizontal complexity of Amer-Anglo republicanism (e.g., the U.S. Constitution) with another kind of complexity, a more vertical complexity suggested to a large degree by the system of federalism adopted in the U.S. Constitution, but going well beyond it. The "secret" of liberty "will be found," Jefferson argues, "in the making [of each man] himself the depository of the powers respecting himself, so far as he is competent to them, and delegating only what is beyond his competence . . . to higher and higher orders of functionaries, so as to trust fewer and fewer powers in proportion as the trustees became more and more oligarchical."[113] What powers can be kept in the hands of each, as a private and individual matter, ought to be so kept. All public power ought to be entrusted to the lowest, most local level capable of exercising it, and each level of government ought to be constructed so as to maximize popular involvement and control. What one does not manage for oneself, one manages with others; where one does not have full control over affairs, one has a share in the management of affairs, so far as is compatible with the affairs being managed at all.

Thus Jefferson spends much space in his later writings detailing the complexity of the allocation of functions and powers among different vertical levels of government, all of which together form one "gradation of authorities."[114] The "national government," Jefferson thinks, should "be entrusted with the defence of the nation, and its foreign and federal relations."[115] Here Jefferson clearly indicates another area of great difference between himself and his friend Madison. In the latter's Amer-Anglo republican constitution, the national government's responsibilities go substantially further. For example, in the plan he drew up for the Constitution, Madison included a provision (to which Jefferson objected) for the Congress of the national government to exercise a veto power over all legislation in the states, a proposal aimed at securing justice and the protection of rights within the states. The Constitution as adopted certainly failed to go as far as Madison hoped, but it did include provisions which went beyond what Jefferson considered appropriate.[116]

Many of the matters Madison would wish to see the national government involved in, Jefferson would leave exclusively to "lower" levels of his system of authorities. The state governments ought to "be entrusted . . . with the civil rights, laws, police, administration of what concerns the state generally; the counties with the local concerns of the counties, and each ward [should] direct the interests within itself."[117] Power remains at the lowest level possible, beginning with each person, his or her self and property, and moves upward only as necessary, only as the lower level proves incompetent. We should trust, he said, "fewer and fewer powers" to each level, as fewer and more distant persons hold the power.[118] The entire "gradation of authorities" would be the means whereby the greatest right to control one's own affairs and to share in the control of one's affairs would remain in the hands of each individual, and at the same time be consistent with the actual needs and tasks of government. Jefferson's later republicanism is not so driven by abstract principle that it does not make place for political needs which require some compromise with the principle that power must be kept entirely in the hands of each citizen.[119]

The most remarkable and probably the most important feature of Jefferson's system is the provision for a system of "ward republics." Each county should be divided into much smaller units, wards, approximately six square miles in size, about one-fourth the size of the average Virginia county.[120] The wards, modeled on the New England township, are the places where Jefferson departs most notably from all adaptations of the English constitution; they are the places where the active will of the people can most make itself felt and effective. They are the places, in other words, where Jefferson's "true republicanism" is to be realized.

Whatever tasks they undertake,[121] Jefferson foresees them fulfilling a number of functions central to the health and survival of republicanism. They are, first, to be loci for the exercise of the right that each possesses to share in political power. "Each ward would be a small republic within itself, and every man in the state would thus become an acting member of the common government, transacting in person a great portion of its rights and duties."[122] Secondly, the wards are to be the vehicle by which (most) public tasks get done better and more effectively.[123] To transfer public business from higher and more distant levels to the wards "will have it better done."[124] People care best for what is of most direct concern to them.

The ward system, thirdly, will importantly contribute to the goal Jefferson had set from his earliest days of a harmonious republic, with the populace attached and well-disposed toward their government. "By making every citizen an acting member of the government, and in the offices nearest and most interesting to him, [the ward system] will attach him by his strongest feeling, to the independence of his country, and its republican constitution."[125] The wards will conduce to political unity; "the whole is cemented by giving to every citizen, personally, a part in the administration of the public affairs."[126]

Enlisting the sentiments and attachments of the people, the wards would be the source of vitality for republican government in America. "These little republics would be the main strength of the great one." The townships of New England have already proved how much energy these "little republics" can generate. "We owe to them the vigor given to our revolution in its commencement in the Eastern States, and by them the Eastern States were enabled to repeal the embargo in opposition to the Middle, Southern and Western States, and their large and lubberly division into counties which can never be assembled."[127] It appears, indeed, to have been his experience of New England opposition to the embargo that first impressed on him the value and significance of the ward organization as a center for political action. "How powerfully did we feel the energy of this organization in the case of the embargo? I felt the foundations of the government shaken under my feet by the New England townships."[128]

The energy unleashed in the wards to some extent also serves negative or checking functions as part of a proper system of divided, and therefore safer, powers. "The way to have good and safe government, is not to trust it all to one, but to divide it among the many." The system of authorities, and especially the wards, "constitutes truly a system of fundamental balances and checks for the government," a system better than the old constitution of horizontal checks and balances modeled on England.[129] The decentralization of government made possible by the ward organization provides the best guard against "what has destroyed liberty and the rights of man in every government which has ever existed under the sun," i.e., "the generalizing and concentrating all cares and powers into one body, no matter whether of the aristocrats of Russia or France, or of the autocrats of a Venetian Senate."[130] Since all governments have ultimately "destroyed liberty and the rights of man," and since the wards promise to fend off this sorry fate, no wonder that Jefferson concluded, "could I once see [the establishment of the ward system] I should consider it as the dawn of the salvation of the republic."[131] "The wit of man," he says almost at the very end of his life, "cannot devise a more solid basis for a free, durable and well-administered republic."[132]

What is perhaps most striking about Jefferson's new natural rights republicanism is the creative way in which he has assimilated the important contributions James Madison had made to American political science. At the time of the drafting of the Constitution Madison had compellingly shown (in *Federalist* 37, among other places) that the dominant approach to politics taken by his countrymen after the Revolution was fundamentally mistaken. Americans had defined the political problem too narrowly, as a problem of *safety* only, that is, as the problem of keeping government from being oppressive of the rights of citizens. Madison had persuasively argued that safety was but one of several qualities that governments must embody; energy and stability were two others which he identified. Madison wondered aloud in the *Federalist* whether the republican form was compatible with these various and partially conflicting requirements, and concluded that it was, but only if republicanism was understood in the relatively lax way he defined it, and only if his ersatz British constitution could be billed as that kind of republic. Jefferson's later republicanism represents an effort to combine the various qualities Madison had identified—safety, competence, energy—with his own more principled, more rigorous definition of republicanism. In doing so, Jefferson set forth the most thoroughgoing conception of what an America, characterized through and through by republican commitments and republican forms, would be.

NATURAL RIGHTS REPUBLICANISM

Jefferson's robust version of democratic republicanism does not bespeak the continued sway over him of classical republican strains of thought as Arendt, Pocock, Wood, Banning, Sheldon, and others would have us believe. Rather it is a specific thinking through of the natural rights philosophy he had given authoritative expression to for America in the Declaration of Independence. Only its connection to the natural rights doctrine allows us to understand the principled, or as some would have it, rigid and inflexible character of Jefferson's republicanism. He declares war on all hereditary power, which had been held to be perfectly acceptable within classical republicanism, and he declares war on all efforts to imitate the effects of hereditary power, as in Madison's much less populist model of republicanism. Republicanism, or, it would now be fair to say, democracy, becomes both the only rightful government and even a personal or individual right. It was this strain of Jeffersonian theory that the Warren Court picked up on, for example, in its reapportionment decisions.

Jefferson's theory is complex because he derives the right to democracy both from an argument of principle and an argument of practice. Principle establishes a right to a democratic republic because government, as a thing made by the contractors—all the persons subject to its authority—belongs to those who made it, and thus, like any piece of jointly owned property, is rightly controlled and managed by the owners, jointly. Far from rejecting a natural right to property in favor of some "higher" form of democracy, Jefferson derives his "higher" democracy from the right to property.

At the same time, he holds the democratic republic to be instrumentally best also. It does better what all governments are to do—secure the rights of its citizens. In modern jargon, Jefferson's case for a right to a democratic republic combines deontological and consequentialist elements. That right is both expressive in itself of a fundamental right and instrumental to other rights. Jefferson thought his theory of the ward republics so important precisely because it combined the competence, safety, stability, wisdom, energy, and allegiance-producing quality required by government in its instrumental role with the principled requirement set by governments as expressions of the rights-bearing quality of human beings.

Jefferson's robust republicanism does not bespeak the sway over him of a counterliberal republicanism, but it does provide a vehicle wherein the American tradition has assimilated to its basic natural rights liberalism elements more intensely political and reminiscent of premodern republicanism. Going beyond the original natural rights liberalism, politics is no longer simply instrumental but is, indeed, a good in itself, an expression of the fundamental character of human beings as rights bearers. Thus, politics in America can not be captured in any utilitarian calculus; the legitimate form is not simply the form that performs best instrumentally. Political participation, too, takes on a meaning somewhat more akin to what it held in earlier forms of republicanism. It is both a good-in-itself and even a civic duty, not merely an interest or private benefit. America has thus been defined in political terms—both Americans and others have traditionally thought, for example, of French culture, but of American democracy. Once again it appears that in America, the natural rights philosophy has been remarkably able to assimilate and reshape premodern elements into a more or less coherent whole. So far as the American political tradition has been unique, it is just in this amalgamation—an amalgamation in which the natural rights commitment has remained senior partner but has brought into its political orbit English Whig historical commitments, Protestant political theology, and premodern political republicanism. It is tempting to say America has had such a remarkable political history precisely because it has developed a political culture that integrates so well politics, religion, history, and philosophy.

Yet the story of the American political tradition is not merely the story of this American amalgam. The elements in the amalgam do not always cohere so effortlessly as some of the classic statements of the amalgam discussed here might suggest. The religious and the liberal elements stand in a certain tension in the mid-90s. The liberal and the historical periodically threaten to come apart, as they do, for example, in Jefferson's more modernist moments, when he believes the past no longer has any lessons for us. Likewise, the amalgam of natural rights liberalism and republican (democratic) politics has not been tensionless or an unmitigated success in American history.

Surely, America as a nation is now only partly defined by republicanism as understood by Jefferson. It is surely not a system in which we find "government by its citizens in mass, acting directly and personally." It would be difficult to say that Americans see themselves, in any significant way, primarily as citizens, or as owners of their governments. Jefferson hoped to see a nation in which "every man is a sharer in the direction of his ward-republic, or of some of the higher ones, and feels that he is a participator in the government of affairs, not merely an election one day in the year"—or one day every four years—"but every day." The kind of self-identification Jefferson's citizens would form is not the kind formed by citizens of America's large, distant, and relatively nonparticipatory republic.

Nonetheless, Jeffersonian republicanism has been deeply transformative of American political life and American political opinion. Over time, we have experienced a synthesis of sorts of the Jeffersonian and Madisonian versions of natural rights republicanism. The large and less strenuously republican Madisonian constitutional system has set the fundamental frame for American politics, but it has been infused with a more Jeffersonian spirit: no longer are the Madisonian institutions as removed from the people as they were under the Madisonian constitution. First, the political parties, then the formal modification of the Constitution, and, finally, the development of the mass media have worked to bridge some of the distance Madison had hoped to establish between governmental institutions and the people. The institutions, to say the least, have been infused with a more popular spirit and thus are far more Jeffersonian.

At the same time, the Jeffersonian popular spirit operates within the Madisonian context of an "elitist" republic, without the vital system of devolution of authority and without the vibrant wards which were to elicit and educate the republican spirit of the people. One is tempted to conclude that contemporary American republicanism is on the whole the poorer for the synthesis, that either the Jeffersonian or the Madisonian version could be superior to the hybrid version we have. The present system does not foster those qualities of deliberation, sobriety, stability, and wisdom that Madison sought, nor does it supply Jefferson's energizing popular spirit, trained in the responsibilities of citizenship and alert to the depredations of government.

Let me conclude somewhat more cautiously, however. Jefferson believed that his theory of ward republicanism represented the one true and authentic working out of the natural rights republican position. He believed that because he believed his version gave full and adequate weight to both the expressive and instrumental dimensions of republicanism. Neither I nor James Madison can entirely agree with Jefferson here, however. Madison's more practical and sophisticated analysis reveals that a tension still remains in Jefferson's system between the expressive and the instrumental dimensions. To mention only the most well-known point: the exercise of the right to control government can, without large stretches of the imagination, produce outcomes that conflict with the rights to be protected. Madison's example of the rights of creditors vs. the political goals of debtors is a sufficient case in point. Madison persisted in his belief that institutional devices supplementary to majority rule remained essential for securing the rights of minorities. Jefferson conceded the principle of minority rights but refused to countenance institutions geared to their protection.

Within the instrumental level Madison also would question whether Jefferson's ward republics and graded authorities would be sufficient to supply all the energy, competence, and prudence required to run a nation successfully. The subsequent course of American history, while it may not definitively settle the matter, certainly suggests that Madison had a point here.

Yet the persistent concern about the quality of democratic life in America more than suggests that Jefferson, too, had a point of continuing value, and that the amalgam for which he stands continues to have power in the political culture. Today, as since the early days of the republic, we live in a tension between Jeffersonian and Madisonian versions of natural rights republicanism, or, put differently, between the expressive and the instrumental dimensions of republicanism. The debate between liberals and communitarians is the contemporary form in which this tension persists. I know of no simple way to resolve this tension—perhaps it should not be resolved. The American amalgam, perhaps, is just such a tension as the Greek philosopher Heraclitus described: it is such a thing as "agrees at variance with itself; it is an attunement turning back on itself, like that of the bow and the lyre."[133]

Notes

Introduction

1. Jefferson to Henry Lee, May 8, 1825, *Writings*, 1501.
2. Pangle, *Ennobling*, 9–10.
3. Cf. ibid., 92–93.
4. Rahe, *Republics*, 336.
5. *The Federalist*, no. 14. cf. Pangle, *Spirit*, 8.
6. Grotius, *On the Law of War and Peace*, Prologue, 57.
7. Locke, *Educational Writings*, 400.
8. Jefferson to Weightman, June 24, 1826, *Writings*, 1516–17.
9. Cf. Pangle, *Spirit*, 2.
10. See also my *Natural Rights and the New Republicanism* as something of a "prequel" to this volume.
11. See, e.g., Sheldon, *Jefferson*, 148–70; Kloppenberg, "Virtues of Liberalism," 12–18.
12. Pangle, *Spirit*, 7–8.
13. Zuckert, *Natural Rights*, ch. 10.
14. Cf. Pangle, *Ennobling*, 93: "In general, the statesman, if not the philosophers, who founded the new constitutional systems were open to the idea that important residues of the earlier—and in their eyes to some extent nobler—traditions could and should be preserved within the new societies they were in the process of creating."

Part I. Introduction

1. Forrest McDonald, *Novus Ordo Seclorum*, 1.
2. Kloppenberg, "Virtues of Liberalism," 21.

1. On the Declaration of Independence

1. On Beard as an attempt to "desacralize" the Constitution and the American Republic, see Ross, *Origins*, 343; for a good but brief account of Beard, setting him in the context of Progressive historiography, see Webking, *American Revolution*, 1–7.
2. Tyler, "Declaration of Independence," 99; cf. Jones, "Declaration," 3.

3. Perry, "Philosophy of the Declaration," 173; cf. Tyler, "Declaration of Independence," 97–101; Jaffa, *How to Think,* ix–x; Diamond, "American Idea," 4–5; Lutz, *Origins,* 121.

4. Tyler, "Declaration of Independence," 100.

5. E.g., Tyler, "Declaration of Independence," 126; Ekirch, *Challenge,* 29; Lynd, *Intellectual Origins.*

6. Eidelberg, *Silence,* xv, 2, 75, 102.

7. Mace, *Hobbes,* 12.

8. Diamond, "Revolution," 67–68; Jaffa, *Conditions,* 58–59; Boorstin, *Lost World,* 181.

9. Lynd, *Intellectual Origins.*

10. Boorstin, *Purpose,* 70; Coleman, *Hobbes,* 71; Shain, *Myth,* 246–59.

11. Boorstin, *Lost World,* 195–96.

12. White, *Philosophy,* 145–228.

13. Wills, *Inventing,* passim; White, *Philosophy,* 107–27; Lynd, *Intellectual Origins,* 17–37; Cf. Raphael, *British Moralists.*

14. For a defense of Locke as an authority for the Declaration, see Zuckert, *Natural Rights,* 15–27; cf. Sheldon: "the Declaration of Independence relies almost exclusively on . . . John Locke's natural rights philosophy," *Political Philosophy,* 140; also cf. 41–52; Kramnick, *Republicanism,* 293: "Garry Wills notwithstanding, Locke lurks behind [the Declaration's] every phrase"; Gerber, "Declaration of Independence," 214–15.

15. Jefferson to Henry Lee, May 8, 1825, *Writings,* 1501.

16. Webking, *American Revolution,* 100.

17. Adams to Rush, July 22, 1816; Ginsberg, *Casebook,* 25; Dana, "Political Principles," 103. Many recent treatments of the American political tradition fail to take note of the parallels among the Declaration and these other documents. See, for example, Shain, *Myth,* who writes as if the only reference to the natural rights social contract philosophy occurs in one sentence in the Declaration of Independence.

18. E.g., Boorstin, *Purpose,* 80–84; also see Reid, *Authority of Rights,* and Shain, *Myth,* discussed in chap. 4 below.

19. Cf. Reid, *Authority,* 90–92; Bailyn, *Ideological Origins,* 155–57; Webking, *American Revolution,* 99; Adler and Gorman, *Testament,* 21; Jones, "Declaration," 3. For alternate accounts of the Declaration's overall structure, see Mahoney, "Declaration," 56–57; Anastaplo, "Declaration," 391–394; Lence, "Declaration" 31; Sheldon, *Jefferson,* 42; for a very similar account, see Mayer, *The Constitutional Thought.* For a failure to appreciate the deductive, structured character of the Declaration, see Arendt, *On Revolution,* 163ff.

Likewise, a clear understanding of the syllogistic structure of the text helps to clarify the confusion Jacque Derrida found in his bicentennial musings on the Declaration. He finds in the Declaration "an indissoluble mix" of "constative and performative moments," or an "obscurity," and "undecidability between . . . a performative structure and a constative structure." Derrida refers here to the distinctions made by the English philosopher J. L.

Austin between different functions served by linguistic statements that may in form appear the same but in meaning are quite distinct. For example, the sentence or phrase, "I do," may in certain contexts function as a constative statement, as a description of some state of affairs. If one is asked, "who washes the dishes in your house," the answer "I do" functions constatively. If on the other hand, one is in the midst of a wedding ceremony and is asked, "Do you take this . . . ," the answer "I do" is not a description of something but is itself a performance—it is the taking or undertaking in question. As Austin puts it, language does not just describe, it "does things," and the concept of a "performative" is his attempt to capture that dimension of linguistic function.

Derrida rightly insists that the Declaration is a performative: it declares independence, it culminates in the claim that "these colonies are . . . free and independent states," with that declaration performing the very function "I do" performs in a wedding ceremony. Derrida also rightly sees that the Declaration is filled with constative elements—the famous "theoretical" paragraph, for example, with its list of "self-evident" truths, or the long list of "abuses" by the king. He finds the copresence of performative and constative to be an "obscurity" pointing, he suggests, to a deeper obscurity in the character of the foundations.

The relation between performative and constative in the Declaration is nowhere so obscure, however, as Derrida professes to find it, if we keep firmly in mind the syllogistic structure of the text. In the light of Derrida's concerns, we may restate the structure as follows: the "theoretical" portion presents a series of propositions which sum up to the following. If certain conditions are met (government fails "to secure these rights"), then the people has a right "to alter or abolish" the government under which it lives. The long list of grievances has the function of establishing the minor premise: the condition required in the major premise (government fails "to secure these rights") does indeed prevail. The document thus concludes that "these colonies . . . ought to be of right free and independent states" and proceeds to call them such. Derrida is correct to see an "indissoluble mix" of performative and constative elelments, but there is nothing obscure about the relation between them. This "mix" does not, of itself, point to difficulties regarding the foundations of the Declaration, as Derrida suggests it does, but this is not to say there are no questions to be raised about the foundations. The Declaration seems to answer that question by declaring the foundation truths to be "self-evident," but this is a claim to which we must return in later chapters.

20. Cf. Adler and Gorman, *Testament*, 35; Diamond, *As Far*, 213.

21. Webking, *American Revolution*, 100; cf. Adler and Gorman, *Testament*, 32.

22. Jefferson to John Adams, October 1813, in *Writings*, 1305–6. On natural aristocracy more broadly for the founding generation, see Morgan, *Inventing*, 245–54.

23. *Two Treatises*, II, 54.

24. *Two Treatises*, II, 95, cf. II, 6, 7.

25. Cf. Mahoney, "Declaration," 60; McDonald, *Novus Ordo*, 53, 63.

26. Cf. Wood, *Creation*, 535; Diamond, *As Far*, 214–15; Webking, *American Revolution*, 101.

27. Cf., e.g. Engeman, "Liberalism, Republicanism and Ideology," 332–33.

28. Sandel, *Liberalism and Its Critics*, 5; cf. Delaney, *Liberalism Debate*, vii–x; Mulhall and Swift, *Liberals and Communitarians*, viii–xiii.

29. Wood, *Radicalism*, 234.

30. On "created," see chap. 3 below.

31. MacIntyre, *After Virtue*, esp. 58, 233–34.

32. Cf., e.g., Lutz, *Origins*, 29, and the link to communitarianism through religion.

33. Kendall and Carey, *Basic Symbols*, 155; also see Lence, "Declaration," 52–53; Reid, *Authority of Rights*, 84, but cf. 85; Shain, *Myth*, 252.

34. See Pangle and Pangle, *Learning of Liberty*, 108–9.

35. To see the natural rights/social contract philosophy as moral history or as rational reconstruction is related to, but much preferable to Morgan's labeling it a fiction. (*Inventing*, passim.)

36. Hooker, *Ecclesiastical Polity*, I, x, 4; Locke, *Two Treatises*, II, 15.

37. An example of the confusion on this issue is Eidelberg, *Silence*, 12–14.

38. E.g., Eidelberg, *Silence*, 4–5, 31; Koch, *Power*, 44.

39. Adler and Gorman, *Testament*, 34–35.

40. Jaffa, *How to Think*, 35, 41–51, 59–60; cf. Sanford Levinson, *Constitutional Faith*, 59–65, 88.

41. Cf. Jones, "Declaration," 10.

42. E.g., White, *Philosophy*, 142–84; Adler and Gorman, *Testament*, 33–34.

43. *Contra* Webking, *American Revolution*, 100: "Natural equality and independence . . . result in human beings' having certain rights"; and Adler and Gorman, *Testament*, 34.

44. Cf. Gerber, "Declaration," 230: "the essential premise of the American Founding is that government exists to secure natural rights, not to cultivate virtue."

45. Cf. Tocqueville, *Democracy*, II, 2; Goldwin and Schambra, eds., *How Capitalistic Is the Constitution?*

46. Diamond, *As Far*, 213–15.

47. *Contra* Arendt, *On Revolution*, 198.

48. Diamond, *As Far*, 214.

49. Locke, *Two Treatises*, II, 119.

50. Jaffa, *How to Think*, 119. For a good account of the ambiguities in the relations between the natural rights philosophy and republican forms, see Pangle, *Ennobling*, 93–97.

51. Jaffa, *How to Think*, 119.

52. Cf. Adler and Gorman, *Testament*, 42.

53. Zuckert, *Natural Rights*, chap. 1; Schochet, *Patriarchalism;* Wood, *Radicalism*, 184.

54. Cf. Zuckert, *Natural Rights*, 19–20; Lynn, "Falsifying"; Jaffa, "Inventing"; cf. the parallel move in Lutz, *Origins*, 29.

55. Cf. Thomas Jefferson to Peter Carr, August 10, 1787, *Writings*, 901.

56. Wills, *Inventing*, 211; cf. 213, 224, 225, 227.

57. Ibid., 210.

58. Ibid., 211.

59. Ibid., 207–9, 228.

60. Eidelberg, *Silence*, 4.

61. Ibid., 5.

62. Ibid., 31.

63. According to Donald Lutz, Burlamaqui did not even register in the top thirty-five most frequently cited secular thinkers during the founding era. (Neither did Hutcheson.) Lutz, *Origins*, 142.

64. White, *Philosophy*, 37.

65. It is thus difficult to see why McDonald calls White's link to Burlamaqui "convincing" (*Novus Ordo Seclorum*, 60n5).

66. White, *Philosophy*, 162.

67. Ibid., 164–65. A derivation of the Declaration's rights very much along the lines of White's version of Burlamaqui is presented by Adler and Gorman, *Testament*, 37–41. The same difficulties beset their account as beset White's.

68. White, *Philosophy*, 165.

69. Ibid., 147–48.

70. Ibid., 145–47.

71. Ibid., 149.

72. Ibid., 149.

73. Ibid., 149.

74. Virginia Bill of Rights, Art. I; Massachusetts Bill of Rights, Pt. I, Art. I.

75. Burlamaqui, *Principles*, I, xi.

76. Ibid., I.iv, 7–8.

2. NATURAL RIGHTS AND THE QUESTION OF SELF-EVIDENCE

1. Mahoney, "The Declaration," 59.

2. Henry Steele Commager, *Jefferson*, xi.

3. Ibid., 82.

4. Levinson, "Self-Evident Truths," 856; cf. Anastaplo, "The Declaration," 398–99; Rahe, *Republicans*, 710; Adler and Gorman, *Testament*, 29–30.

5. Eva Brann, "Concerning the Declaration" 13; cf. Anastaplo, "The Declaration," 396. Also cf. Pangle, *Ennobling*, 10: "The questionableness of modern philosophies of natural rights . . . is today very widely acknowledged."

6. Levinson, "Self-Evident Truths," 858.

7. Jefferson to Henry Lee, May 8, 1825, in Peterson, ed., *Jefferson*, 1501.

8. Jefferson to Roger C. Weightman, June 24, 1826, in ibid., 1517.

9. Morton White is thus almost certainly incorrect in claiming that the presentation of the Americans' argument with the aim of "showing a decent respect to the opinions of mankind" implied that they expected the rest of mankind to be persuaded by their statement or to agree with their action (White, *Philosophy*, 10, 14; cf. Commager, *Jefferson*, 80). Rather, they express respect for the opinion that grave political actions such as they were taking need to be defended, if standards of right and wrong are to have any sway in the world of politics. The Americans followed Locke in not desiring to give "just occasion, to think that all government in the World is the product only of Force and Violence, and that men live together by no other Rules, but that of Beasts, where the strongest carries it, and so lay a Foundation in perpetual Disorder and Mischief, Tumult, Sedition and Rebellion." In giving reasons, the Americans admitted the sway of reason, and of moral and political principle, thereby eschewing mere appeal to force or will. (John Locke, *Two Treatises*, II, 1.)

10. Howell, "The Declaration of Independence," 205–6; cf. Brann, "Concerning," 13.

11. Howell, "The Declaration of Independence," 198–99. Morton White, *Philosophy*, 11–14.

12. Thomas Aquinas, *Summa Theologica*, 1–2, Q. 94, A 2.

13. John Locke, *An Essay Concerning Human Understanding*, I.iii. passim; see esp. sec. 13.

14. Locke, *Essay* I.ii; IV.vi–viii.

15. Howell, "The Declaration," 205–6 (emphasis in original); cf. John Locke, *Essay* IV.vii.1–7.

16. Locke, *Essay* IV.vii.2 (emphasis in the original).

17. Richard Price, *A Review of the Principal Questions and Difficulties in Morals*, quoted in Lynd, *Intellectual Origins*, 28.

18. Martin Diamond, "Revolution," 64. Cf. Jaffa, *How to Think*, 105; Brann, "Concerning," 13–14; Adler and Gorman, *Testament*, 30.

19. Koch, *Power*, 26.

20. Ginsberg, "The Declaration as Rhetoric," 227.

21. Arendt, *On Revolution*, 193.

22. Jefferson to Peter Carr, August 10, 1787, in *Writings*, 430.

23. Cf. White, *Philosophy*, 9–96.

24. Cf. Berns, "Religion and the Founding Principle," 204–29.

25. Webking, *American Revolution*, 100: "the conclusion that people may revolt follows from the other truths."

26. An appreciation of the character of the "we hold" and of the truths so held helps clarify the confusion Hannah Arendt attributes to the Declaration in *On Revolution*, 192.

27. Adler and Gorman, *Testament*, 31.

28. Adler and Gorman concede at the end that "created equal" cannot be self-evident either, for the claim about creation either rests on faith or on complex arguments of natural theology. *Testament*, 33.

29. White (*Philosophy*, pp. 78–94) maintained that Hamilton appealed to self-evident truths, but it is revealing that White cannot produce an actual use of the term by Hamilton. White does cite a passage where James Otis uses the phrase "self-evident," but it is clear Otis is using the term in a different way, for he defended colonial rights by saying these were "self-evident . . . to everyone in the least versed in the laws of nature and nations, or but moderately skilled in the common law." Clearly Otis is not using "self-evidence" in the epistemological sense here; he is speaking loosely of self-evidence, for the truths are not actually said to be "evident in themselves" but evident by reference to other propositions—those of the laws of nature and nations and the common law.

30. Locke, *Two Treatises* II, 54.

31. Arendt, *On Revolution*, 195; on true opinion as the virtue of citizens, see Aristotle, *Politics* 1277.b25–30.

32. It is difficult to identify the "standard account" of self-evident truths in the literature. Many scholars more or less ignore it, and others fall into readily understandable confusions on the subject. An example of the latter is Martin Diamond's otherwise fine work on the Declaration. He concludes at one point that the "truths do not arise by inference one from the other but are each equally and independently self-evident." Yet a few lines later he observes that "the final, self-evident truth . . . is obviously ancillary to" one of the other truths, ancillary here being a softer way of saying, "derivative from." (Diamond, "Revolution," 64–65.) Confused in a similar way is Harry V. Jaffa, *How to Think*, 108, 109, 111, 132.

33. E.g., John Dunn, "Politics of Locke"; Wills, *Inventing America.*

34. White, *Philosophy*, 65 (emphasis added).

35. Ibid. 48, 97; cf. 77, 94.

36. Ibid. 23–53.

37. Locke, *Questions*, 157.

38. Ibid. (emphasis added).

39. White, *Philosophy*, 65. Cf. also Jaffa, *How to Think*, 109.

40. Locke, *Two Treatises*, II, 4 (emphasis added); cf. White, *Philosophy*, 65ff.; Jaffa, *How to Think*, 40, 109–10.

41. White, *Philosophy*, 65; cf. also Jaffa, *How to Think*, 109.

42. Locke, *Essay* II.iv.7.

43. Ibid., IV.x. Cf. Michael P. Zuckert, "An Introduction to Locke's *First Treatise*," 70; William T. Bluhm et al., "Locke's Idea of God," 414–38.

44. Cf. Locke, *Essay*, IV.vii.12–20.

45. White, *Philosophy*, 178, citing Locke, *Essay* I.iii.4.

46. White, *Philosophy*, 14, 164ff.

47. Ibid., 161.

48. Ibid., 77.

49. Ibid., 161.

50. Ibid., 77.

51 Jefferson to Madison, August, 30, 1823, in Ginsberg, *A Casebook,* 30–31. In general, cf. Rahe, *Republics,* 603, 705, 710–11.

52. Thus I cannot accept James Kloppenberg's conclusion that White is our most reliable guide to the philosophy of the Declaration. Kloppenberg, "Virtues of Liberalism," 21.

53. Eva Brann, "Concerning the Declaration," 1. Also cf. her *Paradoxes of Education in the Republic,* chap. 1.

54. Jefferson, "Minutes of the Board of Visitors, University of Virginia, 1822–1825" in Peterson, ed., *Jefferson,* 479.

3. On Nature and Natural Rights

1. See, e.g., Hanson, *The Democratic Imagination* 162, 179–80, 228.

2. J. G. A. Pocock, *Machiavellian Movement;* John Phillip Reid, *The Authority of Rights;* Derrida, *Otobiographies;* Rorty, *Contingency, Irony and Solidarity;* Glendon, *Rights Talk,* 14; Pangle, *Ennobling,* 26–29.

3. *Federalist* 14, p. 104

4. Thomas Jefferson said almost fifty years after the Declaration of Independence, but very much in its spirit, "our Revolution . . . presented us an album on which we were free to write what we pleased. We had no occasion to search into musty records, to hunt up royal parchments, or to investigate the laws and institutions of a semi-barbarous ancestry. We appealed to those of nature, and found them engraved on our hearts." Jefferson to Major John Cartwright, June 5, 1824, in Peterson, ed., *Jefferson,* 1491.

5. Cf. Pangle, *Ennobling:* "the preamble to a piece of legislation or even to a constitution cannot be a treatise on political theory" (129).

6. Peterson, *Thomas Jefferson and the New Nation,* 249.

7. Ibid., 250. Cf. the similar point in Miller, *Jefferson and Nature,* 18, 36–37, and in Mansfield, "Jefferson," 23–50. Wilson, "Jefferson and the Republic of Letters," makes the broader point that Jefferson probably was already planning a work such as *Notes,* and that Marbois's queries merely proved a convenient occasion for him to set down his thoughts (54–55, 57).

8. Jefferson, *Notes,* in Peterson, ed., *Jefferson,* 154.

9. Genesis 7:17–24. Cf. Wills, *Inventing America,* 263.

10. Jefferson, *Notes,* 154; cf. 211. Cf. Jaffa, "Humanizing Certitudes," 116–17.

11. For a statement very much in the spirit of Jefferson's, and probably consciously echoing him, see John Adams's letter to Jefferson of September 14, 1813, in Cappon, ed., *Letters,* 373. Cf. Brann, "Concerning the Declaration"; Jaffa, *How to Think.*

12. Jefferson, *Notes,* 155, and Miller, *Jefferson and Nature,* 23, 26, 92, 94, 156 n. 4, 165. But cf. 32, 50.

13. Jefferson, *Notes,* 155.

14. Jefferson to Peter Carr, August 10, 1787, in Peterson, ed., *Jefferson*, 902. Cf. Anastaplo, "Declaration of Independence," 405.

15. *Notes*, 168–69; cf. 170, 176.

16. Here and elsewhere in his writings Jefferson is quite allusive as to his views on the ultimate relation of God and nature, and on the nature of God: He is clearest in rejecting the biblical notion of a God who acts independently of nature; he accepts neither miracles nor special revelation. On the other hand he tends to distance himself from the atheistic view that nature can be understood entirely self-sufficiently. Behind nature, he often affirms, stands some sort of intelligence and purpose, but this intelligence and purpose operates solely through nature. This is the deism which has often been noted as central to his understanding of God and nature. On at least one occasion, however, Jefferson suggested that gap between his deism (or as he called it, theism), and atheism was not so great. See his letter to Adams of April 8, 1816 (Cappon, ed., *Letters*, 467–68), and the letter to Thomas Law, June 13, 1814 (Peterson, ed., *Jefferson*, 1336). For a general discussion, see Conkin, "Religious Pilgrimmage," 21, 25.

17. Cf. Jefferson to John Cartwright, June 5, 1829 (in Peterson, ed., *Jefferson*), 493–94.

18. Ibid, 289. Cf. Anastaplo, "Declaration," 405–6.

19. For a similar understanding of "Creator," see Brann, "Concerning the Declaration of Independence," 7, 9. Consider Conkin's conclusion that Thomas Jefferson was "one who always saw, as the highest goal of religion, a support for righteousness." "Religious Pilgrimmage," 24; cf. 46.

20. Jefferson to Francis Eppes, January 19, 1829 (in Peterson, ed., *Jefferson*, 1451). Jefferson also knew of "safety" as an issue for writers. See his letter to Adams, October 14, 1816, in Cappon, ed., *Letters*, 491. For an assessment of Jefferson's great debt to Bolingbroke, especially on questions of religion, see Conkin, "Religious Pilgrimmage," 23.

21. See Appendix to this chapter, "On Reading Jefferson."

22. *Notes*, 127.

23. Cf. Miller, *Jefferson and Nature*, 26.

24. *Notes*, 143.

25. Ibid., 148.

26. Ibid.

27. Ibid.

28. Cf. the alternate conventionalist reading in Wills, *Inventing*, 259–72.

29. Pascal, *Pensées*, no. 68. Miller in *Jefferson and Nature* misses this dimension of the experience; see 104–5.

30. See *Notes*, 174, on themes of fear and free government.

31. On Jefferson's own utilitarian attitude toward science, see his letter to Adams, October 14, 1816, in Cappon, ed., *Letters*, 491. *Contra* Miller, *Jefferson and Nature*, 27, 101–4.

32. Jefferson to Adams, April 11, 1823, in Peterson, ed., *Jefferson*, 1467; Conkin, "Religious Pilgrimmage," would do better to cast Thomas Jeffer-

son's religious views in terms of rational theology than in terms of "semitic cosmology" vs. the "specifically Christian" (see, e.g., Conkin, 20–21).

33. Jefferson's statement also needs to be considered in the light of the principles of reading described in the Appendix to this chapter. It is true that Adams and Jefferson by 1823 were intimates, having corresponded regularly and more or less candidly since 1812. But there were definite limits to their candor (see the Appendix for an example). The letter begins with a typical Jeffersonian gesture of agreement with his correspondent: "The being described in [John Calvin's] 5 points is not *the God whom you and I acknowledge and adore . . .*" (emphasis added). This gesture responds to a long-standing expression by Adams of a need for a divinity in whose hands is divine consolation. For at least the previous six or seven years he had been writing to Jefferson of his hopes for another life, for a dualistic universe of spirit and matter, and for a God who could support that hope. For many years Jefferson had noticeably failed to join his voice in reassurance of Adams's hopes, but in 1823 he finally did so.

34. Jefferson to Adams, April 8, 1816, in Peterson, ed., *Jefferson*, pp. 1382–83. Conkin ("Religious Pilgrimmage") pays no heed to this side of Jefferson's thought.

35. On Jefferson's argument from order, consider Locke, *Essay Concerning Human Understanding*, IV x, and Zuckert, "An Introduction to Locke's *First Treatise*," 70–74. Relevant also is Jefferson's materialism (cf. Jefferson to Adams, August 15, 1820) and his epicureanism (Jefferson to William Smith, October 31, 1819).

36. Jefferson to John Trumbull, February 5, 1789, in Peterson, ed., *Jefferson*, 939.

37. *Notes*, 185–86.

38. Ibid., 183.

39. Ibid., 169, 182; *contra* Miller, *Jefferson and Nature*, 63.

40. Cf. to the contrary, ibid., 3, 63, 65.

41. *Notes*, 170. Emphasis in the original.

42. Quoted in *Notes*, 183.

43. Cf. Miller, *Jefferson and Nature*, 64; Matthews, *Radical Politics*, 54.

44. Ibid., 183–88.

45. *Contra* Miller, *Jefferson and Nature*, 12–13, but cf. also 56, 59, 61. Cf. Matthews, *Radical Politics*, 34, 53, 56. Cf. Shklar, "Redeeming American Political Theory," 5.

46. *Notes*, 184–85. Cf. Miller, *Jefferson and Nature*, 64; Matthews, *Radical Politics*, 54.

47. *Notes*, 220. Cf. Jefferson to James Madison, January 30, 1787, in Peterson, *Jefferson*, 882: "[some] societies exist . . . without government, as among our Indians." Also cf. Jefferson to William Ludlow, September 6, 1824, in Peterson, ed., *Jefferson*, 1496: the Indians "live under no law but that of nature."

48. John Locke, *Two Treatises of Government*, II, 87; cf. Miller, *Jefferson and Nature*, 158–59; Jefferson to Thomas Mann Randolph, May 30, 1790, (in Jefferson, *Selected Writings*), ed. Koch and Peden, 496–97.

49. *Notes*, 220; on Locke, cf. Pangle, *Spirit*, chap. 19.

50. Ibid. 185–86.

51. Ibid., (Emphasis added.)

52. Ibid., 186. On the opposition between right and self-love, see Jefferson to Pierre S. Dupont de Nemours, April 24, 1816, in Peterson, ed., *Jefferson*, 1386.

53. The distinction between the moral sense as an epistemological and a practical faculty can be overdrawn, however. According to Jefferson, the moral sense is not purely cognitive, for "every human mind feels pleasure in doing good to another," a feeling deriving from the moral sense, just as the other senses also include pleasure and pain; and pleasure and pain are motives to action. Jefferson to Adams, October 14, 1816, in Cappon, *Letters*, 492; Jefferson to Law, June 13, 1814, in Peterson, ed. *Jefferson*, 1337.

54. *Notes*, 255; on the war of all against all, see also Jefferson to Madison, January 1, 1797, in Peterson, ed., *Jefferson*, 1039. But cf. Jefferson to Samuel Kercheval, July 12, 1816, in ibid., 1401. On Hobbes, see Jefferson to Adams, October 14, 1816, in Cappon, *Letters*, 492.

55. Jefferson to Law, June 13, 1814, in Peterson, ed., *Jefferson*, 1338.

56. *Notes*, 186.

57. Cf. the interesting but very different account of the origins of rights in nature in Larry Arnhart, "Charles Darwin and the Declaration of Independence," unpublished paper, American Political Science Association, 1982, 3, 5, 17–19, 22, 29. Arnhart develops a "biologism" more akin to Buffon than to Jefferson. The same might be said of Jacques Derrida's attempts to undermine natural standards of right in "Racism's Last Word," and of his *Otobiographies*, 13–32. See especially the extension of Derrida's argument to the Declaration in Catherine H. Zuckert's "Derrida and the Politics of Deconstruction."

58. For a clear indication of the degree to which rights supplant the moral sense as the basis for political society, cf. Jefferson's letter to John Norvell, June 11, 1807, in Peterson, ed., *Jefferson*, 1176.

59. Wills, *Inventing*, 215–16, cf. 213. In tracing Jefferson's moral philosophy back to the Scottish Enlightenment, Wills follows Gilbert Chinard, "Jefferson Among the Philosophers," *Ethics* 53:258. As Chinard shows, however, Jefferson more explicitly looked to Lord Kames, who had in turn rejected Hutcheson. Cf. Jefferson to Thomas Law, June 13, 1814, in Peterson, ed., *Jefferson*, 1338.

60. Michael J. Perry, *Morality, Politics, and Law*, 185. Cf. Tibor Machan, *Individuals and Their Rights*, 98, and the summary discussion of the differences between right and rights in Richard Tuck, *Natural Rights Theories*, chap. 1.

The *locus classicus* for the distinction is, of course, Hobbes, *Leviathan*, chap. 13.

61. For Locke, the fundamental natural rights are not themselves surrendered (alienated) when civil society is formed, but rather the "executive power of the law of nature." Locke, *Two Treatises*, II, 89. But on Locke's rights as not inalienable, see A. John Simmons, "Inalienable Rights and Locke's *Treatises*."

62. Wills, *Inventing*, 215.

63. A more comprehensive reconsideration of the moral sense in Jefferson is necessary than can be attempted here. Not only is Jefferson's replacement of the moral sense with the system of rights relevant to this reconsideration, but so is his frequent alignment of himself on moral issues within schools of thought contrary to the moral sense position. Consider especially his self-identification as an Epicurean. (Jefferson to William Short, October 31, 1819; cf. Miller, *Jefferson and Nature*, 98ff.) In general, Jefferson's discussions of the moral sense need to be considered in the light of his attitude toward Bolingbroke. Consider also Pangle, *Spirit*, 117–21; Matthews, *Radical Politics*, 91–92; Diggins, "Slavery, Race, and Equality," 208. A serious attempt to reconcile these various strains of Jefferson's thought is Griswold, "Rights and Wrongs."

64. Jefferson to Madison, January 1, 1797, in Peterson, ed., *Jefferson*, 1039. Cf. Kloppenberg's judgement: "Jefferson was optimistic about the harmonious interaction of individuals only because he believed their inner moral gyroscopes would prevent them from oppressing each other." Kloppenberg, "Virtues," 22.

65. Jefferson to P.S. Dupont de Nemours, April 24, 1816, in Peterson, ed., *Jefferson*, 1387.

66. Jefferson to Weightman, June 24, 1826, in Peterson, ed., *Jefferson*, 1517.

67. Jefferson to Dupont de Nemours, 1387.

68. Ibid.

69. Ibid.

70. For Jefferson's recognition that all human beings are not equally insecure in their rights, and for the role of the invention of gunpowder as the "great equalizer," see his letter to Adams, October 28, 1813, in Peterson, ed., *Jefferson*, 1305.

71. Cf. Morton White, *The Philosophy of the American Revolution*, chaps. 4–5.

72. Cf. Jefferson to Peter Carr, Aug. 10, 1787, in Peterson, ed., *Jefferson*, 903.

73. The document Dupont had sent to Jefferson, to which the latter was replying, was titled, "Mémoire aux Republiques Equinoxiales." On its fate, see Ambrose Saricks, *Pierre Samuel Dupont de Nemours*, 346. This is clearly another case of Jefferson's accommodating style in personal correspondence, as discussed in the Appendix to this chapter. Nonetheless, Jefferson forcefully, if gently, made clear the areas where he disagreed with his friend's

political projection for the new republics of South America. The context may account for his inclusions and omissions, for he introduced the discussion of rights with the phrase, "I believe with you [Dupont,] that. . . ." He appears to have given explicit mention to themes which appeared in the discussion of politics that Dupont had sent to him. We cannot specify with certainty the precise relationship between Jefferson's discussion and Dupont's, however, for the latter's tract has been lost.

74. Jefferson, "Address to the Chiefs of the Cherokee Nation," January 10, 1810, in Peterson, ed., *Jefferson*, 561.

75. Jefferson to Dupont de Nemours, 1387.

76. E.g., Wills, *Inventing*, 229–55; McDonald, *Novus Ordo*, ix–x; White, *Political Philosophy*, 213–28. For other places where Jefferson affirms a right to property, see Jefferson to Adams, October 28, 1813, in Peterson, ed., *Jefferson*, 1306; Jefferson to Kercheval, July 22, 1816, in ibid., 1398; Jefferson to Brother Handsome Lake, November 1, 1802, in ibid., 556; "Address to the Chiefs of the Cherokee Nation," January 10, 1806, in ibid., 561.

77. Matthews, *Radical Politics*, 27; consider also Adler and Gorman's moderate stance on the property right: *Testament*, 38–40.

78. Article I.

79. Part I, Article I.

80. Locke, *Two Treatises* II 26: "The fruit or venison, which nourishes the wild Indian . . . must be his, and so his, i.e., a part of him, that another can no longer have any right to it, before it can do him any good for the support of his life." For discussion, see Zuckert, *Natural Rights*, 252–72. For an account of the right to property that denies the paradox of making the external one's own, see Rasmussen and Den Uyl, *Liberty and Nature*, 115–29.

81. Miller, *Jefferson and Nature*, 200.

82. Jefferson nowhere indicates any doubts about the human practice of treating other animals as property, but he does not accept the principle that other human beings can rightfully be treated as property. Except for the fact that much nonsense is frequently written on the subject, it would be certainly superfluous to mention Jefferson's denial of slavery's congruence with the principles of natural right. Cf. his draft of the Declaration (Peterson, ed., *Jefferson*, 22), *Notes*, (Ibid., 270, 288–89).

83. "Message to the Brothers of the Choctaw Nation," December 17, 1803, in Peterson, ed., *Jefferson*, 559. Cf. Locke, *Two Treatises*, II, 40–46; Zuckert, *Natural Rights and New Republicanism*, chap. 9. An instructive recent exchange over the liberal grounding of property is Ian Shapiro, "Resources, capacities, and Ownership," and James B. Murphy, "The Workmanship Ideal," and Shapiro, "Workmanship Revisited."

84. I have presented here only the broad outlines of Jefferson's doctrine on the right to property. A fuller discussion would need to take account of the implications of inequality in property holdings, and circumstances in which something like a right to welfare might emerge.

85. Jefferson to Dupont de Nemours, in Peterson, ed., *Jefferson*, 1387.

86. McDonald, *Novus Ordo*, ix–xi, cf. also Brann, "Considering," 12, for an Aristotelian reading.

87. Locke, *Essay* II.xxi.62.

88. Ibid., II.xxi.51.

89. *Ibid.*, II.xxi.59.

90. *Ibid.*, II.xxi.57.

91. Cf. Locke, *Two Treatises*, I.86; II.25; consider the intelligent but quite different discussion of "pursuit of happiness" in Adler and Gorman, *Testament*, 40–41.

92. Locke's doctrines of happiness, and of the pursuit of happiness were not developed until he set out to revise his original treatment of free will and necessity for late editions of the *Essay*. The *Essay*'s first edition, not containing the doctrine of happiness, was published in 1690; it is no surprise that the *Treatises on Government* did not contain it. Given the easy fit into his basic way of thinking about politics, however, I speculate that had he undertaken a substantive revision of the *Treatises*, as he did of the *Essay*, he might well have included it among the rights which receive special mention. In other words, Mason and Jefferson's elevation of the pursuit of happiness into one of the basic rights may well accord with Locke's intent. Cf. Strauss, *Natural Right*, 226–27.

93. Hamowy, "Jefferson and the Scottish Enlightenment," 549.

94. *Contra* Miller, *Jefferson and Nature*, 40.

95. Jefferson, "Autobiography," in Peterson, ed., *Jefferson*, 5. Cf. also his "First Inaugural Address," on "the equal rights" of minorities, which "equal law must protect." Ibid., 493.

96. Miller, *Jefferson and Nature*, 167.

97. Reid, *Constitutional History*, chaps. 1–7.

98. *The Federalist*, 51, 322.

99. On the character of the founders' constitutional science as political science rather than constitutional law, see Zuckert, "What Next for Constitutional Studies," pp. 35–38.

100. E.g., Jefferson to Adams, August 22, 1813, in Cappon, *The Adams-Jefferson Letters*, 369.

101. Jefferson to John Taylor, in Peterson, ed., *Jefferson*, 1391.

102. Jefferson to Law, June 13, 1814, in Peterson, ed., *Jefferson*, 1335; Jefferson to Short, October 31, 1819, ibid., 1430.

103. Jefferson to Thomas Jefferson Randolph, November 24, 1808, ibid., 1994. For a very striking case of Jefferson's accommodations to his interlocutor, see Jefferson to Adams, March 14, 1820, in Cappon, *Letters*, 562.

PART II INTRODUCTION

1. Tocqueville, *Democracy*, vol. 1, pt. I, chap. 2.

2. *Zorach v. Clausen* (1952).

3. Cf. Jeffrey Poelvoorde, "American Civil Religion."

4. Tocqueville, *Democracy*. I.1.2.

5. The position taken here is perhaps closest to that developed in Pangle, *Ennobling*. See especially his chapters 7–9. He too pursues the notion of America as an amalgam of natural rights philosophy and other ("nobler") traditions, which are not perfectly harmonious with each other. We differ in our assessments of the natural rights philosophy, both as to its role in the creation of the amalgam and as to its philosophical adequacy. See Pangle, *Ennobling*, 93, 155.

4. NATURAL RIGHTS AND HISTORY: AMERICAN WHIGS AND ENGLISH WHIGS

1. Kendall and Carey, *Basic Symbols*, 26.

2. Randolph Adams, *Political Ideas*, 100, 136; Rossiter, *Seedtime*, 315.

3. On the first claim, consider Daniel Boorstin, *The Genius of American Politics*, 66–98; Lutz, *Origins of American Constitutionalism*, 114; on the second, see Reid, *The Authority of Rights;* "Irrelevance of the Declaration"; Conrad, "Putting Rights-Talk in Its Place."

4. Cf. Pocock, "The Fourth English Civil War," 161–64; Dickinson, "How Revolutionary," 127; Franklin, *Locke and the Theory of Sovereignty*, 87–126.

5. Rahe, *Republics*, 525.

6. Dickinson, *Liberty and Property*, 175; cf. Kenyon, "The Revolution of 1688," 47; Morgan, *Inventing the People*, 112.

7. Quoted in Perry, "The Philosophy of the Declaration," 173; on the contrast between the English and the Americans, see Morgan, *Inventing*, 121.

8. Morgan, *Inventing*, chaps. 5, 10. Also see Pangle, *Ennobling*, 148.

9. Cf. Morgan, *Inventing*, 256: "The English people never, even fictionally, exercised their constituent power outside Parliament."

10. Schwoerer, *Declaration*, 74–78.

11. Straka, *Anglican Reaction to the Revolution of 1688*; Kenyon, *Revolution Principles*, 4–34; Dickinson, "How Revolutionary," 127–28; Rahe, *Republics*, 525.

12. See Zuckert, "Lincoln and the Problem of Civil Religion," 722–23.

13. Tocqueville, *Democracy*, I.2.6.

14. Cf. Morgan, *Inventing*, 116: "the statements of principle were not presented as a new original contract, and William was not asked to accept these as a condition of his accession to the throne." But see Rakove, "Parchment Barriers," 109.

15. Suarez, *De Legibus* I.ii.5.

16. For a fuller discussion of the ancient constitution and its Aristotelian connections, see Zuckert, *Natural Rights*, prologue and chap. 2. Cf. Morgan, *Inventing*, 102, who rightly emphasizes the Whigs' "adherence to the ancient constitution of king, lords, and commons, but he certainly goes beyond the Declaration of Rights when he attaches this to popular sovereignty in any

form (102; see also 108, 113). Morgan's better second thought is on p. 120: "The Convention's restraint meant that England did not achieve—and never would—a formulation and establishment of its constitution by a popular sanction or authority separate from its government." This is not to say contractarian ideas did not put in an appearance at the time of the Declaration of Rights. They did, although except for Locke's *Two Treatises*, the contractarianism of 1688–89 was far different from that of the American Declaration of Independence. See Zuckert, *Natural Rights*, Prologue, chaps. 2–3; Morgan, *Inventing*, 105, 111.

17. Morgan, *Inventing*, 120.

18. Reid, *The Authority of Rights*, 5, 18. Differing only slightly from Reid is Barry Shain, *Myth*, 246ff.

19. Reid, *The Authority of Rights*, 87–92. The last-quoted formulations indicate the point of reference out of which Reid's formulation and questions arise: the twentieth-century debate over whether courts can appeal to nontextual "fundamental rights." The authority for such an appeal is frequently said to be the theory and practice of the founders. Consider Thomas Grey, "Unwritten Constitution," and Suzanna Sherry, "The Founders' Unwritten Constitution." However, also consider Reid's concern to rebut those who see the colonists as "shifting ground" in the course of the prerevolutionary conflict (5, 10, 25, 26, 80).

20. Reid also attaches special importance to the resolves accepted by the Virginia House of Burgesses in May 1765. The resolves, protesting the Stamp Act, constitute "the first official list of claimed rights." (*Authority of Rights*, 18–19.) A very fine discussion of these resolutions can be found in Webking, *American Revolution*, 30–40. I would add but two points to Webking. The fifth resolution insists that all efforts to tax by any authority other than the Virginia Legislature are "illegal, unconstitutional and unjust." (Commager, *Documents*, I, 56.) These are not merely three ways to say the same thing, as Reid concedes regarding the nonlegal character of the constitution. The appeal to justice is, in the context, an appeal to nature, most likely to natural justice as understood in the natural rights philosophy. Likewise, the proposed sixth and seventh resolutions, denying any duty to obey illegally imposed taxes, and declaring those who even claim or defend the right to impose them "enemies" of Virginia, respectively, seem to have the natural right philosophy's right of revolution as conceptual background. Shain's study suffers from many of the same limitations as Reid's. See Shain, *Myth*, 246ff.

21. Stoner, *Common Law and Liberal Theory*, 187.

22. Reid, *Authority of Rights*, 5, 40–46, 94.

23. Cf. Stoner, *Common Law and Liberal Theory* (189): "The influence of Locke on the doctrine of natural rights and revolution is unimpeachable, and Locke's theory, however much it echoed and then influenced English practice, begins as a theory of abstract right. But at least as much as Locke ever intended, into that theory were integrated doctrines and practices of

English common lawyers and their notion of an ancient constitution. . . .The abstract doctrines were assimilated to the well-clothed frame of common law. . . . Jefferson . . . illustrates the ability of the common law mind to assimilate that which demonstrates itself to be reasonable and applicable to settling particular issues of right."

24. See Webking, *American Revolution*, 33. Shain, *Myth*, 249, entirely misses this dimension of the Declaration that goes beyond the affirmation of the community's rights to do what it likes. It could not rightly empower the executive to lay taxes without the approval of a representative legislature, for example. As Jefferson said in *Notes on Virginia*: "it was not an elective despotism that we fought for."

25. Mayhew, "Snare," 245.

26. The Declaratory Act asserted "that the King's majesty, by and with the advice and consent of the lords spiritual and temporal, and commons of Great Britain, in Parliament assembled, had, hath, and of right ought to have, full power and authority to make laws and statutes of sufficient force and validity to bind the colonies and people of America, subjects of the crown of Great Britain, in all cases whatsoever." Commager, *Documents*, I, 61. On the British interpretation of the constitution as the ground of British policy, see Greene, "Posture of Hostility," 6–7.

27. Consider Howard Peckham's survey of the curt dismissal the philosophy of the Declaration received in England in 1776, in "The View from Britain," 24–25: "The first reaction of press and public in Great Britain was contempt for the idealogy of the Declaration expressed in its opening." For a good brief statement of a British reaction to American arguments, one which plays on the ambiguities of the British constitution, see Wesley, "A Calm Address," 411–20. Much of the pamphlet in turn is based on Samuel Johnson's *Taxation No Tyranny*. Stoner, *Common Law and Liberal Theory*, 189.

28. Cf. Julian Boyd, "Jefferson's Expression of the American Mind", 342, 362.

29. See the list of grievances in the Declaration of Independence.

30. McDonald, *Novus Ordo Seclorum*, 58–59. Also see Becker, *Declaration of Independence*, chap. 3, and McIlwain, *American Revolution*, 1–8, 191–196.

31. Reid, *Authority of Rights*, 6, 19, 92; cf. 12 on Blackstone (emphasis in the original).

32. "Declaration and Resolves," in Commager, *Documents*, I, 82–84.

33. See McDonald, *Novus Ordo Seclorum*, 57–58.

34. Thomas Whately, *The Regulations Lately Made*; Daniel Dulany, *Considerations on the Propriety of Imposing Taxes*; Richard Bland, "An Inquiry into the Rights." This last is a particularly clear case of the American use of Lockean natural rights arguments to supply a lens to interpret the British constitution, their rights as Englishmen, and their charters. On the role of natural and legal rights in American thinking, also see Bailyn, *Ideological Origins*, 184–88.

35. In some ways similar to Reid, but even more far-reaching in its attempt to dissociate the revolutionary Americans from rights is Stephen Conrad's essay on Jefferson's 1774 document, *A Summary View of the Rights of British America*. Where Reid insists on the importance of rights, but dismisses as irrelevant natural rights, Conrad challenges the view that rights, natural or otherwise, were central. Like Reid, he takes his point of departure from current discussions of rights, in this case from "critics of the hypostatized American 'rights tradition'." Conrad thinks that analysis of Jefferson's *Summary View* shows that these critics, rather than the rights-thinkers they oppose, are "redeeming an authentic Jeffersonian vision." He goes so far as to conclude that "the basic thought of [Jefferson's] argument does not depend on rights talk at all." ("Putting Rights Talk in Its Place," 273, 274).

Conrad "found himself continually questioning the nature and centrality of [Jefferson's] concern over rights" (272). Jefferson himself is "ambivalent" about "how much store to put in rights talk" (265), an ambivalence that reveals itself in three key features of the *Summary View*: (1) Jefferson expresses or implies serious reservations over the efficacy of rights; they are "feeble" and "ineffective" (261–64); (2) Jefferson at one point in his argument "expressly sets aside rights claims," and reverts to the "larger, ultimate standard of justice"; a "much broader conception" than rights (266–267); (3) Jefferson refers in the *Summary View* to many different types of rights, by no means all of them individual rights, and many of them rights of groups. Jefferson cannot therefore be aligned unequivocally with supporters of individual rights. Conrad goes beyond this to claim that the various uses of "rights" in the *Summary View* amount to "conceptually incoherent talk about rights" (268–71).

Some of Conrad's observations are just and accurate, but none of them justifies his conclusions about the noncentrality of rights in the *Summary View* or about the incoherence of Jefferson's understanding of rights. As to (1): Conrad fails to attend to the distinction between the possession of a right and its security. As the Declaration of Independence makes clear, the former does not produce the latter. If it did, government and political science would be unnecessary. Rights supply the purpose and standards; that they are not self-executing does not derogate from their importance or function (cf. Webking, *American Revolution*, 101; Adler and Gorman, *Testament*, 34). As to (2): Conrad does not attend sufficiently to his own insights into the variety of meanings of "rights" and so quite misunderstands Jefferson's move to "set aside rights claims" and look instead to "justice." The rights claims he sets aside are rights in the sense of legitimate or rightful powers of governing bodies. Jefferson had been considering the power (right) of Parliament to pass certain legislation, which he denied, and then turned to consider the character of the legislation itself (its justice). This is not to set aside "rights," or to appeal to a more important criterion than rights. The theory of rights is itself a theory of justice, and the terms can be used quite interchangeably—justice expresses what one is due or has a right to. Moreover, Jefferson clearly expresses the idea that the rightful arrangement of political authority (rights of governing bodies) is related to and ultimately for the sake of just or rightful policy outcomes (Jefferson, *Summary View*, in Peterson, *Jefferson*, 111–12). As to (3): although Conrad is correct to note that Jefferson uses the term "right" in different ways, yet Conrad has not even begun to make out a case that Jefferson is being "conceptually incoherent." I do not believe such a case can be made out, but I suspend judgment until I hear it made. In any case, in contemporary discourse we speak regularly of the rights of individuals: is it a denial of rights that employers hire according to affirmative action criteria? Is it a violation of a woman's rights to prohibit abortion? We also speak of "rights" or powers of governmental bodies: does the president have the right to send troops to Haiti without prior congressional approval, or does Congress have the right to prevent him from so doing? Likewise we speak of rights as constitutional or statutory or "human" (our equivalent to "natural") and do not seem particularly incoherent in doing all of this. Conrad's nearly final conclusion that "on the evidence of the *Summary View*, there is reason to question whether Jefferson ever formulated—or intended to formulate—a philosophy of rights" is really quite gratuitous. The *Summary View* was a political document, prepared as part of a particular political conflict; it would be quite remarkable for Jefferson or anybody to use this as the occasion to develop or present a "philosophy of rights." Such a philosophy, of course, may be presupposed in the document, as I have shown was the case for the Declaration of Independence; I believe the same can be shown for the *Summary View*. For a concise statement on the *Summary View* which nicely brings out the role of rights in it, see Webking, *American Revolution*, 92–98.

36. Jameson, *American Revolution*; Bailyn, *Ideological Origins*, 232–46; Shain, *Myth*, 247.

37. Rahe, *Republics*, 559.

38. Williams, "Essential Rights," 117. On Williams's Lockeanism, see below, chap. 6.

39. For a fuller account of the Grotian character of Whig thought in the late seventeenth century, see Zuckert, *Natural Rights*, chaps. 4–5.

5. Natural Rights and Portestant Politics: The First Generation

1. McWilliams, *Fraternity*, 112–13.

2. Quoted in Miller and Johnson, *Puritans*, I, 199; John Winthrop, "A Modell of Christian Charitie," 93.

3. Levy and Young, "Preface" in *Puritan Political Ideas*, ed. Morgan, v–vi.

4. Charles McLaughlin, *Foundations of American Constitutionalism*, 67–70; Stanley Gray, "Political Thought of John Winthrop," 682. Nock, *Our Enemy the State*, 54–55, 60; consider Judith Shklar's surmise that the rise of the Puritans in American historiography was a reaction against the

nineteenth-century democratization of American society. "American Political Theory," 9.

5. Power, *Before the Convention*, 2, 15, 38, 54.

6. Pangle, *Spirit of Modern Republicanism*, 21.

7. Pangle, *Ennobling*, 97.

8. Edmund S. Morgan, *Puritan Political Ideas,* xii; also see his "The Puritan Ethic and the American Revolution."

9. Lutz, *Origins,* 10–11, 28, 123; also see 2, 31, 114, 120; also Daniel Elazar, "Political Theory of Covenant," 11.

10. Bernard Bailyn, *Ideological Origins,* 32.

11. Lutz, *Origins,* 7, 11, cf. 3; also see McLaughlin, *Foundations,* 35–36; Simpson, *Puritanism,* 111–13; Sandoz, *Government of Laws,* 100.

12. Gordon Wood, "Virtues," 32.

13. Cf. C. Zuckert, "Not by Preaching."

14. See Kendall and Carey, *Basic Symbols,* 19–26; Lutz, *Origins,* 3, 6; Charles Taylor, *Philosophy,* 32–57.

15. See Power, *Before the Convention,* 13: "The foundation of their new community was set in the Mayflower Compact and Winthrop's *Sermon on Charity.*"

16. McLaughlin, *Foundations,* 17–19; Morgan, *Visible Saints,* 26, 64, 77.

17. William Bradford, *History of Plimoth Plantation,* in Miller and Johnson, *Puritans,* I, 101–2.

18. Quoted in Morgan, *Inventing,* 123.

19. Morgan speaks of the Reformation-generated impulse to contract in both church and state. *Visible Saints,* 29; see also McLaughlin, *Foundations,* 20.

20. Höpfl and Thompson, "The History of Contract as a Motif in Political Thought"; Thompson, *Ideas of Contract*; Zuckert, *Natural Rights and the New Republicanism,* 64–65, 116–18. Lutz presents a version of the "unicontractarian" thesis when he finds direct parallels between the Declaration of Independence, Algernon Sidney, and the Counter-Reformation natural lawyer, Francisco Suarez, who, says Lutz, brought the contract tradition to a "high point of completion." Lutz subscribes to the view that "most of what Locke had to say is found" in Suarez and others of the earlier contract tradition (*Origins,* 118). McLaughlin goes even further back, to Nicholas of Cusa (*Foundations,* 68). For a rebuttal of this version of unicontractarianism, see Zuckert, *Natural Rights and the New Republicanism,* 97–126. McLaughlin (81) indicates one of the chief grounds for the unicontractarian thesis when he contrasts all contract positions with nineteenth-century organic theories.

21. Kendall and Carey, *Basic Symbols,* 8, 151; cf. Lutz, *Origins,* 6–7; McLaughlin, *Foundations,* 28, sees in the Pilgrims compact "the essence of the theory of democracy . . . and the center of free constitutionalism."

22. Kendall and Carey, *Basic Symbols,* 12, 83, 84.

23. For an example of a church covenant, see Lutz, *Origins,* 25.

24. Lutz, (*Origins*, 25–26), gives a detailed and helpful account of the parallels between the standard church covenant and the Mayflower Compact. He sees in the Declaration of Independence many of the same elements (*Origins*, 115–16); also see McLaughlin, *Foundations*, 27; Gough, *Social Contract*, 84; Parrington, *Main Currents*, I, 59–69.

25. Kendall and Carey, *Basic Symbols*, 31, 36, 77; cf. Lutz, *Origins*, 118; Lutz concedes that the invocatory language in the Declaration "stops short" of what would be expected of a theistic covenant (*Origins*, 124).

26. Cf. Wood, "Trials": for Jefferson, "as long as Americans believed certain things [the Declaration's truths], they remained Americans" (408). Also see Wood, *Radicalism*, ix. For the older view, see Rahe, *Republics*, 107.

27. Kendall and Carey, *Basic Symbols*, 32; Lutz, *Origins*, 31; cf. Morgan, *Inventing*, 123: "improvised devices."

28. On the parallel situation for the Pisquataqua combination, see Lutz, *Origins*, 30–31.

29. Cf. ibid., 121: the Declaration "created a new model as well as a universally valid justification for building political societies."

30. Cf. Kendall and Carey, *Basic Symbols*, 39: "Equality in any meaning of the term that would be acceptable to the custodians of our official literature, is wholly absent from the vocabulary of the authors of the compact." See also Gough, *The Social Contract*, 88: The Puritans did not "believe in the equality of all men." An infrequently noted feature of the Compact shows further how little concerned with equality it is. If one peruses the list of signers, one is struck by the odd fact that some signed only their names, while others add "Mr." The latter were indicating their higher social status—not noble, but a cut above the common men who did not rate a "Mr." The differential social status of the signers could be carried over into their very constitutional act. By contrast, the Declaration speaks of abstractly equal prepolitical human beings, reflected in the democracy of the signatures. For an interpretation attributing a notion of "state of nature" and related ideas to the Mayflower Compact, see Arendt, *On Revolution*, 167. For a more "modern" reading on freedom, equality, and consent, see Elazar, "Political Theory of Covenant," esp. 25–26.

31. Thus Kendall and Carey overstate the parallels when they assert that the Declaration's doctrine of consent is "implicitly" affirmed in the Mayflower Compact (*Basic Symbols*, 42).

32. See Rahe, *Republics*, 357, for a similar comparison of the ends of government as revealed in the two documents.

33. Kendall and Carey, *Basic Symbols*, 38.

34. The charter can be found in Commager, *Documents*, I, 16–18. It is notable for the degree of self-government and independence it grants the company, and for its failure to specify that the governing body of the company carry on its business meetings in England. This omission (perhaps secured with this intention) allowed the colonists to take the charter to America, and to become the quasi-independent political entity that they

became (see Morgan, *Puritan Dilemma*, 47). Also worthy of note for its role in later controversy at the time of the agitation leading up to the Revolution was the clear provision that the colonists "shall have and enjoy all liberties and immunities of free and natural subjects within any of the dominions of us [the King]."

35. There is no documentary evidence that Winthrop delivered the sermon, but given its character—and his penchant for sermonizing—it is more than likely that he did deliver it aboard ship. See Schwenninger, *Winthrop*, 42, for conjectures on the circumstances of the sermon. There is general agreement that this sermon is the most important of Winthrop's statements and perhaps the most important American Puritan political statement. Cf. Baritz, *City*, 14; Schwenninger, *Winthrop*, 41.

36. Schwenninger, *Winthrop*, 42–44, shows how Winthop's speech conforms to standard formal patterns of Puritan sermons.

37. Winthrop, "Modell," 76; cf. Miller and Johnson, *Puritans*, 193: "There was no idea of the equality of all men." Gray, "Political Thought," 681, identifies this thesis as "the core" of Winthrop's thinking.

38. Consider the discussion among Lord Say and Seal and John Cotton for an indication of how widespread this beginning point was, but also for its limits in the American context. See Morgan, *Puritan Political Ideas*, 161–73. Also see William Hubbard in the 1670s for the persistence of these conceptions (in Miller and Johnson, *Puritans*, I, 247–49). For discussion, consider Pangle and Pangle, *Learning of Liberty*, 23–25; Wood, *Radicalism*, 11–95; Baritz, *City*, 14–19, 25, 28; Schwenninger, *Winthrop*, 42, 46.

39. Winthrop, "Modell," 93; McWilliams, *Fraternity*, 136.

40. Winthrop, "Modell," 76, 77. Cf. Morgan, *Inventing*, 141, for the prevalence of such views in Puritan social theory as a whole; see Gray ("Political Thought," 684, 692–93), who illustrates well the scholarly confusion when he both emphasizes Winthrop's inegalitarianism and identifies Winthrop with the theory of the Declaration (683); McWilliams, *Fraternity*, 138.

41. Gray, "Political Thought," 685.

42. McWilliams, *Fraternity*, 133; Schwenninger, *Winthrop*, 42; Rossiter, *Political Thought*, 8; Winthrop, *Journal*, 119; Power, *Before the Convention*, 7; Miller and Johnson, *Puritans*, 23; Gray, "Political Thought," 695–98.

43. Winthrop, "Modell," 87–89; cf. Power, *Before the Convention*, 10: Winthrop "placed his primary trust in the presence of charity and love in men's hearts" (also cf. 65).

44. Winthrop, "Modell," 91.

45. Winthrop to Mrs. Winthrop, May 15, 1629, in Miller and Johnson, *Puritans*, II, 467. Morgan, *Puritan Dilemma*, 18–33.

46. McWilliams, *Fraternity*, 136.

47. Winthrop, "Modell," 86; McWilliams, *Fraternity*, 133–34.

48. McWilliams, *Fraternity*, 86, 89; on the role of love, see Baritz, *City*, 15–17, 23. Gray, "Political Thought," 683, is correct to see that Christianity is not "the indispensable basis for the commonwealth," but that it is the only

basis for a successful commonwealth. Consider McWilliams, *Fraternity* (135–36): "Ends and means tend to overlap in Winthrop's analysis."

49. McWilliams, *Fraternity*, 90; Winthrop, "Defense," 146.

50. Calvin, *Institutes*, III, 7, 6.

51. Winthrop, "Modell," 87.

52. Cf. Schwenninger, *Winthrop*, 44: Winthrop's is an "idealistic" attempt to create a "perfect church-state." Also see Baritz, *City*, 13, 17, on Winthrop as attempting to bring the Reformation to "full fruition" and to redeem the world; see also Bercovitch, *Jeremiad*, 9; McWilliams, *Fraternity*, 114–15.

53. Locke, *Letter Concerning Toleration*, 393.

54. Locke, *Two Treatises*, II, 42; Winthrop, "Modell," 92.

55. Winthrop, *Journal*, 138. For a very similar description of liberty, see John Cotton, "An Exposition," 174–76. On Winthrop's "conception" as having the "opposite character" from that in the Declaration, see Gray, "Political Thought," 690.

56. Winthrop, *Journal*, 137. See Pangle and Pangle, *Learning of Liberty*, 24–25. For parallel statement by others, see Miller and Johnson, *Puritans*, I, 189–93.

57. Winthrop, "On Arbitrary Government," 152. Cf. 153, where Winthrop implies that distrust of the judge is equivalent to distrust of God; cf. also his *Journal*, 112; on the Fifth Commandment, see Baritz, *City*, 20. On the authoritarian implications of Winthrop's doctrine, see Gray, "Political Thought," 688.

58. Winthrop, "Modell," 91–92; on the covenant with God in Puritan thought, see more generally, Perry Miller, "The Marrow of Puritan Divinity," in *Errand*, 48–98; on covenant with God in the "Modell," see Schwenninger, *Winthrop*, 44.

59. Winthrop, *Journal*, 138.

60. Ibid., 137, 138.

61. Winthrop made one other statement of a contractarian sort that appears to be much closer to the natural rights position; he says that "no common weale can be founded but by free consent" and affirms that "no man hath lawfull power over another, but by birth or consent" (*Journal*, 144, 145). These claims could be taken to point toward something more like the philosophy of the Declaration, as Gray, for example, sees them, but several considerations speak against reading them this way: (1) these assertions are also consistent with the many different contractarianisms discussed in the text; (2) they are not joined here with any other of the key elements of the natural rights philosophy, particularly natural rights themselves; (3) the context of Winthrop's statement is a speech defending the exclusion of such immigrants as the magistrates conclude will not fit well into the community, "such as come and bring not the true doctrine with them." As we have seen, this is related for Winthrop to the special tasks and possibilities of the Puritan commonwealth, notions entirely foreign to the natural rights philosophy. Examples of the overestimation of the contractarian dimension of

Winthrop's thought abound. See, e.g., McLaughlin, *Foundations*, 33–34; Gray, "Political Thought," 682; Mosse, *Holy Pretence*, 88–89.

62. John Cotton, the important Boston minister of the first Puritan generation in Massachusetts, is often held to have purveyed a fuller-bodied contractarianism than that to be found in Winthrop. (See McLaughlin, *Foundations*, 68.) In a sermon on politics, Cotton stated, for example: "It is fit . . . for the people, in whom fundamentally all power lyes, to give as much power as God in his word gives to men." This is not in fact very different from Winthrop's position, and certainly not the same as the doctrine in the Declaration. The similarity with Winthrop is visible in Cotton's appeal to the same analogy Winthrop had used. "It is good for the Wife to acknowledge all power and authority to the Husband, and for the Husband to acknowledge honour to the Wife, but still give them that which God hath given them, and no more nor lesse." Human beings in their liberty enter into authority relations that God has already ordained and drawn the outlines of. Humans have a secondary power (and task) of ratifying or recognizing the divinely ordained outlines. The source of human knowledge of the divine pattern in these authority relations is "God's word." On all these counts, Cotton essentially agrees with Winthrop and differs from the Declaration. (For an account of the application of the same doctrine to the governance of the church, see Miller, *Errand*, 30–31.) On covenant as a pervasive theme in Puritan thought, see McWilliams, *Fraternity*, 123–26.

The doctrines of Thomas Hooker and the Fundamental Orders of Connecticut contain much the same version of contractarianism. (On Hooker, see Miller, *Errand*, 36–47. For the text of the Fundamental Orders, see Lutz, *Documents of Political Foundation*, 135–41, esp. the preamble.) The great distance between the Fundamental Orders and the Declaration of Independence stands out clearly in the former's statement of the ends of their political association: "enter into combination and confederation together, to mayntayne and preserve the liberty and purity of the gospell of our lord Jesus wch we now prfesse, as also the discipline of the churches, wch according to the truth of the said gospell is now practised among us."

On the application of the same theory of authority to the governance of the church, see Miller, *Errand*, 30–31. For arguments that Hooker and the Fundamental Orders of Connecticut are much closer to the Declaration, see Kendall and Carey, *Basic Symbols*, 43–49; Lutz, *Origins*, 27, 120; McLaughlin, *Foundations*, 68–69. Lutz's views of Hooker do not take account of Miller's strenuous response to the Parringtonian celebration of Hooker as a great democrat, forerunner of Thomas Jefferson and liberal modernity (*Errand*, 16–18). Also cf. the implied critique of Parrington in Delbanco, *The Puritan Ordeal*, 170–83.

63. Power, *Before the Convention*, 19; cf. 79.

64. See Morgan, *Inventing*, 123–24.

6. Natural Rights and Protestant Politics: Lockean Puritans

1. Samuel Langdon, "Government Corrupted by Vice," 361 (emphasis in original).

2. On the jeremiad, see Miller, *From Colony to Province*, 27–39; Bercovitch, *The American Jeremiad*, 23–26; Morgan, "Puritan Ethic," 6.

3. Langdon, "Government Corrupted by Vice," 364–65.

4. Ibid., 365, 367.

5. Ibid., 367–68.

6. Pangle, *The Spirit of Modern Republicanism*, 22–23. For further discussion, see Zuckert, *Natural Rights and the New Republicanism*, 21–22; Baldwin, *The New England Clergy*; Newlin, *Philosophy and Religion*; Dworetz, *Unvarnished Doctrine*, 148–149.

7. Dworetz, *The Unvarnished Doctrine*, 32.

8. Ibid., 135.

9. Ibid., 135–83.

10. Lutz, *Origins*, 143; cf. Dworetz, *Unvarnished Doctrine*, 172.

11. Dworetz, *Unvarnished Doctrine*, 182.

12. Rossiter, *Political Thought*, 8.

13. Ibid., chaps. 6, 7, 9, 10.

14. Ibid., 137.

15. Rossiter perhaps shows the same ambivalence, at times positing Locke as the source of the clerics' political principles, but at other times endorsing a position much more like the strong continuity view. "It was hardly accidental," Rossiter asserts, "that New England ministers gave the first and most cordial reception to the arguments of John Locke and his friends and broadcast from their pulpits the new gospel of government by consent," because various Puritan doctrines anticipated, or at least, prepared the way for Locke. "The Puritan concept of the covenant helped swell the triumph of the social contract. . . . The Puritan theory of the origin of the church in the consent of the believers led directly to the popular theory of the origin of government in the consent of the governed" (*First American Revolution*, 91). I am inclined to see Rossiter as closer to the view that Locke was indeed the source of clerical political theory, but that certain features of Puritanism made them receptive to Locke. This seems to me to be an essentially sound judgment, although it requires fuller treatment than Rossiter gives it. On Locke and Puritanism, consider Quentin Skinner's assertion: "John Locke's *Two Treatises of Government*—the classic text of radical Calvinist politics" *Foundations of Modern Political Thought*, II, 239).

16. On Dworetz's ambiguous language, or even tilt toward convergence, see his *Unvarnished Doctrine*, 147, 154, 179.

17. Ibid., 138.

18. For Locke's official theory, see *Essay Concerning Human Understand-*

ing IV.*xviii–xix; Reasonableness*, paras. 242–245; for discussion, see Zuckert, "Locke and the Problem of Civil Religion."

19. *Two Treatises*, II, 25.

20. See Zuckert, *Natural Rights and the New Republicanism*, chaps. 7–9 for a discussion of the workmanship argument and its tentative role in Locke's larger argument.

21. Ayers, *Locke*, I 121.

22. Locke, "Inspiration," in Wootton, *Political Writings*, 238, 239 (emphasis added).

23. *Two Treatises*, I, 58.

24. Calvin, *Institutes*, I, 3.1; I, 4.1; I, 5.1, 11, 14.

25. Ibid., I, 5.14; I, 6.2, 4.

26. Ibid., II, 8; III, 19; IV, 20.

27. Quoted in Miller, *New England Mind*, 52.

28. Ibid., 52, 54–55.

29. Milton, *Paradise Regained*, IV, 309–13; for further discussion, see Zuckert, *Natural Rights and the New Republicanism*, 83–84.

30. Cf. Calvin, *Institutes*, III, 19.15.

31. Luther, *Soldiers*, 46:95.

32. Ibid., 46:100.

33. Luther, *Temporal Authority*, 45:88.

34. Ibid., 45:111.

35. Ibid., 45:90–91; Luther, *Open Letter on a Harsh Book*, 46:71–73.

36. Luther, *Open Letter on a Harsh Book*, 46:69–70.

37. Luther, *Christian Nobility*, 27.

38. Ibid., 42.

39. See Skinner, *Foundations*, II.

40. See Zuckert, *Natural Rights and the New Republicanism*, 29–94.

41. Power, *Before the Convention*, 7.

42. Ibid., 71.

43. On the tendency to theocracy within Calvinist politics, see Gough, *Social Contract*, 85; Forrester, "Luther and Calvin," 328–29; Morgan, *Puritan Political Ideas*, xxix, xxxi; Baritz, *City*, 23, 24; Gray, "Political Thought," 698–702; for an important caveat, see Morgan, *Puritan Dilemma*, 95–96, 163; on indirect influence of clergy, 163–64.

44. See Miller and Johnson, *Puritans*, I, 128–29, 135, 191–92; Edward Johnson, *Wonder-Working Providence*, 151.

45. Morgan, *Visible Saints*, 101–5; Morgan, *Puritan Dilemma*, 84–100.

46. Cf. Morgan, *Inventing*, 141; Miller, *Errand*, 32–35.

47. Tocqueville, *Democracy*, II,2 (42–43). Also see Massachusetts Body of Liberties, Art. 94. For an account of theocratic tendencies as late as 1773, see Backus, "An Appeal," 339–62; a crusty account is in Nock, *Enemy*, 62 and 62n.

48. Dworetz, *Unvarnished Doctrine*, 142.

49. Morgan, *Puritan Political Ideas*, 331.

50. Locke: "There being nothing more evident than that creatures of the same species and rank promiscuously born to all the same advantages of nature, and the use of the same faculties, should also be equal one amongst another without subordination or subjection. . . ."

Williams: "All men being naturally equal, as descended from a common parent, endowed with like Faculties and Propensities, having originally equal Rights and Properties."

51. Williams, "A Sermon," 334, 337; cf. Locke, *Two Treatises*, II, chap. 5; *Letter Concerning Toleration*, 83.

52. Williams, "A Sermon," 334, 337; Locke, *Two Treatises*, II, 7.

53. Williams, "A Sermon," 337; Locke *Two Treatises*, II, 89.

54. Williams, "A Sermon," 335; also see 336, 337; Locke *Two Treatises*, II, 124.

55. Williams, "A Sermon," 336, 338; Locke, *Letter Concerning Toleration*, 15.

56. Williams, "A Sermon," 341–43; Locke, *Two Treatises*, II, chap. 12. Williams fails to mention one very important Lockean theme, the so-called right of revolution, a doctrine given a featured place in Locke's *Two Treatises* and in Jefferson's Declaration of Independence, to mention but two places. The context of Williams's sermon did not call for a statement on this theme, but it too was a prominent part of the clerical political understanding well before the prerevolutionary troubles began. The best known example is Jonathan Mayhew's, *A Discourse Concerning Unlimited Submission*, delivered in 1750 in protest against the Anglican practice of celebrating Charles II as a blessed martyr. In the context of a consideration of the bearing of Romans 13, Mayhew reiterates the chief points of Lockean political philosophy on the limits of the duty of obedience and the contours of a right of resistance. See esp. 315–17n, and 321, and also his "The Snare Broken," 263. On Mayhew, consider Newlin, *Philosophy and Religion*, 195–96. On his great influence, see Baldwin, *New England Clergy* 9, 44, 91–92.

57. Williams, "A Sermon," 337 (emphasis in the original). Cf. also "The *Law of Nature*, which is the Constitution of the God of Nature, is universally obliging" (Ibid., 348).

58. My conclusions about discontinuity between Lockean and Puritan politics run afoul of the conclusions reached by Quentin Skinner, who finds Locke's *Two Treatises* to be "the classic text of radical Calvinist politics." Skinner's basis for this claim lies in his detailed consideration of pre-Lockean Calvinist thought in Europe, not in the American Puritans. I believe that many of the contrasts I draw between the American Puritans and Locke also hold for the thinkers Skinner considers, but to show that is well beyond the scope of this study. Later in his book, Skinner reconsiders the issue and draws a conclusion far more consistent with the one drawn here. In speaking of the mature "radical Calvinist" doctrine, what Skinner calls "a fully *political* theory of revolution," he says that their position "still differs at two important points from the classic version of modern constitutionalism. Locke not only

vindicates the lawfulness of resistance entirely in the language of rights and natural rights, but goes on to locate the authority to resist with 'the body of the people' and even with 'any single man' if 'deprived of their rights'" (*Foundations of Modern Political Thought*, II, 229, 338).

59. Cf. Dworetz, *Unvarnished Doctrine*, 155–72.

60. West, "On the Right to Rebel," 427.

61. Dworetz, *Unvarnished Doctrine*, 168.

62. Chauncey, "Civil Magistrates Must Be Just," 165; Williams, "A Sermon," 335.

63. A book of this sort is not the place to explore the fine points or depths of Lockean political philosophy. I have made an attempt at this in my *Natural Rights and the New Republicanism*, pt. III, the argument of which lies in the background of my comments here.

64. See Locke, *Reasonableness*. For discussion, see Zuckert, "Locke and the Problem of Civil Religion."

65. Chauncey, "Civil Magistrates Must Be Just," 166.

66. Ibid., 166–67.

67. Williams, "A Sermon," 338. Emphasis in the original.

68. Locke, *Letter Concerning Toleration*, 17–23.

69. An excellent example from later American history of the bridging function of Locke's workmanship argument occurs in the "Annual Report" of the New England Anti-Slavery Society. The Garrisonian abolitionists begin with a paraphrase of Locke's workmanship argument and move on to list many of the rights that follow from his grasp of rights as grounded in self-ownership. The document is reprinted in William Pease and Jane Pease, eds., *The Anti-Slavery Argument*, 60–64.

70. Elisha Williams, "Essential Rights and Liberties," 55, 56, 59, 83.

71. For a review of some of the evidence of Locke's early popularity in America, see my *Natural Rights and the New Republicanism*, 18–25.

72. Williams, "Essential Rights," 59, 60. Emphasis in the original.

73. Ibid., 61, 91, 92. Emphasis in the original.

74. Ibid., 92, 93, 94. Emphasis in the original.

75. Ibid., 94, 95, 96. Emphasis in the original.

76. Ibid., 61–62. Emphasis in the original.

77. Ibid., 73; also see 86.

78. Locke, *Letter Concerning Toleration*, 17, 23.

79. Williams, "Essential Rights," 67, 68, 69, 70, 71.

80. Ibid., 62.

81. Ibid., 63.

82. Ibid., 67, 68, 69, 70, 71.

83. Ibid., 72, 82, 83.

84. Ibid., 79.

85. Ibid., 79.

86. Ibid., 80.

87. Ibid., 92–93, cf. 77, 91; Locke, *Essay Concerning Human Understanding*, IV, 16.3–4.

88. McWilliams, *Fraternity*, 142.
89. Heinrich Bullinger, *The Decades*, 22, 23.
90. Ibid., 23.
91. Calvin, *Institutes*, IV, 20.9.
92. Cambridge Platform, Arts. 6,8,9, in Commager, *Documents*, I, 30–31.
93. John Rawls, *Political Liberalism*, I, 2.2.
94. Cambridge Platform, Art. 6, in Commager, *Documents*, I, 30.
95. Miller, *From Colony to Province*, esp. 3–15.
96. Ibid., 82–104; Morgan, *Visible Saints.*
97. Miller, *From Colony to Province*, 395–481.
98. Newlin, *Philosophy and Religion.*
99. See McWilliams, *Fraternity*, 156.
100. Locke, *The Reasonableness of Christianity*, pars. 242–43.
101. Jefferson, *Notes on Virginia*, Query XVIII, 289.

7. The Natural Rights Republic

1. Bailyn, *Ideological Origins*, 152–56; Bailyn also mentions in passing the condemnation of slavery contained in Jefferson's draft of the Declaration (237, 246).
2. Ibid., 188.
3. Ibid., 34.
4. Ibid., 34, 45.
5. Bailyn, "Central Themes," 7–8.
6. Ibid., 34, 45.
7. Pocock, "Virtue and Commerce in the Eighteenth Century," 122. For a fuller account, complete with relevant citations, see Zuckert, *Natural Rights and the New Republicanism*, 159–64; 166–70.
8. Pocock, "Between Gog and Magog," 340; idem, *Virtue, Commerce, and History*, 68.
9. Kramnick, *Republicanism and Bourgeois Radicalism*, 630.
10. Wood, *Creation*, 47.
11. For a fuller account, complete with fuller citations, see Zuckert, *Natural Rights and the New Republicanism*, 155–59.
12. Kramnick, *Republicanism*, 167.
13. This point bears also on Shain's peculiar interpretation of liberal modernity. *Myth*, xiv, 10, 13–15, 17, 324–25.
14. See C. Zuckert, "Aristotle on the Limits and Satisfactions of Political Life;" Pangle, *Spirit of Modern Republicanism*; Rahe, *Republics*, pt. I.
15. See Sullivan, "Machiavelli's Momentary 'Machiavellian Moment.'"
16. See Davis, "Pocock's Harrington"; Goodale, "Pocock's Neo-Harringtonians"; Mansfield, *Taming the Prince*, 183–86; Sullivan, "Civic Humanist Portrait"; Rahe, *Republics*, 408–26.
17. See Goodale, "Pocock's Neo-Harringtonians"; Zuckert, *Natural Rights and the New Republicanism*, 166–83; Rahe, *Republics*, 429–40.

18. See Pangle, *Spirit;* Diggins, *Lost Soul;* Appleby, *Capitalism and a New Social Order;* Rahe, *Republics,* bk. III. (for all the topics covered in notes 12–18 here, Rahe has excellent bibliographic references in his *Republics*); Dworetz, *Unvarnished Doctrine.*

19. Banning, "The Republican Hypothesis: Errors, Contributions, and Misunderstandings" in Klein et al., eds., *Republican Synthesis Revisited.*

20. Gerber, "Whatever Happened to the Declaration of Independence?" 219. Also see Schmitt and Webking, "Revolutionaries," Webking, *American Revolution,* 10–15.

21. Leinisch, *New Order of the Ages;* Sheldon, *Thomas Jefferson;* Banning, "Republican Hypothesis"; Banning, "Some Second Thoughts on Virtue"; for a sketch of the legal profession's flirtation with the republican thesis and of its efforts to move beyond "either/or," see Miriam Galston, "Taking Aristotle Seriously," 331–39. Consider also Pangle's notion of an "American synthesis of republicanism and individual rights," in his *Ennobling,* 98.

22. Thomas Jefferson, "Epitaph" (1826), in Peterson, ed., *Jefferson,* 706–7.

23. Jefferson to Roger Weightman, June 24, 1826, in Peterson, ed., *Jefferson,* 1517. Cf. Jefferson to John Adams, October 28, 1813, in ibid., 1309.

24. Jefferson, "A Bill for Establishing Religious Freedom," in Peterson, ed., *Jefferson,* 347.

25. Jefferson, "A Bill for the More General Diffusion of Knowledge," in Peterson, ed., *Jefferson,* 365.

26. Jefferson to Adams, July 15, 1814, in Peterson, ed., *Jefferson,* 1341; cf. Jefferson to Short, October 31, 1819, in ibid., 1431–32, and especially, Jefferson to Short, August 4, 1820, in ibid., 1438.

27. Jefferson to Tiffany, August 26, 1816, in Jefferson's *Selected Writings,* 87–88.

28. Jefferson to Brazier, August 24, 1819, in Peterson, ed., *Jefferson,* 1424. As printed, the punctuation of Jefferson's letter is ambiguous, but the passage makes sense only as applying to ancient ethical science.

29. Jefferson to Adams, February 28, 1796, in Peterson, ed., *Jefferson,* 1034.

30. Jefferson, *Notes on the State of Virginia,* in Peterson, ed., *Jefferson,* 254.

31. Ibid., 252.

32. Ibid., 254.

33. Jefferson was not entirely hostile to Rome. Cf. Jefferson to Adams, February 28, 1796, in Peterson, ed., *Jefferson,* 1034.

34. Machiavelli, *Discourses,* I.2.

35. Jefferson, *Notes on Virginia,* 254.

36. *Discourses,* I.4, 6.

37. *Notes,* 252.

38. Jefferson to George Washington, April 16, 1784, in Peterson, ed., *Jefferson,* 791.

39. Ibid. On opposition to hereditary rule as the core of early American republicanism, and on how far that stands from the tradition, see Pangle, *Ennobling,* 99–100.

40. Cf. *Jefferson*, 148–49.

41. Jefferson, *Notes*.

42. Jefferson, "Draft Constitution for Virginia," in Peterson, ed., *Jefferson*, 337, 338.

43. Ibid., 345.

44. Jefferson to Edmund Pendleton, August 26, 1776, in Peterson, ed., *Jefferson*, 755–56.

45. *Notes*, 254.

46. "Draft Constitution," 343.

47. Note "Autobiography," 44.

48. Ibid., 32, 45. Cf. Tocqueville, *Democracy in America*, I.3.

49. Cf. Lerner, *Thinking Revolutionary*, 63.

50. *Notes*, 290. Cf. Jefferson to Adams, in Peterson, ed., *Jefferson*, 1034.

51. *Notes*, 290.

52. Alexander Hamilton, James Madison, and John Jay, *The Federalist*, no. 9.

53. *Notes*, 243.

54. Ibid., 275.

55. Ibid., 243.

56. Ibid., 244.

57. Ibid.

58. Ibid., 274.

59. "Draft Constitution," 338.

60. Jefferson to Pendleton, in Peterson, ed., *Jefferson*, 756.

61. *Notes*, 245.

62. *Federalist*, no. 47.

63. Montesquieu, *De l'Esprit des Lois*, bk. XI.

64. *Notes*, 245.

65. Ibid.

66. Ibid.

67. Ibid., 246.

68. Jefferson to Pendleton, 756. Cf. Machiavelli, *The Prince*, chap. 9; Melancton Smith, Speech in New York Ratifying Convention, in Herbert J. Storing, ed., *The Complete Anti-Federalist*, VI, 148–76.

69. Jefferson to Pendleton, 756.

70. Ibid., 755.

71. Ibid.

72. "Autobiography," 32; *Notes*, 274; Jefferson to Adams, 1306; on natural aristocracy as the true principle of classical republicanism, see Pangle, *Ennobling*, 107.

73. *Notes*, 245.

74. *Federalist*, no.10.

75. *Notes*, 274. Cf. Jefferson to Littleton Waller Tazewell, January 5, 1805, in Peterson, ed., *Jefferson*, 1149; Jefferson to John Wyche, May 14, 1809, in ibid., 1207; Jefferson to John Tyler, May 26, 1810, in ibid., 1226.

76. *Notes*, 273.

77. Ibid., 274.

78. Pangle and Pangle, *Learning of Liberty*, 110–11.

79. *Notes*, 273. Cf. Pangle and Pangle, *Learning of Liberty*, 287.

80. *Notes*, 274.

81. Jefferson to P. S. Dupont de Nemours, April 24, 1816, in Peterson, ed., *Jefferson*, 1337. The implication of Jefferson's discussion of the necessity of education should be considered in relation to his position on the moral sense.

82. "Bill for Diffusion of Knowledge," in Peterson, ed., *Jefferson*, 365.

83. *Notes*, 274.

84. "Bill for Diffusion of Knowledge," 365. Cf. Pangle and Pangle, *Learning of Liberty*, 117.

85. Jefferson to Adams, in Peterson, ed., *Jefferson*, 1308.

86. *Notes*, 246.

87. Ibid., 251.

88. Ibid.; cf. Jefferson to Kercheval, July 12, 1816, in Peterson, *Jefferson*, 1396.

89. Jefferson to John Taylor, May 28, 1816, in Peterson, ed., *Jefferson*, 1394.

90. Jefferson to Major John Cartwright, June 5, 1824, in Peterson, ed., *Jefferson*, 1491.

91. Jefferson to Taylor, 1394.

92. Jefferson to Kercheval, 1397.

93. Ibid.

94. Jefferson to James Madison, December 20, 1787, in Peterson, ed., *Jefferson*, 915.

95. Jefferson to Kercheval, 1886–97, 1400.

96. Jefferson to Madison, 914–18; Jefferson to Taylor, 1394.

97. Jefferson to Adams, 1306.

98. Ibid., 1305–6.

99. Ibid., 1306.

100. Jefferson to James Madison, September 6, 1789, in Peterson, ed., *Jefferson*, 964.

101. Jefferson to Elbridge Gerry, January 26, 1799, in Peterson, ed., *Jefferson*, 1056); Jefferson to Dr. Benjamin Rush, January 16, 1811, in Peterson, ed., *Jefferson*, 1235.

102. Jefferson to Kercheval, 1396.

103. Jefferson to Taylor, 1392.

104. Ibid., 1393.

105. *Federalist*, no. 39; cf. Jefferson to Taylor, 1392.

106. *Federalist*, no. 39.

107. Arendt, *On Revolution*, 255.

108. Jefferson to Taylor, 1395.

109. Jefferson to Kercheval, 1398.

110. Jefferson to Cartwright, 1494; cf. Pangle, *Ennobling*, 149.

111. Jefferson to Dupont de Nemours, 1385.

112. Ibid.

113. Jefferson to Joseph C. Cabell, February 2, 1816, in Peterson, ed., *Jefferson,* 1380.

114. Ibid.

115. Ibid., cf. Jefferson to Kercheval, 1399.

116. Cf. Charles F. Hobson, "The Negative on State Laws" Zuckert, "Federalism and the Founding," 187–98; Zuckert, "A System Without Precedent," 145–49; Lance Banning, "The Practicable Sphere of a Republic," 162–87.

117. Jefferson to Cabell, in Peterson, ed., *Jefferson,* 1380; cf. Jefferson to Cabell, in ibid., 1399–1400.

118. Jefferson to Cabell, 1380.

119. Cf. Jefferson's frequent animadversions against Montesquieu's small repubicanism, and his endorsement of Madison's federalism: Jefferson to Francois D'Ivernois, February 6, 1765, in Peterson, ed., *Jefferson,* 1024. Cf. Jefferson to Cartwright, 1493.

120. Jefferson to Cartwright, 1492.

121. See Jefferson to Cabell, 1380; Jefferson to Kercheval, 1399.

122. Jefferson to Cartwright, 1492.

123. Jefferson to Cabell, 1379–80.

124. Jefferson to Kercheval, 1399. Cf. Jefferson to Adams, 1308.

125. Jefferson to Kercheval, 1399. Consider the critique of Jefferson offered by Pangle and Pangle, *Learning of Liberty:* "We note with unease the absence . . . of any reference to the virtues of obedience to and reverence for law" (113–14). Jefferson sees such reverence emerging from the educative functions of republican institutions.

126. Jefferson to Kercheval, 1400.

127. Jefferson to Tyler, in Peterson, ed., *Jefferson,* 1227.

128. Jefferson to Cabell, 1381.

129. Ibid., 1380.

130. Ibid.

131. Jefferson to Cabell, 1227.

132. Jefferson to Cartwright, 1493; cf. Jefferson to Kercheval, 1399.

133. Heraclitus, Fragment 78 (Kahn numeration).

Bibliography

Adams, Randolph G. *The Political Ideas of the American Revolution.* New York, 1958.

Adler, Mortimer J., and William Gorman. *The American Testament.* New York, 1975.

Anastaplo, George. "The Declaration of Independence." *St. Louis University Law Journal* 9 (1965).

Appleby, Joyce. *Capitalism and a New Social Order: The Republican Vision of the 1790s.* New York, 1984.

Arendt, Hannah. *On Revolution.* New York, 1963.

Ayers, Michael. *Locke.* 2 vols. London and New York, 1991.

Backus, Isaac. "An Appeal to the Public for Religious Liberty." In *Political Sermons of the Founding Era,* ed. Ellis Sandoz. Indianapolis, 1991.

Bailyn, Bernard. "The Central Themes of the American Revolution: An Interpretation." In *Essays on the American Revolution,* ed. Stephen G. Kurtz and James Hudson. Chapel Hill, N.C., 1973.

———. *The Ideological Origins of the American Revolution.* Cambridge, Mass., 1967.

Baldwin, Alice. *The New England Clergy and the American Revolution.* Durham, N.C., 1928.

Banning, Lance. "The Practicable Sphere of a Republic: James Madison, the Constitutional Convention, and the Emergence of Revolutionary Federalism." In *Beyond Confederation,* ed. Richard Beeman, Stephen Botein, and Edward Carter III. Chapel Hill, N.C., 1987.

———. "The Republican Hypothesis: Errors, Contributions, and Misunderstandings." In Klein, Milton M., et al., eds., *The Republican Synthesis Revisited.* Worchester, Mass., 1992.

———. "Some Second Thoughts on Virtue and the Course of Revolutionary Thinking." In *Conceptual Change and the Constitution,* ed. Terrence Ball and J. G. A. Pocock. Lawrence, Kan., 1988.

Baritz, Loren. *City on a Hill.* New York, 1961.

Becker, Carl. *The Declaration of Independence.* New York, 1942.

Bercovitch, Sacvan. *The American Jeremiad.* Madison, 1978.

Berns, Walter. "Religion and the Founding Principle." In *The Moral Foundations of the American Republic,* ed. Robert Horwitz, 3d ed. Charlottesville, Va., 1986.

Bland, Richard. "An Inquiry into the Rights of the British Colonies." In *Tracts of the American Revolution,* ed. Merrill Jensen. Indianapolis, 1967.

Bluhm, William T., et al. "Locke's Idea of God." *Journal of Politics* (1980): 414–38.

Boorstin, Daniel. *The Lost World of Thomas Jefferson.* Boston, 1948.

———. *The Genius of American Politics.* Chicago, 1952.

Boyd, Julian P. "Jefferson's Expression of the American Mind." *Virginia Quarterly Review* 50 (1974).

Brann, Eva. "Concerning the Declaration of Independence." *The College* (of St. John's College) 28 (1973): 1–17.

———. *Paradoxes of Education in the Republic.* Chicago, 1979.

Bullinger, Heinrich. *The Decades.* In *Puritan Political Ideas,* ed. Edmund S. Morgan, 15–35. Indianapolis, 1965.

Burlamaqui, Jean Jacques. *Principles of Natural Law,* trans. Thomas Nugent. London, 1748.

Calhoun, John C. "Speech on the Oregon Bill." In *Union and Liberty,* ed. Ross Lence, 539–70. Indianapolis, 1992.

Calvin, John. *Institutes of the Christian Religion* (1559), ed. John T. McNeill. 2 vols. Philadelphia, 1960.

Cappon, Lester. *The Adams-Jefferson Letters: The Complete Correspondence between Thomas Jefferson & Abigail and John Adams.* Chapel Hill, N.C., 1959.

Chauncey, Charles. "Civil Magistrates Must be Just, Ruling in the Fear of God." In *Political Sermons of the American Founding Era,* ed. Ellis Sandoz, 137–77. Indianapolis, 1991.

Coleman, Frank M. *Hobbes and America.* Toronto, 1977.

Commager, Henry Steele. *Documents of American History.* 2 vols. New York, 1963.

———. *Jefferson, Nationalism, and the Enlightenment.* New York, 1975.

Conkin, Paul K. "The Religious Pilgrimage of Thomas Jefferson." In *Jeffersonian Legacies,* Peter Onuf, 19–49. Charlottesville, Va., 1993.

———. *Self-Evident Truths.* Bloomington, Ind., 1974.

Conrad, Stephen. "Putting Rights Talk in Its Place." In *Jeffersonian Legacies,* ed. Peter Onuf. Charlottesville, Va., 1993.

Cotton, John. *An Exposition Upon the Thirteenth Chapter of the Revelation.* In *Puritan Political Ideas,* ed. Edmund S. Morgan. Indianapolis, 1965.

Dana, William F. "The Political Principles of the Declaration of Independence." In *A Casebook on the Declaration of Independence,* ed. Robert Ginsberg. New York, 1966.

Davis, J. C. "Pocock's Harrington: Grace, Nature, and Art in the Classical Republicanism of James Harrington." *Historical Journal* 24 (1981): 683–98.

Delaney. C. F., ed. *The Liberalism-Communitarianism Debate.* Lanham, Md., 1994.

Delbanco, Andrew. *The Puritan Ordeal.* Cambridge, Mass., 1989.

Derrida, Jacques. *Otobiographies.* Paris, 1988.

Diamond, Martin. "The American Idea of Equality." *Review of Politics,* July 1976.

———. *As Far as Republican Principles Will Admit.* Ed. William A. Schambra. Lanham, Md., 1991.

————. "The Revolution of Sober Expectations." In *The American Revolution: Three Views*, 57–85. New York, 1975.

Dickinson, H. T. "How Revolutionary Was the 'Glorious Revolution' of 1688?" *British Journal of Eighteenth Century Studies* (1988): 125–42.

————. *Liberty and Property*. New York, 1977.

Diggins, John P. *The Lost Soul of American Politics: Virtue, Self-Interest, and the Foundations of Liberalism*. New York, 1984.

————. "Slavery, Race, and Equality: Jefferson and the Pathos of the Enlightenment." *American Quarterly* 28 (1976).

Dulaney, Daniel. *Considerations on the Propriety of Imposing Taxes on the British Colonies, for the Purpose of Raising a Revenue by Act of Parliament*. In *Tracts of the American Revolution*, ed. Merrill Jensen, 94–107. Indianapolis, 1967.

Dunn, John. "The Politics of Locke in England and America." In *John Locke: Problems and Perspectives*, ed. John Yolton. Cambridge, 1969.

Dwortez, Steven. *The Unvarnished Doctrine: Locke, Liberalism, and the American Revolution*. Durham, N.C., 1990.

Eidelberg, Paul. *On the Silence of the Declaration of Independence*. Amherst, Mass., 1976.

Ekirch, Arthur A. *The Challenge of American Democracy*. Belmont, Calif., 1973.

Elazar, Daniel. "The Political Theory of Covenant: Biblical Origins and Modern Developments." *Publius*, Fall 1990: 3–30.

Engeman, Thomas. "Liberalism, Republicanism, and Ideology." *Review of Politics* 55 (Spring 1993).

Fitzhugh, George. *Sociology for the South* (1854). In *Ante-Bellum*, ed. Harvey Wish. New York, 1960.

Forrester, Duncan. "Luther and Calvin." In *A History of Political Philosophy*, ed. Leo Strauss and Joseph Cropsey. Chicago, 1982.

Franklin, Julian. *John Locke and the Theory of Sovereignty*. Cambridge, Mass., 1978.

Galston, Miriam, "Taking Aristotle Seriously: Republican-Oriented Legal Theory and the Moral Foundation of Deliberative Democracy." *California Law Review* 82 (March 1994).

Gerber, Scott D. "Whatever Happened to the Declaration of Independence . . ." *Polity* 26 (1993): 207–31.

Ginsberg, Robert. *A Casebook on the Declaration of Independence*. New York, 1966.

————. "The Declaration as Rhetoric." In *A Casebook on the Declaration of Independence*, ed. Robert Ginsberg. New York, 1966.

Glendon, Mary Ann. *Rights Talk*. New York, 1991.

Goldwin, Robert A., and William Schambra, eds. *How Capitalistic Is the Constitution?* Washington, D.C., 1982.

Goodale, J. F. "J. G. A. Pocock's Neo-Harringtonians: A Reconsideration." *History of Political Thought* 1 (June 1980): 237–60.

Gough, J. W. *The Social Contract*. Oxford, 1957.

Gray, Stanley. "The Political Thought of John Winthrop." *New England Quarterly* 3 (1930): 681–705.

Greene, Jack P. "A Posture of Hostility." In *Preachers and Politicians*, ed. Jack P. Greene and William G. McLoughlin, 5–46. Worcester, Mass., 1977.

Grey, Thomas C. "Origins of the Unwritten Constitution: Fundamental Law in American Revolutionary Thought." *Stanford Law Review* 30 (1978): 843–93.

Griswold, Charles J., Jr. "Rights and Wrongs: Jefferson, Slavery, and Philosophical Quandaries." In *A Culture of Rights*, ed. Michael J. Lacey and Knud Haakenssen. New York, 1988.

Hamilton, Alexander, James Madison, and John Jay, *The Federalist*. Ed. Clinton Rossiter. New York, 1961.

Hamowy, Ronald. "Jefferson and the Scottish Enlightenment." *William and Mary Quarterly*, 3d series, 37, 1979.

Harrington, James. *Oceana*. Ed. J. G. A. Pocock. Cambridge, 1992.

Hobson, Charles F. "The Negative on State Laws: James Madison, the Constitution, and the Crisis of Republican Government." *William and Mary Quarterly*, 3d ser., 36: 215–35.

Hooker, Richard. *Of the Laws of Ecclesiastical Polity*. London, 1907.

Höpfl, Harro, and Marilyn P. Thompson. "The History of Contract as a Motif in Political Thought." *American Historical Review* 84 (1979): 919–44.

Howell, Wilbur Samuel. "The Declaration of Independence and Eighteenth Century Logic." In *A Casebook on the Declaration of Independence*, ed. Robert Ginsberg. New York, 1966.

Jaffa, Harry V. *The Conditions of Freedom*. Baltimore, 1975.

———. *Equality and Liberty*. New York, 1965.

———. *How to Think about the American Revolution*. Durham, N.C., 1978.

———. "Humanizing Certitudes and Impoverishing Doubts." *Interpretation*, Fall 1988.

———. "Inventing the Past." *The Saint John's Review* 33 (1981): 3–19.

Jameson, J. Franklin. *The American Revolution Considered as a Social Movement*. Princeton, N.J., 1926.

Jefferson, Thomas. "Autobiography." In Merrill D. Peterson, ed., *Thomas Jefferson Writings*. New York, 1984.

———. *The Life and Selected Writings of Thomas Jefferson*, ed. Koch and Peden. New York, 1944.

———. *Notes on the States of Virginia*. In Merrill D. Peterson, ed., *Thomas Jefferson Writings*. New York, 1984.

———. *Selected Writings*. Ed. Harvey Mansfield, Jr. Arlington Heights, Ill., 1979.

Johnson, Edward. *Wonder-Working Providence* (1654). In *The Puritans*, ed. Miller and Johnson, I: 143–62. New York, 1938.

Jones, Howard Mumford. "The Declaration of Independence: A Critique." In *The Declaration of Independence*, ed. Howard Mumford Jones and Howard Peckham, 3–20. Worcester, Mass., 1976.

Kahn, Charles H. *The Art and Thought of Heraclitus: An Edition of the Fragments with Thranslation and Commentary.* Cambridge, 1979.

Kendall, Willmoore, and George Carey. *The Basic Symbols of the American Political Tradition.* Baton Rouge, La., 1970.

Kenyon, J. P. "The Revolution of 1688: Resistance and Contract." In *Historical Perspectives in Studies in English Thought and Society in Honour of J. Plumb,* ed. Neil McKendrick. London, 1974.

———. *Revolution Principles: The Politics of Party, 1689–1720.* Cambridge, 1979.

Kloppenberg, James T. "The Virtues of Liberalism: Christianity, Republicanism, and Ethics in Early American Political Discourse." *Journal of American History* 74 (1987): 9–33.

Koch, Adrienne. *Power, Morals, and the Founding Fathers.* Ithaca, N.Y., 1961.

Kramnick, Isaac. *Republicanism and Bourgeois Radicalism.* Ithaca, N.Y., 1990.

Langdon, Samuel. "Government Corrupted by Vice, and Recovered by Righteousness." In *Puritan Political Ideas,* ed. Edmund Morgan, 352–72. Indianapolis, 1965.

Lence, Ross. "The American Declaration of Independence." In *Founding Principles of American Government: Two Hundred Years of Democracy on Trial,* ed. George J. Graham, Jr., and Scarlett G. Graham. Bloomington, 1977.

Lerner, Ralph. *The Thinking Revolutionary.* Ithaca, N.Y., 1987.

Levinson, Sanford. *Constitutional Faith.* Princeton, N.J., 1988.

———. "Self-Evident Truths in the Declaration of Independence." *Texas Law Review* 57 (1979).

Lienisch, Michael. *The New Order of the Ages: Time, the Constitution, and the Making of Modern American Political Thought.* Princeton, N.J., 1988.

Locke, John. *An Essay Concerning Human Understanding* (4th ed., 1700). Ed. Peter H. Nidditch. Oxford, 1990.

———. *A Letter Concerning Toleration.* In *Political Writing of John Locke,* ed. David Wootton, 390–436. New York, 1993.

———. *Questions Concerning the Law of Nature.* Ed. Robert Horwitz, et al. Ithaca, N.Y., 1990.

———. *The Reasonableness of Christianity* (1962). Ed. George W. Erwing. Chicago, 1965.

———. *Two Treatises of Government* (1690). Ed. Peter Laslett. Cambridge, 1960.

Lundberg, David, and Henry F. May. "The Enlightened Reader in America." *American Quarterly* 28 (1976).

Luther, Martin. *Open Letter Concerning the Hard Book against the Peasants.* In *Works of Martin Luther* IV, trans. C. M. Jacobs, 259–81. Philadelphia, 1931.

———. *An Open Letter to the Nobility of the German Nation.* In *Three Treatises,* ed. and trans. C. M. Jacobs, A. T. H. Steinhaeuser, and H. A. Lambert. Philadelphia, 1947.

———. *Secular Authority: To What Extent It Should Be Obeyed.* In *Works of Martin Luther* III, trans. J. J. Schindel, 228–73. Philadelphia, 1931.

———. *Whether Soldiers, Too, Can Be Saved.* In *Works of Martin Luther* V, trans. C. M. Jacobs, 32–74. Philadelphia, 1931.

Lutz, Donald. *The Origins of American Constitutionalism.* Baton Rouge, La., 1988.

———, ed. *Documents of Political Foundation.* Philadelphia, 1986.

Lynd, Staughton. *Intellectual Origins of American Radicalism.* New York, 1969.

Lynn, Kenneth. "Falsifying Jefferson." *Commentary,* October 1978.

Mace, George. *Hobbes, Locke and the Federalist.* Carbondale, Ill., 1979.

Machan, Tibor. *Individuals and Their Rights.* La Salle, Ill., 1989.

Machiavelli, Nicolo. *Discourse on the First Ten Books of Titus Livius* (1532). Ed. Bernard Crick, trans. Leslie J. Walker. Harmondsworth, Middlesex, 1970.

MacIntyre, Alasdair. *After Virtue.* Notre Dame, Ind., 1981.

Mahoney, Dennis. "The Declaration of Independence." In *The Framing and Ratification of the Constitution,* ed. Leonard Levy and Dennis Mahoney. New York, 1988.

Mansfield, Harvey Jr. "Jefferson." In *American Political Thought,* ed. Martin Frisch and Richard Stevens, 23–50. 2d edition. Chicago, 1971.

———. *Taming the Prince: The Ambivalence of Modern Executive Power.* New York, 1989.

———, ed. *Jefferson's Selected Writings.* Arlington Heights, Ill., 1979.

Matthews, Richard. *The Radical Politics of Thomas Jefferson.* Lawrence, Kans., 1984.

Mayer, David N. *The Constitutional Thought of Thomas Jefferson.* Charlottesville, Va., 1994.

Mayhew, Jonathan. *A Discourse Concerning Unlimited Submission.* In *Puritan Political Ideas,* ed. Edmond S. Morgan. Indianapolis, 1965.

———. "The Snare Broken" (1776). In *Political Sermons of the American Founding Era, 1730–1805,* ed. Ellis Sandoz, 231–64. Indianapolis, 1991.

McDonald, Forrest. *Novus Ordo Seclorum.* Lawrence, Kans., 1985.

McIlwain, Charles H. *The American Revolution: A Constitutional Interpretation.* New York, 1958.

McLaughlin, Charles. *The Foundations of American Constitutionalism* (1932). New York, 1961.

McLoughlin, William G. "Enthusiasm for Liberty: The Great Awakening as the Key to the Revolution." In *Preachers and Politicians,* ed. Jack P. Greene and William G. McLoughlin, 47–73. Worcester, Mass., 1977.

McWilliams, Wilson Carey. "The Bible in the American Political Tradition." In *Religion and Politics,* ed. Myron J. Aronoff. New Brunswick, N.J., 1984.

———. *The Idea of Fraternity in America.* Berkeley, 1973.

———. "In Good Faith: On the Foundation of American Politics." *Humanities in Society* 6 (1983): 19–40.

Miller, Charles A. *Jefferson and Nature.* Baltimore, 1988.

Miller, Perry. *Errand into the Wilderness.* Cambridge, Mass., 1956.

———. *The New England Mind,* vol. 2: *From Colony to Province.* Cambridge, Mass., 1953.

————, and Thomas H. Johnson, eds. *The Puritans, A Sourcebook of the Their Writings.* 2 vols. New York, 1938.

Milton, John. *Paradise Regained* (1671). In *Complete Poems and Major Prose,* ed. Merritt Y. Hughes. New York, 1957.

Montesquieu, Charles Secondat. *On the Spirit of the Laws* (1748). Ed. and trans. Anne M. Cohler, Basia Carolyn Miller, and Harold S. Stone. Cambridge, Mass., 1989.

Morgan, Edmund S. *Inventing the People.* New York, 1988.

————. *The Puritan Dilemma—The Story of John Winthrop.* Boston, 1958.

————. "The Puritan Ethic and the American Revolution." *William and Mary Quarterly* 64 (January 1969): 3–43.

————. *Visible Saints: the History of a Puritan Idea.* Ithica, N.Y., 1965.

————, ed. *Puritan Political Ideas.* Indianapolis, 1965.

Mosse, George. *The Holy Pretence: A Study in Christianity and Reason of State from William Perkins to John Winthrop.* Oxford, 1957.

Mulhall, Stephen and Adam Swift. *Liberals and Communitarians.* Oxford, 1992.

Murphy, James B. "The Workmanship Ideal: A Theologico-Political Chimera?" *Political Theory* 20 (1992): 319–26.

Newlin, Claude M. *Philosophy and Religion in Colonial America.* New York, 1962.

Nock, Albert Jay. *Our Enemy, the State.* Delavan, Wis., 1963.

Onuf, Peter, and Nicholas Onuf. *Federal Union, Modern World: The Law of Nations in an Age of Revolution, 1776–1814.* Madison, 1993.

Pangle, Lorraine S., and Thomas. *The Learning of Liberty.* Lawrence, Kans., 1993.

Pangle, Thomas. *The Ennobling of Democracy.* Chicago, 1992.

————. *The Spirit of Modern Republicanism.* Chicago, 1988.

Parrington, V. L. *Main Currents in American Thought.* 2 vols. New York, 1927.

Pease, William, and Jane Pease, eds., *The Anti-Slavery Argument.* Indianapolis, 1965.

Peckham, Howard H. "Independence: The View from Britain." In *The Declaration of Independence,* ed. Howard Mumford Jones and Howard H. Peckham, 21–37. Worcester, Mass., 1976.

Perry, Ralph Barton. *Morality, Politics, and Law.* New York, 1988.

————. "The Philosophy of the Declaration." In *A Casebook on the Declaration of Independence,* ed. Robert Ginsberg. New York, 1966.

Peterson, Merrill D. *Thomas Jefferson and the New Nation: A Biography.* London, 1970.

————, ed. *Thomas Jefferson Writings.* New York, 1984.

Pocock, J. G. A., "Between Gog and Magog: The Republican Thesis and *Ideologica Americana.*" *Journal of the History of Ideas* 68 (1987): 325–46.

————. "The Fourth English Civil War." *Government and Opposition* 23 (1988): 151–66.

————. *The Machiavellian Moment.* Princeton, N.J., 1975.

———. "Virtue and Commerce in the Eighteenth Century." *Journal of Interdisciplinary History* 3 (1972): 119–34.

———. *Virtue, Commerce and History.* Cambridge, 1985.

Poelvoorde, Jeffrey. "American Civil Religion." In *How Does the Constitution Protect Religious Freedom?* ed. Robert A. Goldwin and Arthur Kaufman. Washington, D.C., 1979.

Power, M. Susan. *Before the Convention: Religion and the Founding.* Lanham, Md., 1984.

Rahe, Paul A. *Republics Ancient and Modern.* Chapel Hill, N.C., 1992.

Rakove, Jack N. "Parchment Barriers and the Politics of Rights." In *A Culture of Rights*, ed. Michael J. Lacey and Knud Haakenssen. Cambridge, 1991.

Raphael, D. D., ed. *British Moralists, 1650–1800.* 2 vols. Oxford, 1969.

Rasmussen, Douglas, and Douglas Den Uyl. *Liberty and Nature.* La Salle, Ill., 1991.

Rawls, John. *Political Liberalism.* New York, 1991.

Reid, John Phillip. *Constitutional History of the American Revolution: The Authority of Rights.* Madison, 1986.

———. "The Irrelevance of the Declaration." In *Law in the American Revolution and the Revolution in Law: A Collection of Review Essays on American Legal History*, ed. Hendrik Hartog, 46–89. New York, 1981.

Reid, Thomas. *Essays on the Intellectual Powers of Man.* In *Works*, ed. Hamilton. Edinburgh, 1863.

———. *Essays on the Active Powers of the Human Mind.* In *Works*, ed. Hamilton. Edinburgh, 1863.

Robbins, Caroline. *The Eighteenth Century Commonwealthmen.* New York, 1968.

Rorty, Richard. *Contingency, Irony and Solidarity.* Cambridge, 1989.

Ross, Dorothy. *The Origins of American Social Science.* Cambridge, 1991.

Rossiter, Clinton. *The First American Revolution.* New York, 1956.

———. *The Political Thought of the American Revolution* (Pt. III of *Seedtime of the Republic*). New York, 1963.

Sandel, Michael J., ed., *Liberalism and Its Critics.* New York, 1984.

Sandoz, Ellis. *A Government of Laws.* Baton Rouge, La., 1990.

Saricks, Ambrose. *Pierre Samuel Dupont de Nemours.* Lawrence, Kans., 1965.

Schmitt, Gary, and Robert Webking. "Revolutionaries, Anti-Federalists, and Federalists: Comments on Gordon Wood's Understanding of the American Founding." *Political Science Reviewer* 9 (1979): 195–229.

Schochet, Gordon. *Patriarchalism in Political Thought.* New York, 1975.

Schwenninger, Lee. *John Winthrop.* Boston, 1990.

Schwoerer, Lois J. *The Declaration of Rights, 1698.* Baltimore, 1981.

Selden, Richard Ely. "Criticism in the Declaration of Independence as a Literary Document." In *A Casebook on the Declaration of Independence*, ed. Robert Ginsberg. New York, 1966.

Shain, Barry Alan. *The Myth of American Individualism: The Protestant Origins of American Political Thought.* Princeton, N.J., 1994.

Shalhope, Robert E. "Toward a Republican Synthesis." *William and Mary Quarterly* 29 (1972): 49–81.

Shapiro, Ian. "Resources, Capacities, and Ownership." *Political Theory* 19 (1991): 47–72.

————. "Workmanship Revisited: Reply to Professor Murphy." *Political Theory* 20 (1992): 327–31.

Sheldon, Garrett Ward. *The Political Philosophy of Thomas Jefferson.* Baltimore, 1991.

Sherry, Suzanna. "The Founders' Unwritten Constitution." *University of Chicago Law Review* 54 (1987), 1127–77.

Simpson, Alan. *Puritanism in Old and New England.* Chicago, 1955.

Shklar, Judith. "Redeeming American Political Theory." *American Political Science Review* 85 (1991): 3–15.

Sigmund, Paul E. *Natural Law in Political Thought.* Cambridge, Mass., 1971.

Simmons, A. John. "Inalienable Rights and Locke's *Treatises.*" *Philosophy and Public Affairs,* Summer 1983.

Skinner, Quentin. *The Foundations of Modern Political Thought.* 2 vols. Cambridge, 1978.

Stoner, James R., Jr. *Common Law and Liberal Theory.* Lawrence, Kans., 1992.

Storing, Herbert J., ed. *The Complete Anti-Federalist.* 7 vols. Chicago, 1981.

Straka, Gerald M. *Anglican Reaction to the Revolution of 1688.* Madison, 1962.

Strauss, Leo. *Natural Right and History.* Chicago, 1954.

Suarez, Francisco. *Selections from Three Works.* Ed. James Brown Scott. Oxford, 1944.

Sullivan, Vickie. "The Civic Humanist Portrait of Machiavelli's English Successors." *History of Political Thought* 15 (Spring 1994): 73–96.

————. "Machiavelli's Momentary 'Machiavellian Moment.'" *Political Theory* 20 (May 1992): 309–18.

Taylor, Charles. *Philosophy and the Human Sciences.* Cambridge, Mass., 1985.

Thomas Aquinas. *Summa Theologica.* Translated by Fathers of the English Dominican Province. New York, 1947.

Thompson, Martyn. *Ideas of Contract: English Political Thought in the Age of John Locke.* New York, 1987.

Tocqueville, Alexis de. *Democracy in America.* Ed. J. P. Mayer. Garden City, N.Y., 1969.

Tuck, Richard. *Natural Rights Theories.* Cambridge, 1979.

Tyler, Moses Coit. "The Declaration of Independence in the Light of Modern Criticism." In *A Casebook on the Declaration of Independence,* ed. Robert Ginsberg. New York, 1966.

Vossler, Otto. "The American Argument." In *A Casebook on the Declaration of Independence,* ed. Robert Ginsberg. New York, 1966.

Webking, Robert. *The American Revolution.* Baton Rouge, La., 1989.

Wesley, John. "A Calm Address to Our American Colonies." In *Political Sermons of the American Founding Era, 1730–1805,* ed. Ellis Sandoz. Indianapolis, 1991.

West, Samuel. "On the Right to Rebel Against Governors" (1776). In *American Political Writing During the Founding Era, 1760–1805*. 1:410-48. Indianapolis, 1983.

Whately, Thomas. *The Regulations Lately Made Concerning the Colonies and the Taxes Imposed on Them, Considerations*. In *Prologue to Revolution: Sources and Documents on the Stamp Act Congress*. Chapel Hill, N.C., 1959.

White, Morton. *The Philosophy of the American Revolution*. New York, 1981.

Williams, Abraham. "An Election Sermon" (1762). In *American Political Writing During the Founding Era*, ed. Charles S. Hyneman and Donald S. Lutz, 2 vols, 1: 3–18. Indianapolis, 1983.

Williams, Elisha. "The Essential Rights and Liberties of Protestants." In *Political Sermons of the American Founding Era*, ed. Ellis Sandoz. Indianapolis, 1991.

Wills, Garry. *Inventing America*. Garden City, N.Y., 1978.

Wilson, Douglas. "Jefferson and the Republic of Letters." In *Jeffersonian Legacies*, ed. Peter Onuf. Charlottesville, Va., 1993.

Winthrop, John. "A Declaration in Defense of an Order of Court Made in May, 1637." In *Puritan Political Ideas*, ed. Edmund S. Morgan. Indianapolis, 1965.

———. "Journal." In *Puritan Political Ideas*, ed. Edmund S. Morgan. Indianapolis, 1965.

———. "A Modell of Christian Charitie." In *Puritan Political Ideas*, ed. Edmund S. Morgan. Indianapolis, 1965.

———. "On Arbitrary Government." In *Puritan Political Ideas*, ed. Edmund S. Morgan, 149–60. Indianapolis, 1965.

Wood, Gordon. *The Creation of the American Republic*. Chapel Hill, N.C., 1969.

———. *The Radicalism of the American Revolution*. New York, 1992.

———. "The Trials and Tribulations of Thomas Jefferson." In *Jeffersonian Legacies*, ed. Peter S. Onuf, 395–417. Charlottesville, Va., 1993.

Wootton, David, ed. *The Political Writings of John Locke*. New York, 1993.

Zuckert, Catherine. "Aristotle on the Limits and Satisfactions of Political Life." *Interpretation* 11 (1983): 185–206.

———. "Derrida and the Politics of Deconstruction." *Polity* 3 (Spring 1991): 335–56.

———. "Not by Preaching: Tocqueville on the Role of Religion in American Democracy." *Review of Politics* 42 (April 1981).

Zuckert, Michael P. "Federalism and the Founding: Toward a Reinterpretation of the Constitutional Convention." *Review of Politics* 48 (1986): 166–210.

———. "An Introduction to Locke's *First Treatise*." *Interpretation* 7 (1979).

———. "Lincoln and the Problem of Civil Religion." In *Law and Philosophy: The Practice of Theory*, ed. John A. Murley, Robert L. Stone, and William T. Braithwaite. Athens, Ohio, 1992.

———. "Locke and the Problem of Civil Religion." In *The Moral Foundations of the American Republic*, ed. Robert Horwitz, 3d ed. Charlottsville, Va., 1986.

————. *Natural Rights and the New Republicanism.* Princeton, N.J., 1994.

————. "Of Wary Physicians and Weary Readers." *Independent Journal of Philosophy* 1977.

————. "The Recent Literature on Locke's Political Philosophy." *Political Science Reviewer* 5 (1975).

————. "A System without Precedent: Federalism in the Constitutional Convention." In *The Framing and Ratification of the Constitution,* ed. Leonard Levy and Dennis Mahoney. New York, 1988.

————. "What Next for Constitutional Studies?" *Constitutional Commentary* 5 (1988).

Zyskind, Harold. "How to Read the Declaration of Independence." In *A Casebook on the Declaration of Independence,* ed. Robert Ginsberg. New York, 1966.

Index